EXISTENTIALISM AND CONTEMPORARY CINEMA

EXISTENTIALISM AND CONTEMPORARY CINEMA

A Sartrean Perspective

Edited by

Jean-Pierre Boulé and Enda McCaffrey

Berghahn Books
New York • Oxford

Published in 2011 by

Berghahn Books

www.berghahnbooks.com

©2011 Jean-Pierre Boulé and Enda McCaffrey

Library of Congress Cataloging-in-Publication Data

Existentialism and contemporary cinema : a Sartrean perspective / edited by
Jean-Pierre Boulé and Enda McCaffrey.
   p. cm.
Includes bibliographical references and index.
ISBN 978-0-85745-320-4 (hardback : alk. paper) -- ISBN 978-0-85745-321-1
(ebook)
1. Existentialism in motion pictures. 2. Philosophy in motion pictures.
   3. Sartre, Jean-Paul, 1905-1980--Philosophy. 4. Sartre, Jean-Paul,
   1905-1980--Influence. I. Boulé, Jean-Pierre. II. McCaffrey, Enda.

PN1995.9.E945E94 2011
791.43'684--dc23

2011019539

British Library Cataloguing in Publication Data

A catalogue record for this book is available from
the British Library.

Printed in the United States on acid-free paper

ISBN 978-0-85745-320-4 (hardback)

ISBN 978-0-85745-321-1 (ebook)

CONTENTS

ACKNOWLEDGEMENTS

We would like to thank our colleagues Matt Connell and Martin O'Shaughnessy, the Editorial Manager at Berghahn Books, Mark Stanton, and all our contributors for their patience and diligence.

INTRODUCTION

Movies exercise a hold on us, a hold that, drawing on our innermost desires and fears, we participate in creating. To know films objectively, we have to know the hold they have upon us. To know the hold films have on us, we have to know ourselves objectively. And to know ourselves objectively, we have to know the impact of films on our lives. No study of film can claim intellectual authority if it is not rooted in self-knowledge, our knowledge of our own subjectivity. In the serious study of film, in other words, criticism must work hand in hand with the perspective of self-reflection that only philosophy is capable of providing.

(Rothman and Keane 2000: 17–18)

At the heart of this volume is the understanding that Sartrean existentialism, most prominent in the 1940s particularly in France, is still relevant as a way of interpreting the world today. And film, by reflecting philosophical concerns in the actions and choices of characters, continues and extends a tradition in which art exemplifies the understanding of this philosophy. This book, therefore, seeks to revalidate the Sartrean philosophical project through its application to film.

'I am an existentialist.' What does this statement mean? What kind of existentialism is one talking about? There are a variety of philosophical tenets held by those who call themselves existentialists, some of whom are phenomenologists, a philosophy that deals with consciousness and that goes 'back to the things themselves', asking the question: what does existing mean? Existentialism is a philosophy derived from the Danish and German philosophers Kierkegaard and Heidegger; the former was Christian and the latter an atheist. In France, the philosopher Gabriel Marcel was influenced by the ideas of Kierkegaard and Jean-Paul Sartre (whose existentialism is the primary focus of this volume) by the ideas of Heidegger. William Shearson, in highlighting the differences amongst philosophers who would define themselves as existentialists, defines existentialism as based on two principles: knowledge that is gained through experience, and the self defined not as substance but as a lived relation to that which situates it (Shearson 1975: 135, 138).

Existentialism emerged in France at the end of the Second World War, which had seen France occupied by Germany (see McBride 1996; Webber 2008). A philosophy of freedom and responsibility resonated particularly in

France and in Western Europe before crossing the Atlantic and finding an echo in North America which had also suffered from the war. This context is paramount to the success of Sartrean existentialism in France (Boschetti 1985; Galster 2001). After the end of the Second World War, as Sartre became more prominent in the media, he was continually asked to explain existentialism (Boulé 1992). Sartre says that existentialism is a doctrine according to which existence precedes essence (and not the converse which would be the definition of determinism). His thesis is that human beings exist first and in choosing themselves, they create themselves. In acting, they define themselves; in short, therefore, there is no difference between being and doing. Furthermore, human beings' acts and choices are always defined within a given situation, and within that situation (which is simply one of the aspects of the human condition) human beings are free and therefore responsible.

In most newspaper articles and interviews at the time, Sartre explained existentialism in terms one can find in his work *Existentialism Is a Humanism*.[1] This slim and accessible volume started as a public lecture given on 29 October 1945 which the publisher Nagel published as a small booklet in 1946. It was only ever intended as a lecture designed on the one hand to popularise Sartre's thought and on the other hand to respond to accusations from French Communists and Christians alike that his philosophy was having a corrupting influence on French youth. *Existentialism Is a Humanism* does not represent a complete picture of Sartrean philosophy (Keefe 1972). As an early insight into Sartre's thinking, it is a condensed version of his existentialist philosophy which is why it was chosen as the key reference text for all contributors to this collection. It is inevitable, therefore, that some central existentialist themes will be repeated across chapters. This adds focus to the volume and should not detract from the originality of each chapter, conceived as each is to stand alone on its own merits. *Existentialism Is a Humanism* also has a distinctly un-nuanced moral dimension that does not feature prominently in Sartre's bigger and more theoretical work *Being and Nothingness* (1943), sub-titled 'Essay in Phenomenological Ontology', which features a more in-depth and ontological approach to existentialist thought. As for Sartrean ethics, this is given a thorough treatment in his *Notebooks for an Ethics* (1983). Because this volume focuses on the early period of Sartrean existentialism, it may be viewed that existentialism – at least as it is elaborated in this introduction – is more in tune with the hegemonic ideology of liberal democracy, as espoused especially in the USA today. For example, what Falzon in his chapter calls 'the affirmation of the sovereign individual' in existentialism could be seen as equally applicable to the American Dream of self-realisation as to existentialism. However, it should be stressed that Sartre's insistence on the individual has to be constantly resituated within the context of the Second World War and of the Occupation of France by Germany. Once Sartre discovered Marxism in the late 1940s (Poster 1979), his philosophical focus shifted away from liberal democracy and the denouncement of alienation and oppression towards a greater acknowledgement of the collective:

As soon as there will exist *for everyone* a margin of *real* freedom beyond the production of life, Marxism will have lived out its span; a philosophy of freedom will take its place. But we have no means, no intellectual instrument, no concrete experience which allows us to conceive of this freedom or of this philosophy.

(Sartre 1960b: 34)

McBride reminds us in an article entitled 'Sartre at the Twilight of Liberal Democracy' that Sartre never attempted to elaborate on this philosophy but that 'it remained the inspiration for all that he wrote in this area' (McBride 2005: 312), and that he regarded the electoral system, seen as the pinnacle of 'real' democracy, as 'a profound mystification' (McBride 2005: 312).

Sartre insisted that *Existentialism Is a Humanism* represents a philosophy of optimism, which was not how it was generally received. The day after his public lecture in 1945, Sartre gave a lengthy interview to the journalist Christian Grisoli in which he expressed dismay at the way his version of existentialism was being received as a 'philosophy of despair', particularly when he had gone to such lengths in this lecture to emphasise that human beings are the choices they make, that they choose to be good or bad and are always responsible for their acts. In Sartrean existentialism, he stressed, there is no predetermined path that takes human beings to salvation. People have to invent their own path. And in inventing it, they are free, responsible and have no excuses; all hope is therefore within them. If human beings are free, they are also responsible for themselves and for the world in which they live. Through their choices, they decide what sense the world has: they cannot refuse to choose since this refusal is itself a choice. And they must choose alone, without any recourse or help from any religion or system of pre-established values. The accompanying feeling of 'dread' experienced in choice is itself the awareness of freedom and an acknowledgement that one's future is one's possibility (Sartre 1981: 1913). Freedom, for Sartre, is not a property of our human essence. Human existence is synonymous with freedom; we are free because *we are*. There is, therefore, no distance between our being and our freedom (Sartre 1981: 1914). Human beings are condemned to be free (Sartre 1981: 1916). One is not born a hero or a coward. One chooses to be a hero or a coward, and this choice can always be questioned and changed. In short, there is no absolute meaning in Sartrean existentialism. Sartre's last liberating move in this interview was to state that it is the future that decides the meaning of the past.

After the existentialist trend of the late 1940s, Sartre's reception and reputation, in France and abroad, suffered various fortunes. From the 1960s onwards, Sartre is sidelined by structuralism and post-structuralism. Michel Foucault declared: '*The Critique of Dialectical Reason* is the magnificent and pathetic attempt by a man of the nineteenth century to think the twentieth century. In that sense, Sartre is the last Hegelian and, I would say, the last Marxist' (Flynn 2005: 2). Sartre is also sidelined by influential Marxist thinkers such as Louis Althusser: 'At best, I saw him as one of those post-Cartesian and post-Hegelian "philosophers of history" whom Marx detested' (Flynn 2005: 2).

In a reversal of fortune, Sartre returns to the spotlight over May '68 (and Althusser himself is ironically and temporarily sidelined). *The Critique of Dialectical Reason* (Sartre 1960a), with its analysis of the French revolution and of 'groups-in-fusion' (people brought together by a common cause) resonates positively with his philosophical contemporaries. Epistémon, the pseudonym for Didier Anzieu, declared that Sartre's *Critique* was an apocalyptic work which allowed one to *think* the revolution of May '68 (Boulé 2009: 5). Daniel Cohn-Bendit acknowledged that the militants at the instigation of the students' revolt had more or less all read Sartre (Contat and Rybalka 1970: 462). Flynn reminds us that the shock of May '68 is seen as 'Sartrean social philosophy in praxis' (2005: 2). Sartre lends students his support, creating the concept of the 'new intellectual' who is at the service of the masses as opposed to the 'universal intellectual' who speaks in the name of the masses. Sartre was to subsequently become involved with the revolutionary left in France (*la gauche prolétarienne*).

As a philosopher, Sartre soon fell out of fashion and out of favour post '68 with the rise of the 'new philosophers' and the emerging dominance of an anti-totalitarian strand in French intellectual life (for example, André Glucksmann and Bernard-Henry Lévy). According to Galster, by 1987 there was a perception that intellectuals had lost faith in Sartre's political stance. Philosophers grew indifferent to his philosophy and students no longer felt it relevant (Galster 1987: 244). And yet by the time of his death in 1980, the day of his funeral is acknowledged as the last demonstration of May '68 and tributes are paid to his work and legacy. In 2000, Bernard-Henry Lévy, one of the 'new philosophers', repays his debt by publishing *Le Siècle de Sartre*, a vibrant homage to Sartre. And in 2005, on the occasion of Sartre's centenary, a plethora of books is published (see for instance Cohen-Solal 2005). However, it is Ronald Aronson who sums up the significance of Sartre's centenary in *The New York Times*: 'Meanwhile: Jean-Paul Sartre at 100: Still troubling us today'. Here, Aronson points to Sartre's true legacy, the relevance and subtlety of his views on free will against determinism, and his insistence on our responsibility in a globalised world (Aronson 2005).

Today, Sartre has gained recognition as a thinker whose philosophy can be used to address contemporary issues. His association in the public mind with Simone de Beauvoir, whose feminist legacy in particular is alive and thriving, adds to the perennial appeal of existentialism. Likewise, themes such as authenticity and responsibility continue to hold sway and underpin some postmodernist ethics (Emanuel Levinas). A recent symposium, held following the events of September 11 2001, invoked the memory of Sartre when the organiser Kenneth Anderson said in his introduction that this kind of event 'called for [a Sartrean] philosophical consideration' (Anderson 2003: 3). Sartre's relevance continues to appeal to scholars researching into Sartre and race, for example (Judaken 2008),[2] and Sartre and decolonisation (Arthur 2010).[3] Flynn in the aptly titled 'Sartre at One Hundred – a Man of the Nineteenth Century Addressing the Twenty-First?' argues that in as far as existentialism reflects the experience of Western Europe in the 1940s, it is tied to its own facticity, but to the extent that Sartre's philosophy addresses the human condition, its relevance transcends the historical values attached to these variables. He states: 'The drama may shift with the dramatis personae, but … "the plot" remains the same: people trying to make sense of an increasingly complex, threatening, and impersonal world' (Flynn 2005: 11). Flynn concludes that existentialism is primarily a way of life, a form of what the Greeks called 'care of the self' (Flynn 2005: 11). Based on these observations, it is not an exaggeration to claim that Sartre's philosophy transcends time and place.

With a volume entitled *Existentialism and Contemporary Cinema: A Sartrean Perspective*, readers may be curious to know more about Sartre's relationship to film. During the war, Sartre worked briefly as a scriptwriter for Pathé. He was hired, thanks to the director Jean Delannoy. The latter was so disappointed by the film scripts he had been given that he went to see Sartre to ask him to write film scripts (Contat and Rybalka 1970: 486). In 1943–1944, Sartre wrote *Les Jeux sont faits* (*The Chips are Down*), *Typhus*, *La Fin du monde* (*The End of the World*) (Contat and Rybalka 1970: 29) as well as *Les Faux Nez* (*The False Noses*) and *L'Engrenage* (*In the Mesh*). Two of these would become films: *The Chips are Down* which came out in 1947 and *Typhus* in 1953. In an interview given in 1944, Sartre said that the film scripts for *The Chips are Down* and *Typhus* were those of committed films, reflecting life's eternal problems and the complexity of human relationships through the lens of daily existence (Contat and Rybalka 1970: 106). *The Chips are Down* picks up elements of the short story 'The Room' in *The Wall* and proposes the sort of problematical situation found in *No Exit* (also translated as *In Camera*), written at about the same time. The film version of *Typhus* is only partly derived from Sartre's original script. However, the same misadventure that befell *Typhus* comes at the conclusion of Sartre's film script on Freud (Sartre 1984). In 1958, Sartre wrote a first draft of the Freud script but it was too long (almost 800 pages). After meeting with John Huston, he wrote a second version which was even longer. Exasperated, Huston ditched Sartre's services and hired Hollywood scriptwriters. Unsurprisingly, Sartre withdrew his name from the film credits (he refused to have his name associated with the film *Les Orgueilleux* (*The Proud Ones*)), even though the film was described by a critic in *Cahiers du cinéma* in 1951 as a phenomenological film (Contat and Rybalka 1970: 490). In 1976, there was a film made about Sartre by Alexandre Astruc and Michel Contat called *Sartre by Himself* (1976) which was autobiographical and based on a series of interviews given by Sartre. There have been seven films made from Sartre's work including *Les Sorcières de Salem* (1957), an adaptation of Arthur Miller's *The Crucible*.[4]

Sartre also tried his hand as a film critic and wrote an article on *Citizen Kane* which, whilst recognising the technical merits of the film, raises doubts about its value as an example for French cinema to follow (Contat and Rybalka 1970: 125); in keeping with his growing 'new intellectual' credentials, Sartre would reproach Welles for having made a film as an intellectual for intellectuals rather than for the masses. The nature of this critique highlights one of the key functions of film for Sartre. In an interview given in 1947, he claimed that film offers a broader horizon than theatre, pointing out that one can embrace more realistically in film the collective and the crowd; film, he believed, also intensifies the simultaneity of images and he compares changes of scenes on screen to the rapidity of thought processes (Contat and Rybalka 1970: 156). Sartre used to say that the art of cinema was born with him. With the Lumière Brothers' first films appearing at the end of the nineteenth century, cinema was in effect in its infancy as Sartre was growing up: 'We had the same mental age: I was seven and I could read; it was twelve and could not speak ... I thought we could grow up together' (Sartre 1964: 77). When he held his first teaching job in Le Havre in 1931, Sartre made a speech at the annual prize-giving ceremony praising cinema as an art form (Contat and Rybalka 1970: 546–52). Addressing a group of eighteen-year-old students, he told them that film cannot be reduced to nor compared to the theatre. Rather, film must be seen as a cultural experience on a par with Greek art or Philosophy and that, of all the art forms, it most resembles the real world.[5]

These links between film and theatre are apposite because they raise some existential concerns relating to both, and hint indirectly at the direction of this volume, conceived for students seeking to apply the philosophy of existentialism to film. Sarah Cooper reminds us that Sartre works through his philosophy within an aesthetic dimension, and his characters play out existentialist dilemmas, sometimes exposing thorny issues that philosophy cannot resolve. In a similar vein and echoing Sartre's views on the 'descriptive' power of the absurd in the novel and in art, William Pamerleau states:

> ... film, precisely because of its concrete depictions, can convey insights that inform even the abstract ideas of theoretical philosophy. Generally speaking, there are two ways in which it does so: through its ability to deliver realistic narratives and through the expressive nature of visual imagery.
>
> (Pamerleau 2009: 85)

As Michelle R. Darnell argues in her chapter on 'Being – *Lost in Translation*', Sartre held theatre in great esteem because it was for him a 'true event' in which words and the language of gesture point to something else, a reality not given but one to be perceived through an act of freedom. For Sartre, cinema, it would appear, was more contrived in the way actors and actions were 'ready-canned' and where the interpretative function (meaning) was lost as a vital element of freedom. In the same way that a 'theatre of situations' was part of the template for Sartre's literary exploration of existentialism in the post-war period, a 'film of situations' may signal the illustration of Sartrean philosophy in contemporary film.

In the second part of *Existentialism Is a Humanism* (namely 'A Commentary on *The Stranger*'),[6] Sartre's study of Camus's 'novel' informs us that philosophy has an interpretative and instructive purpose in relation to fiction (art and potentially film). Cohen-Solal points to the integral link between philosophy and fiction in her description of the 'deft enunciation of philosophy at the very heart of fiction' (Cohen-Solal 2007: 6). Sartre also tells us that this relationship is a unique one in that the absurd (for Camus) and contingency (for Sartre) operates without justification or explanation: 'Camus is not concerned about justifying what is fundamentally unjustifiable' (Sartre [1946] 2007: 79). Sartre's implication is that the 'descriptive' power of the absurd is enough to convey a philosophy of the absurd. Philosophy, therefore, has a positive role to play in art and film (in the tradition of epistemological inquiry) but in the specific context of the absurd/contingency, this role is decidedly passive and 'descriptive', even post-epistemological in that the absurd and the contingent are by definition explainable phenomenologically, in no need of 'proof', more a matter of 'silence' and as Sartre says more 'in the realm of what is not said' (Sartre [1946] 2007: 80). Likewise, film can illustrate philosophical points in a way that renders accessible obscure philosophical concepts. For Pamerleau, film does so in two ways, firstly 'through its ability to deliver realistic narratives' and secondly 'through the expressive nature of visual imagery' (Pamerleau 2009: 85). And films 'evoke a variety of intellectual and emotional reactions' (40). For Sartre, philosophy in the novel and in art generally instructs the absurd descriptively, using 'substance', 'content', 'presentation', 'image' and 'perception' to convey 'idea' or 'meaning'. This is the template that could transfer legitimately to the screen where the apparatus of film production is deployed to capture the 'truth' of philosophy: 'the outraged acknowledgement of the limitations of human thought' (Sartre [1946] 2007: 81).

The eleven chapters in this volume were not written with a narrow brief but they share the common thread of treating films as narrative texts, as scenarios wherein the actions and interactions of the protagonists are taken to be telling exemplars of the kinds of existential modes that Sartre talks of in his works. As exemplars, they do not engage fully or directly with the filmic object on its own terms. Filmic, fictional representations can inform an understanding of actual character formation and human agency, the model of the 'real' against which this fictional representation is judged being Sartre's existentialist analyses of human behaviour as expounded in his philosophical and fictional texts. Some contributors rely more heavily on Sartre's philosophy in their studies of film, whilst others draw parallels between the films they are studying and Sartrean plays and/or novels. A priori, one might have expected films from the 1950s and 1960s to fall within the scope of this volume, particularly given the coincidence of the emergence of existentialism and the French New Wave, and more broadly the influence of philosophical themes and ideas on classic noir and neo-noir films internationally. Of course, these connections have been established and enriched by a range of scholars, notably Mary Litch (2002), Mark Conard and Robert Porfirio (2007), Chris Falzon (2007), Daniel Shaw (2008), Stephen Faison (2008) and Pamerleau (2009). However, we lay claim to the distinctiveness of our volume in two ways. Firstly, it seeks to engage with contemporary film from an exclusively Sartrean perspective, which distinguishes our approach from volumes with broader frames of philosophical reference, or from volumes which engage with the filmic object on its own terms. Secondly, it aims to look not at how existentialism underpinned the philosophical outlook of directors in the post-war period in France, Europe and the US, but how we might approach contemporary films using Sartrean existentialism. The focus of this volume lies in the articulation of Sartre's philosophy with the individual filmic texts; how certain philosophical conceptualisations of human behaviour find exemplary models in a select range of filmic texts.

Whilst one is not surprised to see Michael Haneke or Jean-Pierre and Luc Dardenne as existentialist filmmakers, other filmmakers such as Cédric Klapisch are more unexpected. One may well ask to what extent, and in what ways, are the films under study 'existentialist' films? We do not claim that these filmmakers deliberately address issues central to Sartre's philosophy. Some, such as Mike Leigh, make films known more for their social relevance. For others, it is more the case that there are fortuitous parallels with existentialism. But, in the broad brush of film history, which films do not deal with existence or the human condition in some form or another? Drawing a parallel with existentialism, Robert Lapsley and Michael Westlake point out that the heroes and heroines of countless Hollywood movies, when faced with choices and confronted by a crisis, have to make decisions and choose a course of action that define their beings (Lapsley and Westlake [1998] 2006: xi). We also acknowledge the fact that some of the contributors use existentialism as a tool to read films that were never intended to be interpreted as existentialist films by their creators in the first place. In the light of these qualifications, what we feel sure of laying claim to in this volume is that there is a valid case to be made for an application of the philosophy of existentialism to film.[7]

The films have been chosen for their relative contemporaneity and international provenance, and have been grouped broadly into two interconnecting sections: 'The Call to Freedom' and 'Films of Situation'. There is of course no exhaustive inventory of existentialist themes but we believe that the above categories incorporate some of the more specific aspects of existentialism, including phenomenology, theories of consciousness, existential crisis, selfhood and subjectivity, identity and authenticity, determinism and predestination, time, commitment, responsibility, ethics, bad faith, despair and dread. We want to stress that our approach in this volume is not to simply reduce existentialism to a checklist of stereotypical themes and motifs. As Hugo Münsterberg has argued, film is an art form that creates its own reality. He characterises cinema as 'overcoming the causal requirements of the outer world to more accurately capture the reality of the inner world', going on to claim that this is the most important reason why film can contribute to existentialism (cited in Pamerleau 2009: 222). Films are seen to have their own concrete realities. Films reflect life on their own terms, and as Sartre has inferred, they represent an opportunity for characters in real life situations to be called to freedom. Although readers will clearly not identify fully with the characters, there will be situations or aspects of the film narratives to which she/he can relate.

The Call to Freedom

Christopher Falzon in his treatment of Peter Weir's *The Truman Show* (1998) underlines the importance of individual freedom as a condition of 'existential awakening' and of its capacity for self-determination. Kevin L. Stoehr's analysis of Michael Haneke's film corpus highlights the radical freedom implied by human subjectivity, but also cautions against the complacency caused by bad faith that 'kills' genuine freedom. In this vein, Mark Stanton's examination of Mike Leigh's *Naked* (1993) demonstrates how characters deny freedom by adopting prescribed social roles through bad faith. In this respect, he focuses on expressions of bad faith by individuals towards themselves and attitudes of bad faith directed towards others. In Tom Martin's study of The Coen Brothers' *The Man Who Wasn't There* (2001), bad faith is expressed in the form of a distancing (transcendence) in the case of Ed Crane. Specifically, Crane's choice of dry cleaning offers him the possibility (illusion) of escaping hands-on engagement with the ambiguity of worldly objects. Sarah Cooper reads the Dardenne Brothers' film *Lorna's Silence* (2008) from a Sartrean perspective of characters on the road to freedom and responsibility. Specifically, she uses the atheistic overtones of Sartre's existential humanism to illustrate how the Dardennes' 'godless world' calls forth human beings to embrace their freedom and take responsibility for their actions. The call to freedom is also broached by Michelle R. Darnell in her discussion of Sofia Coppola's *Lost in Translation* (2003) and her chapter provides the ideal transition to 'Films of Situation'.

Films of Situation

Darnell revisits the language of the theatre of situations as a site from which meaning is derived, not from one word but from a contextual whole. The situatedness of language becomes the context for both a calling forth of freedom for the main protagonist and a broader assessment of a hypothesis based on a 'film of situation'. In her chapter on Neil Jordan's *The Crying Game* (1992), Tracey Nicholls acknowledges that life, for the existentialist, is a product of choice and that, in making choices, one's life becomes a path for others. Sartre says as much in his statement: 'Every man realizes himself in realizing a type of humanity' (Sartre [1946] 2007: 43). The link, therefore, between individual subjectivity/choice and collective responsibility is at the heart of the Sartrean project and this cluster of films. Enda McCaffrey explores the tensions in this link in his study of gratuitous murder and crimes of passion in the Coen Brothers' *No Country for Old Men* (2007), and particularly in the contrast drawn between the Hegelian terrorism embodied in the character Anton Chigurh and the protagonist Paul Hilbert in Sartre's short story *Erostratus*. Patrick Williams underscores the political dimensions of existentialist choice in his chapter on Ousmane Sembene's film *Moolaadé* (2004). Taking individual subjectivity as a starting point, he argues that an individual decision to protect girls in Africa from genital excision is seen to have an inescapable, collective and ethical dimension, which extends beyond the film to involve the commitment of the filmmaker himself. Drawing parallels with Roquentin in Sartre's novel *Nausea* (1938), Jean-Pierre Boulé charts Xavier's quest for authenticity in Cédric Klapisch's duology *The Spanish Apartment* (2002) and *Russian Dolls* (2005). Accentuating the link between freedom and the freedom to make choices, Boulé traces Xavier's journey from his fear of commitment to choose love (a state of having freedom as an unrealised potential) to the exercise of his freedom in the choice to write as the ultimate expression of his commitment to a project of self-discovery. *Nausea* also forms the backdrop to Alistair Rolls' study of Baz Luhrmann's adaptation of *William Shakespeare's Romeo + Juliet* (1996). Rolls demonstrates how the modernisation of the film parallels Sartre's development of the philosophical novel in *Nausea*. By focusing on auto-antonymic comparisons and a mutual recourse to the mechanics of Freudian fetishism, Rolls highlights common points of articulation between key poetic tropes of modernisation and the world-view of Sartrean existentialism. In this way, it is argued that Sartrean philosophy can be used not only to explain diegesis and the psychology and/or motivation of individual characters but also, and importantly, to illuminate filmic and literary process.

These two sections reflect two distinct but interconnected pathways to understand existentialism in the context of Contemporary Cinema, and to engage with the world. The first section represents a theoretical approach and the second provides more concrete examples of situations. Sartre argued 'For a Theatre of Situation' (Sartre [1947] 1973: 3–5). We believe that the contributors to this volume have argued the case 'For a Film of Situation'. Collectively, we hope that these essays make a case for existentialism and its relevance to understanding today's society, whilst keeping at the forefront the elements of freedom, choice and responsibility.

Notes

1. Readers of this volume may benefit from reading this seminal text alongside this book.
2. 'The first book to systematically interrogate Jean-Paul Sartre's antiracist politics and his largely unrecognised contributions to critical race theories, postcolonialism, and African existentialism' (back cover blurb).
3. 'In this major re-reading of Sartre's life and work, Paige Arthur traces the relationship between the philosopher's decades-long commitment to decolonization and his intellectual thought. Where other commentators have focused on the tensions between Sartre's Marxism and his account of existential freedom – usually to denigrate one in

favour of the other – Arthur shows that Sartre's political engagement with global liberation movements and his philosophical framework were inextricably intertwined' (back cover blurb).
4. *Dirty Hands, The Respectful Prostitute, No Exit, Kean: Genius or Scoundrel, The Crucible, The Condemned of Altona, The Wall*. See filmography.
5. Beauvoir recounts in her memoirs that Sartre ranked cinema almost as high as literature (Beauvoir 1960: 48).
6. Translated as *The Outsider* in the USA.
7. Economy of space prevented us from commissioning more counter-intuitive examples – for instance, popular genre cinema – but we believe that there is a wide applicability of existentialism to cinema. In preparation is *Existentialism and Contemporary Cinema: A Beauvoirian Perspective*, Jean-Pierre Boulé and Ursula Tidd (eds), Berghahn Books. For a more general treatment of commitment in contemporary French cinema, see Martin O'Shaughnessy (2007).

Bibliography

Anderson, K. 2003. 'Introduction', *Sartre Studies International* 9(2): 3–25, 'Sartre on Violence', Symposium on 'Sartre and Terror'.
Aronson, R. 2005. 'Meanwhile: Jean-Paul Sartre at 100: Still Troubling Us Today', *The International Herald Tribune*, 22 June, http://www.nytimes.com/2005/06/21/opinion/21iht-edaronson.html (accessed 27 October 2010).
Arthur, P. 2010. *Unfinished Projects*. London: Verso.
Beauvoir, S de. 1960. *La Force de l'âge*, I and II. Paris: Gallimard.
Boschetti, A.-M. 1985. *Sartre et 'Les Temps Modernes': Une entreprise intellectuelle*. Paris: Minuit.
Boulé, J.-P. 1992. *Sartre médiatique*. Paris: Minard.
———. 2009. 'May '68, Sartre and Sarkozy', *PhaenEx* 4(2): 1–25. http://www.phaenex.uwindsor.ca/ojs/leddy/index.php/phaenex/article/viewFile/2912/2332 (accessed 27 October 2010).
Cohen-Solal, A. 2005. *Sartre, un penseur pour le XXIème siècle*. Paris: Gallimard.
———. 2007. 'Introduction', *Existentialism Is a Humanism* (including A Commentary on *The Stranger*), J. Kulka (ed.), trans. C. Macomber. New Haven, CT: Yale University Press, pp. 3–15.
Conard, M. and R. Porfirio. 2007. *The Philosophy of Film Noir*. Lexington, KY: University of Kentucky Press.
Contat, M. and M. Rybalka (eds). 1970. *Les Ecrits de Sartre*. Paris: Gallimard.
Faison, S. 2008. *Existentialism, Film Noir, and Hard-Boiled Fiction*. New York: Cambria Press.
Falzon, C. 2007. *Philosophy Goes To The Movies: An Introduction To Philosophy*. London: Routledge.
Flynn, T. 2005. 'Sartre at One Hundred – a Man of the Nineteenth Century Addressing the Twenty-First?', *Sartre Studies International* 11(1/2): 1–14.
Galster, I. 1987. 'Images actuelles de Sartre', *Romanistische Zeitschrift für Literaturgeschichte* 11(12): 215–44.
———. 2001. *La Naissance du phénomène Sartre: Raisons d'un succès 1938–1945*. Paris: Seuil.
Judaken, J. (ed.). 2008. *Race after Sartre*. New York: New York University Press.
Keefe, T. 1972. 'Sartre's *L'Existentialisme est un humanisme*', *Philosophical Journal* 9(1): 43–60.

Lapsley, R. and M. Westlake. 1998. *Film Theory. An Introduction*. 2nd ed. [2006]. Manchester: Manchester University Press.

Lévy, B.-H. 2000. *Le Siècle de Sartre*. Paris: Grasset.

Litch, M. 2002. *Philosophy through Film*. London: Routledge.

McBride, W. 1996. *The Development and Meaning of Twentieth-Century Existentialism*. London: Routledge.

———. 2005. 'Sartre at the Twilight of Liberal Democracy', *Sartre Studies International* 11(1/2): 311–18.

Münsterberg, H. 1916. *The Photoplay: A Psychological Study*. New York: D. Appleton and Company.

O'Shaughnessy, M. 2007. *The New Face of Political Cinema: French Film since 1995*. Oxford: Berghahn Books.

Pamerleau, W.C. 2009. *Existentialist Cinema*. London: Palgrave Macmillan.

Poster, M. 1979. *Sartre's Marxism*. London: Pluto Press.

Rothman, W. and M. Keane. 2000. *Reading Cavell's 'The World Viewed': A Philosophical Perspective on Film*. Detroit: Wayne State University Press.

Sartre, J.-P. 1938. *La Nausée (Nausea)*. Paris: Gallimard.

———. 1939. *Le Mur (The Wall)*. Paris: Gallimard.

———. 1943. *L'Etre et le néant (Being and Nothingness)*. Paris: Gallimard.

———. 1945. *Huis Clos* suivi de *Les Mouches (The Flies* followed by *No Exit/In Camera)*. Paris: Gallimard.

———. 1946. *L'Existentialisme est un humanisme (Existentialism Is a Humanism)*. Paris: Nagel.

———. 1947. *Les Faux nez, La Revue du cinéma*. No. 6, 3–27.

———. 1960a. *Critique de la raison dialectique (The Critique of Dialectical Reason)*. Paris: Gallimard.

———. 1960b. *Questions de Méthode (Search for a Method)*. Paris: Gallimard.

———. 1962. *L'Engrenage (In the Mesh)*. Paris: Nagel.

———. 1964. *Les Mots (Words)*. Paris: Gallimard, trans. I. Clephane, London: Penguin Books.

———. 1973. *Un Théâtre de Situations*. Paris: Gallimard (M. Contat and M. Rybalka (eds), *Sartre on Theater*, trans. F. Jellinek. New York: Pantheon Books).

———. 1981. *Œuvres Romanesques*. Paris: Gallimard, Pléiade, 'Entretien avec Jean-Paul Sartre' by C. Grisoli, pp. 1912–17.

———. 1983. *Cahiers pour une morale (Notebooks for an Ethics)*. Paris: Gallimard.

———. 1984. *Le Scénario Freud*. Paris: Gallimard. Ed. used 1985, *The Freud Scenario*, trans. Quintin Hoare, Chicago: University of Chicago Press.

———. 2007. *Typhus*. Paris: Gallimard.

———. [1946] 2007. *Existentialism Is a Humanism* (including A Commentary on *The Stranger*), J. Kulka (ed.), trans. C. Macomber. New Haven, CT: Yale University Press.

Shaw, D.C. 2008. *Film and Philosophy: Taking Movies Seriously*. London: Wallflower Press.

Shearson, W. 1975. 'The Common Assumptions of Existentialist Philosophy', *International Philosophical Quarterly* 15: 131–47.

Webber, J. 2008. *The Existentialism of Jean-Paul Sartre*. London: Routledge Studies in Twentieth-Century Philosophy.

Filmography

Allégret, Y. (dir.). 1953. *Les Orgueilleux* (*The Proud Ones*). Chrysage Films.

Astruc, A. and M. Contat. (dirs.). 1976. *Sartre par lui-même* (*Sartre by Himself*). Institut National de l'Audiovisuel.

Audry, J. (dir.). 1954. *Huis Clos* (*No Exit*).

Delannoy, J. (dir.). 1947. *Les Jeux sont faits* (*The Chips are Down/Second Chance*). Les Films Gibé.

Gassman, V. (dir.). 1956. *Kean* (*Kean: Genius or Scoundrel*). Lux Film.

Huston, J. (dir.). 1962. *Freud: The Secret Passion*. Universal International Pictures.

Pagliero, M. and C. Brabant. (dir.). 1952. *La P. Respectueuse* (*The Respectful Prostitute*). Artès Films.

Rivers, F. (dir.). 1951. *Les Mains sales* (*Dirty Hands*). Les Films Fernand Rivers.

Rouleau, R. (dir.). 1957. *Les Sorcières de Salem* (*The Crucible*). Films Borderie.

Roullet, S. (dir.). 1967. *Le Mur* (*The Wall*). Les Films Niepce.

Sica, V. de. (dir.). 1962. *Les Séquestrés d'Altona* (*The Condemned of Altona*). Société Générale de Cinématographie.

Welles, O. (dir.). 1941. *Citizen Kane*. Mercury Productions, RKO Radio Pictures.

Part I

The Call to Freedom

1

PETER WEIR'S *THE TRUMAN SHOW* AND SARTREAN FREEDOM

Christopher Falzon

In Peter Weir's *The Truman Show* (1998), Truman Burbank (Jim Carrey) gradually discovers that since birth he has been the unwitting star of a reality television show, watched by a global audience. His home town of Seahaven is in fact an enormous studio set filled with hidden cameras; all those around him, including his wife Meryl (Laura Linney) and best friend Marlon (Noah Emmerich), are really actors; and his life is being orchestrated from behind the scenes by the show's producer and director, Christof (Ed Harris). A series of unusual events lead him to question his situation, and he makes increasingly bold attempts to escape. Finally he takes to the sea, and, surviving a storm that Christof throws at him, arrives at the edge of the huge sky-painted dome that surrounds his world. Christof announces himself and tries to convince him to stay, but the film ends with Truman walking through the door marked 'Exit' that leads to the real world outside.

Weir's perhaps most widely praised film has been read in a number of ways. As an urban paranoia film it re-envisions the creeping fear that one's social world has been taken over by strange forces, memorably articulated against the background of McCarthyite anti-communist hysteria in *Invasion of the Body Snatchers* (Don Siegel, 1956). It does so in terms of a more contemporary anxiety, that we might be part of a media-engineered spectacle, being watched by an unseen audience. And while such thinking might be dismissed as delusional (there are even documented psychological conditions featuring such beliefs), it can also play a role in establishing truth. After all, doesn't Descartes put forward the ultimate paranoid scenario – that there might be an all-powerful evil demon intent on deceiving us, such that everything we believe about the world could be false – as a step in his programme of critically assessing beliefs, in order to determine what he can be sure of? *The Truman Show* offers its own version of the possibility of systematic deception, with the all-powerful Christof standing in for the evil demon. Its challenge to unexamined beliefs about our situation has in turn informed the film's reception as a critique of the media-driven fabrication of reality (see e.g., Frost and Banks 2001: 82–4); as well as an updated version of Descartes' critique of what we take for granted in our thinking (see e.g., Blessing 2005).

This chapter is going to focus on another theme that has been associated with the film, the manner in which it engages with existentialist concerns, and Sartre's existentialism in particular. At its heart is a Sartrean affirmation of individual freedom. This turn to the individual also has connections with the film's Cartesian questioning of ordinary presuppositions about the world. Such questioning inevitably robs us of a stable framework for living, and throws us onto our own resources. Descartes himself finds that the only thing he can be sure of is his own existence, and has to use only what he can find within himself to rebuild knowledge. Sartre follows in Descartes' footsteps by questioning whether there are any external grounds for the values we live by. In the absence of external support or justification, Sartre's self has to determine its purpose, the meaning of its existence, through its own choices. At the same time, Sartre understands this lonely self-determination to be central to our humanity. An authentic human existence requires subjective isolation, the rejection of any attempt to subordinate individuals to external determination, authority or coercion. This means a rejection not only of a God who might provide our existence with purpose and direction, but also of social rules and constraints that might give our life an orienting framework. To submit to such constraints is to have security, but to lose oneself.

As Jonathan Rayner notes, an abiding theme in Weir's work is this very idea, that integration into society amounts to a loss of personality and authority (Rayner 2003: 27). Weir's American films in particular 'predominantly remain narratives of individual struggles against authority, constraint, mundanity, and conformity' (Rayner 2003: 229). These are struggles typically undertaken for the sake of personal realisation and self-affirmation. Thus in *Dead Poets Society* (1989), a constraining institutional milieu is challenged in the name of individual self-expression and a fully lived life. In *Fearless* (1993) the protagonist, having survived a plane crash, is moved to reject his old life, family and friends in order to find a new meaning for his existence. And in *The Truman Show*, the individual finds self-affirmation in determining the meaning and direction of his life, in the face of a constraining and repressive social situation. This affirmation begins with Truman's questioning of everything he has hitherto relied on to structure his existence. His Cartesian-style questioning leads directly to the realisation that these forms are the product of external determination, through which his life has been controlled. It is a comfortable, secure life, but not ultimately his own. It falls upon him to reject these impositions, assert his freedom and establish a meaningful life for himself.

This is where the film reveals a strong, Sartrean commitment to the individual's capacity for self-determination. Sartre is also recalled in so far as Truman's rejection of external determination includes both a repudiation of God, or at least Christof now viewed as a God-like figure; and of social constraints and demands, with Christof in this case as locus of social control. We will be examining these Sartrean themes in the film in more detail. However, there are also aspects of the film that seem to undermine its own commitment to individual freedom, that pose questions concerning the extent of social situatedness and influence on the individual that the later Sartre himself was to pose with regard to his existentialism. This will be addressed towards the end of the discussion.

Individual Freedom

The first theme, then, is the film's Sartrean affirmation of individual freedom, in the face of external influences and pressures to conform. As Rayner notes, the film poses existential questions 'through its concentration on an isolated individual, who is subject to others' demands but who seeks individual meaning' (Rayner 2003: 243). It also offers an account of 'existential awakening', from a life of unthinking conformity to the requirements of one's role and the expectations of others, to a recognition of one's capacity for self-determination. Truman's initial state of integration and conformity is emphasised in the opening scenes of the film. The setting in which Truman finds himself has the look of an idyllic fifties-style community, clean, manicured and orderly, but inevitably also self-enclosed, conservative and fixed in its ways. Truman's first appearance is as an apparently ideal member of such a community. He is conservatively dressed, and his life is one of routine, reliability and responsibility. His greeting to his neighbours is evidently part of a routine that has been going on for a long time, he takes a set route to work, and his life is bound by the conventional requirements of house, marriage, car and desk job.

These routines and responsibilities effectively conspire to keep Truman tied down. The conceit of the film, that he is living in a huge studio set where it is important that he remain predictable and constrained, means that his confinement in conventional patterns of life is also a literal means of imprisonment, engineered to ensure his compliance. Yet even if his situation were not really one of large-scale imprisonment, it would still provide an ideal setting for existential rebellion. Such rebellion is by no means absent even at this stage. Truman already has misgivings about his situation, associated with dreams of travel and his yearning for Sylvia (Natascha McElhone), the object of a brief 'unscripted' college romance that ended with her apparent move to Fiji (in reality the actress has been banished from the set). But his current circumstances, including his marriage to Meryl, have been arranged to keep these yearnings in check. This confinement is successful to the extent that Truman continues to live his life within conventional patterns. It is only a series of external events, anomalies he encounters, that bring him to seriously question his situation and initiate the main action of the film.

Truman has something in common with Sartre's protagonist Roquentin in *Nausea* (1938). Roquentin similarly finds himself in a small town, a closed, rather stifling setting. Certainly he is not as constrained by role, demands and expectations as Truman. He is not tied to family or friends, and he does not need to work for a living because he can rely on an inheritance. He does, however, have various presuppositions about the world, in terms of which the world and his own existence are seen as meaningful and justified, and which come into question in the course of the novel. Through Roquentin, Sartre invites us to shake off our ordinary presuppositions about the world and ourselves (see Falzon 2005). In Roquentin's case, no specific event moves him down this path. There is simply a growing sense of unease about his environment, in which things and people around him, and eventually his own existence, come to appear strange, disturbing, nauseating. Ultimately he comes to realise that his feeling of nausea is the apprehension of the contingency of things and of his own existence, their utter lack of point and purpose, external justification or necessity (Sartre [1938] 2000: 188).

Both Roquentin and Truman, then, enact a kind of Cartesian questioning of their situation, through which the presuppositions that formerly structured their existence and gave it meaning come to be challenged. In Roquentin's case, his existence turns out to be meaningless, in the sense of lacking necessity. His nausea represents an awakening from the illusion of meaning, a 'revealing of the world' (Beauvoir 1984: 207). For Truman, the most radical of Descartes' sceptical considerations, the supposition that there might be an evil demon bent on deceiving him, turns out to be a reality in the figure of Christof who has been secretly orchestrating Truman's existence. He finds that he has not only been labouring under an illusion, but has been in reality the plaything of external forces. His existence lacks meaning because it does not derive from him, because he has been playing a role scripted and determined by someone else (see Blessing 2005: 8). Both Sartre and *The Truman Show* also follow in Descartes' footsteps in that this process of questioning leads to the affirmation of a sovereign self.

Sartre's re-enactment of Cartesian doubt in *Nausea* at first seems to be simply destructive, robbing his existence of justification. He does encounter himself in the process, but not as the chastely disembodied Cartesian self, the 'thinking thing'. Rather it is as an embodied being whose thinking is permeated by corporeal existence. Existence, as Roquentin puts it, 'takes my thoughts from behind and gently expands them from behind' (Sartre [1938] 2000: 148; see Manser 1966: 11), and 'this is only to say that I too am infected by the nauseating lack of necessity that afflicts all existence'. However, what is primarily a destructive process in *Nausea* also clears the way for the human being to take centre stage as the sovereign source of meaning in *Being and Nothingness* (1943). Now, without any external support whatsoever, through wholly free choices, we choose our purposes and give meaning to our existence. As with Descartes, the self is affirmed as the starting point. It is worth noting, however, that Sartre still distances himself from Descartes in that the self is never seen as disembodied. It is situated in relation to the world (the 'in-itself'), and to its own corporeal existence (its 'facticity'). In addition, Sartre locates this self in a world of others, a social situation. Nonetheless, he also affirms the primacy of the free self, in the face of any kind of external determination or coercion. The self is never determined by the world or its own facticity. However constraining our situations might be, no matter how much they impact on us, we are always free to escape them, to transcend them and freely define ourselves (Fox 2003: 11).

This detour through Sartre's development might seem to have taken us far from *The Truman Show*, but in fact Sartre arrives at a position quite close to it. Broadly speaking, the film's trajectory is also a journey towards the affirmation of the sovereign individual, capable of self-determination, in this case directly in the face of any kind of external determination or coercion. Truman's questioning of the forms that structure his existence involves the recognition that these have been determined by others, and ultimately by Christof. To that extent, Truman has been deprived of personality and identity. However, the film also affirms his capacity to escape these imposed forms, to exercise his freedom, and to determine the meaning and direction of his existence for himself. In this way *The Truman Show* embraces a Sartrean freedom of self-definition in the face of external determination and coercion. Nevertheless, there is also a certain divergence from Sartre here. Sartre insists on a self that although free always remains situated, and which also longs for determination even as it escapes it. *The Truman Show*'s affirmation of freedom is more straightforward; it involves a complete, and regret-free, repudiation of situation. Truman can escape entirely from his circumstances, and happily does so. As we pursue the film's engagement with Sartrean themes in more detail, this divergence will be evident at a number of points.

Freedom and God

Roquentin's questioning of the presuppositions that give meaning to his existence is also bound up with the rejection of a God, a being who might 'overcome contingency', provide ultimate justification, and give human existence purpose and direction (Sartre [1938] 2000: 188). That Sartre's subsequent affirmation of the free self also presupposes this rejection is made explicit in *Existentialism Is a Humanism* (1946). There he argues that the notion of God stands in the way of freedom. For Christianity in particular, Sartre argues, there is a conception of what a human being essentially is that dwells in the divine understanding, and which is realised when God creates human beings – just as an artisan has a conception of a paper knife before bringing one into existence. Made to a formula, human beings would automatically have certain values and pursue certain goals. However, 'if God does not exist there is at least one being in whom existence precedes essence, a being who exists before he can be defined by any concept of it' (Sartre [1946] 2007: 22). In short, dispensing with God means that human beings, without a pre-ordained essence to define them, are free to make themselves.

In *The Truman Show* freedom is similarly construed in terms of rejecting God, or at least escaping from Christof in so far as he can be seen as a God-like figure. He certainly occupies a God-like position in the film. Sitting high above Seahaven in the 'Omnicom Sphere' that masquerades as the moon, he is the architect of Truman's world, observing, scripting and guiding his life. The film does not miss the opportunity to allude to his elevated status. At the end of the film when he finally announces himself to Truman it is as a booming voice in the sky, and he tells him that he is 'the creator ... of a television show'. Christof's role as the creator-artist behind the scenes recalls Sartre's characterisation of God as a 'superlative artisan' in *Existentialism Is a Humanism* (Sartre [1946] 2007: 21). Christof wants to fashion Truman as if he were a kind of artefact, 'designing' him according to a pre-arranged script. In *The Truman Show*, God is a real presence, but this does not mean that freedom is excluded. Rather, Christof is a God who insists that his creature is free to leave 'at any time'; and the rejection of God here takes the form of revolt, rebellion against a controlling figure.

This is also the case with Sartre in some of his formulations, where God becomes a real presence for dramatic purposes. Freedom becomes overt revolt against God in Sartre's play *The Flies* ([1944] 1989). In this reworking of the Greek legend, Orestes returns to Argos to avenge the murder of his father, the king, by killing his usurper. In the original play by Aeschylus, Orestes had no choice but to avenge his father's murder; it was a destiny he could not escape, the result of a curse. In Sartre's version, however, Orestes is no longer the victim of a curse, but freely decides to do his duty and commit this act. In so doing he defies Zeus, who as Hazel Barnes suggests may be taken to represent the traditional concept of God in Christianity (Barnes 1959: 85). Towards the end, Zeus reveals himself to Orestes as the creator of all things, and demands he conform to his will. In response, Orestes makes a distinction between things that are determined, and human beings who are free: 'You are the king of the gods, king of stones and stars, king of the waves and the sea. But you are not the king of man ... I am my freedom. No sooner had you created me than I ceased to be yours' (Sartre [1944] 1989: 117). Human freedom thus means rebellion against God; and this, as Zeus acknowledges, is the beginning of the end of the rule of the Gods over humanity. As Barnes puts it: 'Orestes knows fully all that his rebellion involves. It means that he accepts for himself no standard, law, excuse or remedy which comes from either God or Nature. He must decide alone and find his right way, must determine his own goal' (Barnes 1959: 94).

The Truman Show embraces this idea of freedom as rebellion in the face of God, the rejection of divine authority. When Truman leaves the world of Seahaven at the very end of the film, it is the final rejection of Christof's rule in favour of self-determination, open possibilities and an uncertain future. Interestingly, Zeus as an image of God-like authority also suggested itself to Weir, for whom 'Christof is Zeus, in the sense that he's trying to control the mortals ... He could do other God-like things, including controlling the weather, but he cannot, as Christof/Zeus does, begin to interfere with the decisions his creature has taken, which is to leave' (Weir 1998: 22). The value that the film gives to freedom is further emphasised in that the world Truman leaves is comfortable and secure, a virtual Eden, insulated from the harshness of the external world. His world has, after all, been created as an ideal world, 'the way the world should be', as Christof puts it while defending himself from Sylvia's criticisms when she rings during an on-air interview. It is the outside world, he thinks, that is the 'sick place'. In his final encounter with Truman he points out that the world Truman is trying to escape from is much more desirable than the real thing. But the film clearly values independence and freedom over a controlled, imprisoned life, however comfortable and secure that life might be.

Famously these are the alternatives – freedom versus happiness in a controlled world – presented by the Grand Inquisitor in Dostoevsky's *Brothers Karamazov*. In Ivan Karamazov's parable, Christ returns to Earth only to be arrested by the Inquisition. The Inquisitor visits him in his cell in order to justify his position. He insists that people want to be subjected to authority, the domination of himself and his kind, because freedom is too great a burden for mortal human beings to bear. It only brings them disorder, uncertainty and unhappiness. The first thing people want to do is to give it away, and it is unrealistic and cruel to expect anything else from them. Out of 'love and pity', the Inquisitor and the Church will take on the responsibility that the rest of humanity so desperately wants to escape. In this story it is Christ who stands on the side of freedom. Christ expects people to freely choose to follow him, which the Inquisitor insists is asking too much. Had Christ respected man less he would have loved him more (Dostoevsky 2003: 334). Here Sartre can be aligned with Christ in expecting individuals to embrace their freedom, even if it is a cause of unhappiness. Christof's position is of course closer to that of the Grand Inquisitor. Like the Inquisitor, Christof thinks he is helping Truman by providing him with a secure if controlled environment; and similarly believes that Truman does not want to be free. As he claims during Sylvia's phone call, 'he can leave at any time ... what distresses you really, caller, is that ultimately, Truman prefers his "cell", as you call it'.

But if *The Truman Show* rejects Christof's controlled world, we can also discern a divergence from Sartre's account, because of the film's relatively straightforward affirmation of freedom. Particularly in *Being and Nothingness*, Sartre is willing to acknowledge that freedom, while central to our humanity, is also a terrible burden. Utterly responsible for our choices, without any support or guidance, we experience our freedom in the form of anguish. We yearn for the security of a fixed, determined identity, and are constantly tempted to disown freedom, to hide from anguish in forms of self-deception or 'bad faith'. In *Existentialism Is a Humanism*, although Sartre finds in the absence of a controlling God the opportunity for human beings to make their own existence, he also speaks of humanity as having been 'abandoned' by God, leaving us without any guiding values or direction. Truman in contrast does not feel any sense of loss when he parts ways with Christof. Freedom is not a burden or the source of anguish for Truman. To that extent the film departs from Sartre's view of freedom. It does have affinities with Sartre's largely sunny characterisation of freedom in *The Flies*, where the burdensome aspect is absent and freedom is simply something exhilarating, to be rejoiced in. But *The Flies* is atypical of Sartre's existentialism; the 'dark' side of freedom is more usually evident.

Freedom and the Other

Freedom for Sartre is asserted not only in the face of God, but also in the face of others, of social circumstances. Indeed Sartre suggests God is merely the concept of the other pushed to the limit (Sartre [1943] 1958: 266). But whereas Sartre's God is primarily an absent figure, one who has left the scene, the other is an inescapable part of our situation. Sartre as mentioned is keen to see the self as situated. As one commentator puts it: '[t]he whole strategy in *Being and Nothingness* is to consider the consciousness or for-itself first and situate it gradually in its concrete situation in the world, starting with the in-itself' (Shearson 1980: 158). And this concrete situation includes our location in a world of other people, a social world. Freedom thus needs to be asserted in the face of other people, who continually threaten to undermine it, to steal it from us. At the same time it remains the case for Sartre that no matter how oppressive or constraining our social circumstances, we are always free to rise above them, to exercise our capacity for self-determination.

This turn from God to the other brings Sartre's trajectory even closer to that of *The Truman Show*. Truman's freedom above all involves confrontation with a world of social control and constraint, a repudiation of patterns of life manufactured by others, and ultimately by Christof. Christof does not only play the part of a God-like figure. He is also the locus of social control, designing and regulating the world in which Truman is required to play his role. Christof's omniscience involves the eyes and ears of the townspeople along with an extensive network of hidden cameras, and is instrumental in maintaining control. At the same time the film affirms the individual's essential freedom in the face of social constraint and control. It remains confident in Truman's ability to reject imposed forms and patterns, and to determine the direction of his existence for himself. As with Sartre, individuals remain free no matter how oppressive or constraining their social circumstances.

Sartre provides a 'scopic' account of our relations with others, which accords well with the film's emphasis on observation as a key element in social control. In *Being and Nothingness*, Sartre's account of our intersubjective relations is primarily in terms of 'being seen', of my being the object of 'the look'. The other's look, which makes me aware of myself as I appear to the other, is a threat to my freedom that needs to be overcome. *The Truman Show* has its protagonist as the object of near-continual surveillance, both by the people around him and by Christof behind the scenes. Occasionally the film itself adopts the viewpoint of one of the concealed cameras, vignetting the edges of the frame and adopting an awkward framing. The main action of the film is precipitated by Truman's becoming aware of being looked at, and seeking to escape from that look. Initially he is not aware of being an object of observation. Not only is he entirely unaware of Christof at this stage; he doesn't seem to be especially troubled by those around him. He certainly wants to hide away from them occasionally, as he does at one point in order to secretly assemble a picture of Sylvia from magazine clippings. But amongst others he does not seem to be especially aware of himself as an object of their gaze, and does not moderate his behaviour. He seems to be un-self-consciously engaged in his activities, and integrated into his social environment.

Truman's existence is transformed by the sudden awareness that he is being observed by others. This becomes evident when he hears voices on his car radio detailing his progress to work. From this point on he becomes concerned that he is being watched and followed. He becomes suspicious of everyone around him, noticing signs of observation everywhere: the slight glance of the passerby in his direction, the car mirrors that seem to turn towards him. What are the consequences of being looked at? As Sartre suggests, it means that I am no longer the centre of the world, un-self-consciously immersed in my projects. I am alienated from myself, aware of myself as an object in the other's world. The other, says Sartre, is my 'original fall' (Sartre [1943] 1958: 288–89). With Seahaven as a kind of Eden, the characterisation is especially apt for Truman's situation; through the appearance of the other, Truman has been dislodged from his privileged position. Sartre also points to a number of feelings through which the other's look is revealed to me; shame in the first instance, but as one commentator notes, '[a]longside shame can be listed such related phenomena as guilt, embarrassment and paranoia' (Cox 2006: 46). It is above all through feelings of paranoia that Truman experiences his object status. He confides to his friend Marlon that people seem to be talking about him, and that he is definitely being followed, though it's hard to say by whom as they 'look like ordinary people'.

Two further aspects of Sartre's description of being looked at are evident in the film. First, once we are aware of the other's gaze, we realise that we are no longer masters of our situation. As Mary Warnock puts it, paraphrasing Sartre:

[t]here is something in it that in principle eludes one, namely the Other's thoughts. Things may be done to me that I do not understand; there can be a kind of Kafkaesque quality in real life, but only when I think of myself under the gaze of the other.

(Warnock 1965: 79)

This is Truman's experience. He finds that people around him are acting strangely, keeping an eye on him for some unknown reason. Even those closest to him, like his wife Meryl, have become mysterious. He notices in a photo that she was crossing her fingers during their wedding. Secondly, no longer able to control my situation, 'I am in the eyes of the other an object not of perception but of appraisal' (Warnock 1965: 79). That is, I can be judged and labelled by others, given a 'character', cast in a role not of my choosing. And this becomes Truman's overwhelming sense of himself, that he is playing a role determined by others who expect him to behave in 'normal' ways. Those closest to him now seem to be imposing expectations upon him, as in the scene where he sits uncomfortably between his wife and mother, both none-too-subtly hinting that it is time for him to embrace fatherhood.

How are we to react to these impositions of the other, the judgemental look that robs us of our freedom? Truman's overriding response is to challenge the expectations about who he is and how he should behave. He wants to repudiate these imposed forms, to act spontaneously and unpredictably. Instead of going into the office he ducks into the building next door, steps into the road and stops traffic, and takes off in his car with a reluctant Meryl in search of a way out of Seahaven. Up to a point this conforms to Sartre's account. Since the freedom of the other robs me of my freedom, affirming my freedom requires that I escape the sway of the other. However, here the film once again diverges from the Sartrean account. To return to this account for a moment, Sartre insists, as we have seen, that the self is situated in relation to the world and facticity, and in relation to other people. We depend on the look of others to experience feelings like shame and paranoia; and more broadly, Sartre's account acknowledges the extent to which my self-image depends on how others regard me. At the same time he sees this dependence in essentially negative terms. To be defined by others is a threat to my freedom. Affirming my freedom requires that I free myself from the hold of the other, making them in turn the object of my defining gaze. Thus I may always exist in situation, in a world of others, but as a free being my belonging takes the form of endless conflict with those others (Sartre [1943] 1958: 364), in a world where everyone is committed to negating the freedom of their fellows.

Sartre also describes various concrete relations with the other, in which we try, though always fruitlessly, to overcome this conflict. We may try to reduce the other entirely to an object, the attitude of sadism, which fails in so far as the other always remains free and can at any time 'return the look', as in the defiant look of the torture victim. Alternatively, we can try to be no more than an object for the other, to surrender to their freedom, in the attitude of masochism. This fails because we cannot truly deny our freedom, and are in any case freely using the other as a means of giving ourselves a determinate identity. Or we can try to assimilate the other's freedom to ours while simultaneously preserving them as free subjects, in the attitude of love. Here we want to be defined by the other, but in the way we choose to be, as we ideally see ourselves. This fails since we are seeking, impossibly, to both control the other and maintain them as free (Sartre [1943] 1958: 367). In practice, the other can always revoke their consent to define us as we want to be defined, and we can still be at the mercy of their freedom, their whims or sadism. Love strives for the impossible synthesis of determination through the other and freedom in the face of the other, and cannot succeed.

Where *The Truman Show* diverges from Sartre is once again in its relatively straightforward affirmation of freedom. Here, the free self is not understood to be inherently situated amongst others, so that freedom involves endless conflict. Truman's freedom is expressed solely through escape, through the rejection of others in order to enjoy unlimited self-determination. His response to the discovery that he is being watched is pure flight, attempts to escape by car, plane and bus; and then there is the final, successful escape by boat under cover of night. The response from the other side is equally one-sided, the essentially sadistic attempt to overcome Truman's freedom and reduce him to a compliant object, whatever the cost. This is evident in Truman's encounter with Christof himself in the final stages of the film. Christof's response to Truman's bid for freedom borders on the murderous. Once Truman is located, far out at sea, Christof engineers a storm to crush him, perhaps even to kill him.

It is when Truman has survived the storm and reached the limits of his world, the side of the dome surrounding the studio set, that Christof reveals himself directly to Truman. As Truman stands before the door marked 'Exit', Christof announces himself as the creator of the show Truman has been unknowingly starring in. He tells him he has been watching him all his life, and knows him better than he knows himself; and that while he cannot stop him, he does not think he will leave to go into an uncertain world. Christof clearly has affection for Truman – at one point we see him tenderly stroking Truman's sleeping face on the television monitor – but this does not amount to love, at least not as Sartre defines it. Christof acknowledges Truman's freedom, but does not seek to possess it as freedom. Rather, he wants Truman to agree to stay in Seahaven, to submit to him, to become once more a compliant object. This is more like a continuation of Christof's sadism. If it is love, it is closer to the love that Dostoevsky's Grand Inquisitor has for humanity. Out of love, Christof wants to relieve Truman of the burden of freedom, to take it on for himself, so that Truman can have security and happiness in the controlled world of Seahaven. It is a paternalistic, stifling love.

For his part, Truman has no love for Christof. He does not need Christof to affirm him as the kind of person he wants to be, does not require external definition in any form. In that respect we can contrast him with the characters in Sartre's 1944 play *In Camera* (also known as *No Exit*), who find themselves in a drawing room in what turns out to be Hell. Each of them is concerned for the look of the other, so as to confirm them as having the character they ideally want to have. Of course, to the extent that they are dependent on the other's look, they are also at the mercy of their sadistic whims. Thus *In Camera*'s Garcin looks to Inez to regard him as he wants to be regarded, as a hero; but he is thereby exposed to her harsh judgements, as she pronounces him a coward. Yet even when the door to the room springs open, and it is possible for Garcin to escape, he does not do so. There is no exit. If he leaves without convincing Inez, her judgemental look will continue to haunt him. As he says: 'it's you whom I have to convince; you are of my kind. Did you suppose I meant to go? No, I couldn't leave you here, gloating over my defeat, with all those thoughts about me running in your head' (Sartre [1944] 1989: 42). He needs to convince her to see him as heroic. Truman, however, is under no such constraint. He does not need the affirmation of others; and by the same token, he is not at the mercy of Christof's judgement, or his sadism. Not dependent on others, he can go through the door; he can make his escape.

So Truman asserts his freedom by escaping from Seahaven, and the film offers a ringing affirmation of the human capacity for freedom and self-determination in the face of demands for conformity. There is nonetheless an aspect of the film that also subverts the straightforward affirmation of freedom. A back story is alluded to, which indicates that Truman has been profoundly shaped by his environment, shaped from birth to be a certain kind of person; and that it is this, rather than overt force, that ensures his continuing imprisonment. We can see in flashback how his adventurous impulses have been tamed by his upbringing and education. His on-set father tells the young Truman that he needs to know his limitations, his teachers discourage exploration since there is nothing new to discover. Specific associations have also been established to constrain him, such as a fear of water instilled by being made to witness his father's apparent drowning. The film also makes much of the ongoing messages in the media promoting conformity and discouraging transgression; newspapers name the town the best place to live, television shows extol the virtues of small town life. Those close to him, his wife, mother and best friend, reinforce these messages. There has evidently been an ongoing process of indoctrination, over a long time, designed to give Truman the right kind of character and outlook, to render him docile and compliant.

We might even speak here of the inculcation of a 'submissive consciousness', characterised by Simone de Beauvoir in terms that seem peculiarly appropriate to Truman:

> [t]here are beings whose life slips by in an infantile world because, having been kept in a state of servitude and ignorance, they have no means of breaking the ceiling which is stretched over their heads. Like the child, they can exercise their freedom, but only within a universe which has been set up before them, without them.
>
> (Beauvoir 1948: 37)

Seeing Truman as having been shaped by a long process of education and indoctrination makes it possible to account for his utter predictability when we first meet him, and the way he seems to be seamlessly integrated into his social environment. We might similarly account for his failure to question his circumstances over such a long period of time. And it becomes clearly disingenuous of Christof to claim that Truman can leave any time, that ultimately he 'prefers his cell', since a great deal of work has been done to promote that compliant state of mind.

Christof also claims that while Truman's world is counterfeit there is nothing fake about Truman, implying as Michael Bliss notes, that there is 'a part of the personality that is independent of the effect of culture and the media' (Bliss 2000: 175). But as Bliss points out, the level of cultural influence is so high in *The Truman Show* that it is difficult to believe this is true. Indeed, the film's allusion to the force of circumstances stands in some tension with its main theme, its strong affirmation of individual freedom. Truman repudiates everything that structures his world and escapes in order to determine himself, but can he escape his circumstances and persona so decisively, given that he has been so thoroughly influenced by his environment? The emphasis on environmental influences seems to undermine the film's celebration of radical autonomy. This tension is never confronted since the aspect of indoctrination is marginalised, alluded to mainly in flashback, as something that occurred before the struggle for freedom that the film focuses on. Nonetheless it remains in the background; and it also poses a more general question about the individual's capacity for self-determination, given that they exist in and are inevitably shaped by their social circumstances.

Sartre also encounters this problematic in his existentialism. In his strong affirmation of individual freedom, he arguably downplays the force of circumstances. As noted, he certainly wants to situate the self, to locate it in relation to the world, facticity, and other people. But he insists that we also remain entirely free; no matter how constraining our circumstances, we are always free to escape them, to transcend them and freely define ourselves. This aspect of his account has led to accusations that he remains tied to an abstract, Cartesian conception of the self, ultimately untouched by its immersion in the world (Fox 2003: 11–14). In his later, post-existentialist thinking, Sartre was to modify his position to take social circumstances more fully into account. For the later Sartre we are all, to some extent, formed by the cultures in which we are born – formed by our prescribed value in that culture, by our class position, our sex, our race, our language, our means of providing for our subsistence, and so on. And we are no longer free regardless of circumstances. Some situations are more limiting, more oppressive than others, and oppressive circumstances can even condition the way we think, limiting our capacity to envisage alternatives to our current situation. Nonetheless, Sartre doesn't want to say that we are completely a product of our social and political circumstances. As he puts it in a late interview:

human beings can always make something out of what is made of them. This is the limit I would today accord to freedom – the small movement which makes a totally conditioned human being someone who does not simply render back completely what his conditioning has given him.

(Sartre [1969] 1983: 35)

The later Sartre, then, can be seen as attempting to reconcile freedom and determination, to acknowledge social circumstances without losing the notion of freedom. As such he seeks to go beyond the abstract freedom of his earlier existentialist thought, his downplaying of social influence. He also goes beyond *The Truman Show*, which similarly affirms a capacity for self-determination, but more straightforwardly, by repudiating any dependence on situation. While the film does acknowledge the influence of social circumstances on Truman's formation, it avoids confronting the apparent conflict between freedom and determination by marginalising the latter, placing it outside the main action of the film. It is thus able to affirm its strong notion of individual freedom, at the cost of failing to take its own acknowledgement of social influence seriously. In the last analysis we can say that *The Truman Show* is existentialist not only in its affirmation of individual freedom but also in so far as it shares the limitations of Sartre's existentialism.

Bibliography

Barnes, H. 1959. *Humanistic Existentialism: The Literature of Possibility*. Lincoln, NE: University of Nebraska.

Beauvoir, S. de. 1948. *The Ethics of Ambiguity*, trans. B. Frechtman. New York: Citadel.

———. 1984. *Adieux: A Farewell to Sartre*, trans. P. O'Brien. Harmondsworth: Penguin.

Blessing, K. 2005. 'Deceit and Doubt: The Search for Truth in *The Truman Show* and Descartes' *Meditations*', in Kimberley A. Blessing and Paul J. Tudico (eds), *Movies and the Meaning of Life*. Chicago and La Salle, IL: Open Court, pp. 3–16.

Bliss, M. 2000. *Dreams Within a Dream: the Films of Peter Weir*. Carbondale, IL: Southern Illinois University Press.

Cox, G. 2006. *Sartre: A Guide for the Perplexed*. London and New York: Continuum.

Dostoevsky, F. 2003. *The Brothers Karamazov*, trans. D. McDuff. Harmondsworth: Penguin.

Falzon, C. 2005. 'Sartre and Meaningful Existence', in A. Rolls and E. Rechniewski (eds), *Sartre's Nausea: Text, Context, Intertext*. Amsterdam and New York: Rodopi, pp. 105–20.

Fox, N.F. 2003. *The New Sartre*. London: Continuum.

Frost, M. and R. Banks. 2001. *Lessons from Reel Life: Movies, Meaning and Myth-Making*. Adelaide: Open Book.

Manser, A. 1966. *Sartre: A Philosophic Study*. London: Athlone.

Rayner, J. 2003. *The Films of Peter Weir*. New York and London: Continuum.

Sartre, J.-P. [1938] 2000. *Nausea*, trans. R. Baldick. Harmondsworth: Penguin.

———. [1943] 1958. *Being and Nothingness*, trans. H. Barnes. London: Methuen.

———. [1944] 1989. 'The Flies', in *No Exit and Three Other Plays*, trans. S. Gilbert. New York: Vintage International.

———. [1946] 2007. 'Existentialism is a Humanism', in J. Kulka (ed.), *Existentialism Is a Humanism*, trans. C. Macomber. New Haven, CT and London: Yale University Press.

———. [1969] 1983. 'The Itinerary of a Thought', in *Between Existentialism and Marxism*. London: Verso, pp. 33–64.

Shearson, W. 1980. *The Notion of Encounter*. Ottowa: Canadian Library of Philosophy.

Warnock, M. 1965. *The Philosophy of Sartre*. London: Hutchinson.

Weir, P. 1998. 'Designing Visions', interview with Paul Kalina, *Cinema Papers* (127) October: 18–22, 56.

Filmography

Weir, P. (dir.). 1998. *The Truman Show*. Paramount Pictures. Scott Rudin Productions.

2

MICHAEL HANEKE AND THE CONSEQUENCES OF RADICAL FREEDOM

Kevin L. Stoehr

Many of the feature films and television productions of screenwriter-director Michael Haneke explore the individual's unsuccessful attempts in coming to terms with his or her innate autonomy. Many existentialist thinkers, including Jean-Paul Sartre in his lecture *Existentialism Is a Humanism*, suggest a kind of radical freedom that is implied by human subjectivity and that provides opportunities for creative individuality. Yet such freedom also poses serious challenges that may lead a person away from the path to genuine self-realisation and instead to a life of untruthfulness or inauthenticity, to a slavish type of conformism, or to a pathological form of life-negation. This is particularly the case when the recognition of such freedom is joined with an acknowledgement of the contingent circumstances in which individuals continually find themselves.

Sartre and other existentialist thinkers such as Martin Heidegger typically refer to these contingent conditions of freedom in terms of a human being's 'facticity'. In general, this idea refers to the fact that humans already exist in a world of concrete and immediate particularities with which we must cope, long before we begin to become conscious of and make sense of these immediate conditions. And through the specific visual and narrative strategies employed in a majority of his films, Haneke recurrently emphasises the facticity of human existence and the ways in which freedom is realised or not realised within the constraints of an individual's specific 'situatedness'. In Haneke's recent film *The White Ribbon* (2009), for example, he explores the ways in which children growing up in a rigidly disciplined Protestant village in northern Germany circa 1913 become psychologically repressed by the strict mores of that society and subsequently use their limited freedom to take vengeance against the community's oppressive elders. The children react violently against a situation in which they already find themselves, into which they have been born, and though they appear to be partially dehumanised by the rituals and practices of their village, the children take action (however negative) in response to their unwilling, unchosen membership in this community.[1]

Sartre emphasises the inherent freedom of the human being in the following excerpt from his above-mentioned lecture. A basic pre-condition of our belief in radical freedom is the kind of 'godless' existentialism that Sartre professes as his adopted worldview:

> Atheistic existentialism, which I represent, is more consistent. It states that if God does not exist, there is at least one being in whom existence precedes essence – a being whose existence comes before its essence, a being who exists before he can be defined by any concept of it. That being is man, or, as Heidegger put it, the human reality. What do we mean here by 'existence precedes essence'? We mean that man first exists: he materializes in the world, encounters himself, and only afterward defines himself. If man as existentialists conceive of him cannot be defined, it is because to begin with he is nothing. He will not be anything until later, and then he will be what he makes of himself. Thus, there is no human nature since there is no God to conceive of it. Man is not only that which he conceives himself to be, but that which he wills himself to be, and since he conceives of himself only after he exists, just as he wills himself to be after being thrown into existence, man is nothing other than what he makes of himself. This is the first principle of existentialism ... Man is indeed a project that has a subjective existence, rather unlike that of a patch of moss, a spreading fungus, or a cauliflower. Prior to that projection of the self, nothing exists, not even in divine intelligence, and man shall attain existence, only when he is what he projects himself to be ... If, however, existence truly does precede essence, man is responsible for what he is. Thus, the first effect of existentialism is to make every man conscious of what he is, and to make him solely responsible for his own existence.
>
> (Sartre [1946] 2007: 22–23)

The freedom suggested by Sartre entails responsibility for the individual who comes to terms with the proposition that human reality (what Heidegger calls 'Da-Sein' or 'being-there') is not pre-defined or pre-determined like some artificially designed invention or God-given landscape. According to this view, being human is inherently subjective and thus self-creating in a dynamic, open-ended manner. At the same time, human reality is always finite, perspectival, and context-dependent, since our perceptions and experiences are shaped by given or chosen points of orientation that inevitably fluctuate. We are always free, according to Sartre, but always within certain restrictions established by the resistance of reality. And in the sense that a human individual is responsible for his or her own existence after a certain point in life, through the very choices in actions and attitudes that constitute one's self-creation, there may emerge a feeling of angst or despair on the part of some individuals when they realise that there are no absolute guarantees or fixed foundations in a life that is saturated by chance and contingency. This is the type of dread about one's own existence that is expressed by the title of Sartre's famous novel *Nausea* and that is also suggested by characters in a good number of Haneke's films.

One problem that is associated with the responsibility implied by the task of 'choosing oneself' is the possibility of one's outright refusal to accept, on a consistent basis, the basic freedom that is integral to human reality. This is related to the problem of inauthenticity. The inauthentic person is one who typically denies the truth of his or her freedom to self-create in an individuating manner and who chooses instead to lead a life that is chiefly conditioned by others (society, religion, government, etc.). In his *On the Genealogy of Morals*, Sartre's intellectual forebear Friedrich Nietzsche refers to such an inauthentic person as a 'slave'. The slave is a weak-willed conformist who resents the creative individuality of any person (a 'master') who does not similarly live life in strict accordance with external conditions or structures (Nietzsche [1887] 1989).[2] To be authentic, on the other hand, is to acknowledge that one is free to respond in various ways – and not merely in ways that are pre-established by God or Nature or Society – to the given situations into which one has been 'thrown' (to use another Heideggerian term).[3]

Apart from a slavish type of conformism, another problem that is connected with a consciousness of one's autonomy and self-responsibility involves the spectre of moral indifference and even nihilism. Human freedom entails that an individual *should* view himself or herself as a self-legislator and a values-creator who is engaged in his or her own self-creation. According to this view, values should *not* be determined by others and handed down to one as if set in stone. It is always a choice as to whether one accepts, rejects, modifies, or creates certain values that are in question. But the possible anguish that can result from a person's difficulty in acknowledging this kind of freedom and accountability may drive certain individuals to a loss of conviction in *any* values, whether they be imposed by others or self-determined. This loss of conviction results in moral apathy toward external sources of value-determination and, when directed toward oneself as a values-legislator, results in the overall attitude that *nothing* has intrinsic value, including one's own being. In his unpublished writings, Nietzsche refers to the individual who maintains consistently that nothing matters or nothing makes a difference as a 'pathological' or 'passive' nihilist, one who negates life in general, including one's own power of constructing new values (Nietzsche [1901] 1968).[4]

Haneke's works deal on a regular basis with problems of inauthenticity, moral indifference, and outright nihilism. He is a filmmaker who, especially in his choices of subject matter, summons his viewers to consider the consequences of acknowledging or not acknowledging their radical freedom and its accompanying responsibilities. While Haneke typically avoids the kind of moralising and psychologising that are frequent features of those select mainstream movies dealing with serious issues of human existence, his movies and television productions do present recurring situations in which characters suffer either from a malaise that is bred by the refusal to live a self-determined life or from a loss of faith in values that could otherwise nourish and enhance one's existence. Most especially, Haneke presents his characters and their contexts in ways that emphasise the contingency and concreteness of everyday life, precisely the type of conditioning or facticity that leads some individuals to flee from the responsibilities and opportunities occasioned by their inherent autonomy. One way that Haneke accomplishes this is through a direct focus on such characters and situations, typically through an intentionally detached cinematic style that tends to mirror the kind of emotional detachment that is made thematic in his narratives. Another way he does so is through an intentional fragmentation of both storyline and montage, along with an accompanying emphasis on the discrepancies between various characters' perspectives and situations. Haneke's use of fragmentation draws attention to the brute immediacy, concreteness, and particularity of a character's 'being-in-the-world'.[5]

Haneke's works tend to evoke the kind of emotional estrangement that is often engendered by the impersonal conditions and forces of a modern consumer society. Furthermore, his movies address the ways in which our inauthentic, apathetic, and even nihilistic responses to the contemporary world can lead to violence against others and ultimately against ourselves. Underlying these themes, as we propose here, is Haneke's basic concern with the responsibility that is entailed by a human's ever-present freedom to change and undertake self-transformation, no matter the consequences – and particularly in a multicultural, bureaucracy-governed, technology-driven culture in which change seems to be pre-given and not self-propelled. In making such a recurring emphasis clear in his body of work, Haneke echoes the lessons of his intellectual and cultural forebears, the Existentialists, and most especially those like Nietzsche, Sartre, and Heidegger who stress the implications of being radically free in a world of contingency and impermanence.

An individual may exercise his or her freedom inauthentically, as a denial of one's true self or as a repression of the changing realities and corresponding possibilities that are currently shaping one's life. In his *Existentialism Is a Humanism*, Sartre criticises the type of individual who rejects the basic freedom that underlies his very existence. This person practises a form of self-deception by shifting responsibility for his decisions and actions onto such 'scapegoats' as emotional drives, biological or social conditioning, and divine providence. Sartre refers to this kind of self-deception as 'bad faith' ('*mauvaise foi*') and maintains that we are justified in judging others (and ourselves) if they (or we) commit such acts of existential inconsistency. He explains:

> We may also judge a man when we assert that he is acting in bad faith. If we define man's situation as one of free choice, in which he has no recourse to excuses or outside aid, then any man who takes refuge behind his passions, any man who fabricates some deterministic theory, is operating in bad faith. One might object by saying: 'But why shouldn't he choose bad faith?' My answer is that I do not pass moral judgments against him, but I call his bad faith an error. Here, we cannot avoid making a judgment of truth. Bad faith is obviously a lie because it is a dissimulation of man's full freedom of commitment. On the same grounds, I would say that I am

also acting in bad faith if I declare that I am bound to uphold certain values, because it is a contradiction to embrace these values while at the same time affirming that I am bound by them ... That does not mean that he wills it in the abstract; it simply means that the ultimate significance of the actions of a man of good faith is the quest of freedom in itself.

(Sartre [1946] 2007: 47–48)

Sartrean 'bad faith', as a denial of one's own inherent autonomy as a subjective agent, is a type of personal untruthfulness that may sometimes be chosen because of an unhealthy concern (or even obsession) with the illusory comforts of one's personal status quo. Haneke's films reveal that he is quite attuned to the dangers of this type of concern.

In *Hidden* (2005), Georges (Daniel Auteuil) reveals during a rare visit to his mother (Annie Girardot) that his life appears to be continuing in its normal tracks, with nothing occurring that is much better or worse than his life in the past. He tells her that he and his wife Anne (Juliette Binoche) work too much and hardly see each other, that his television talk show is going well, that his son Pierrot (Lester Makedonsky) is battling puberty, etc. Our feeling of continuing in the same rut lies at the heart of Haneke's critique of modern society's monotony and mediocrity. Haneke's willingness to dwell upon the 'et cetera' of contemporary bourgeois (i.e. mainstream) culture is evident in this scene where Georges' mother senses that something is wrong and voices her concern, detecting that her son appears to be hiding a problem, but Georges insists nonetheless that all is well.

It is a touching scene, and Georges' mother conveys genuine concern through her eyes but she also conveys her pride as well: she likewise insists on her part that she is not 'unwell', as Georges believes she is, but rather quite 'well' for her age. Her eyes tell all and they express different emotions, though this mother's love and compassion always manage to supersede her implicit regret about Georges' long absence. She occasionally pushes a smile upon her face so that Georges will not feel any more of a burden than he is obviously already feeling, despite his own objections to that point. They are alike in that they both express concern for each other's welfare while resisting any attempts at the truth, assuring the other that all is fine and that life continues, whether through work or TV-watching or whatever else makes up their seemingly conventional lives. They succumb to mutual deception, all for the sake of maintaining the status quo, even though the purpose of Georges' visit is connected with a recent disruption in the fabric of his seemingly comfortable life. Haneke shows us how humans tend to really behave in such situations, and he gives the scene a sense of realism not so much by what is disclosed but by what is concealed. As in real life, the moral situation is rarely a simple one and there is a tension here between truth-seeking and untruthfulness.

The one sign that Georges does risk stirring things up a bit is when he tells his mother that he has had a dream about a distant childhood incident. Majid, the young son of Georges' parents' former Algerian servants, had been adopted by the family after Majid's mother and father were killed by the French police during a protest in Paris in 1961. The corpses of two hundred Algerians wound up floating in the Seine after this tragic mass killing. While it may seem that Georges' willingness to share his recent dream about Majid reveals a willingness to reverse his earlier decision to disguise any of his problems, we soon realise that there is really no great change here, especially in emotional terms. He asks his mother about the incident, but he clearly wants his mother to confirm what he already feels, as if to explain away the dream. He wants her to tell him that the childhood incident and his parents' subsequent abandonment of Majid did not constitute some great tragedy that should suddenly haunt him at midlife.

The decision to be truthful or deceptive has consequences for an individual's character as well as for one's search for meaning (whether subjective or objective) in life.[6] Even the 'little' everyday choices that we make in dealing with changing situations and the lives of others become significant when they lead to the creation of an authentic or inauthentic 'self'. One of Haneke's recurring concerns in his film narratives has to do with an individual's refusal to recognise the negative and cumulative effects that distortions or omissions of the truth can engender. In the case of *Hidden*, these decisions are typically motivated by a desire to maintain the illusory status quo of a comfortable life, even when reality (not to mention one's own subconscious) signals that things are not running as smoothly as they seem. Similarly, in *Variation* (1983), Haneke's production for Austrian/German television earlier in his career, the marriage of a couple slowly disintegrates as the husband cultivates an adulterous relationship. The husband then becomes highly resistant to discussing matters with his wife when she begins to suspect the truth and then demands some dialogue about the issue. He refuses to respond, not merely because of a desire for deception but, more importantly, because of a growing indifference to his wife's emotional concerns. Here, freedom is exercised in terms of a rejection of personal truthfulness, leading to a sense of inauthenticity and even apathy.

Another form of inauthenticity that involves self-denial and/or self-deception is that of a slavish, weak-willed conformism in which the individual clings to social norms, traditional values and external authority rather than exercising his or her autonomy in a more individuating way. This type of conformism is another form of Sartrean 'bad faith' that can lead to the psychologically damaging effects of self-repression. An example occurs in Haneke's German television production *The Rebellion* (1993), in which the director explicitly depicts the aftermath of the grim *fin de siècle* Viennese culture that had been defined in large part by Emperor Franz Joseph's obsessive conservatism. *The Rebellion* is based on a novel by Joseph Roth and, in its concluding section, includes a brief homage to F.W. Murnau's landmark silent classic *The Last Laugh* (1924), a film about an ageing hotel doorman (Emil Jannings) who loses his job and consequently his sense of dignity. *The Rebellion*'s Andreas Pum (Branko Samarovski) is a former soldier who has sacrificed one of his legs, not to mention years of personal happiness, in military service during World War One. After the war his society now classifies him as an invalid and he continues to live a dreary existence by maintaining subservience to almost everyone around him. When Pum finally explodes and protests against an insulting injustice done to him by a social superior on the street tram, Andreas is punished for his expression of sudden anger. His anger is the culmination of his long repressed resentment against those who have looked down upon him and against a cold-hearted society that he has unquestioningly served.

Pum then finally rebels against God Himself, given his unhappy life and the ways in which he has been consistently 'punished', despite his willingness to do right by adhering to his duties. Pum represents the stifling realities of Franz Joseph's Vienna – the same culture in which Sigmund Freud first formed his psychological theory of instinctual repression. But in the last section of the movie, with the unleashing of his repressed resentment, Pum symbolises in some ways those *fin de siècle* artists and thinkers who reacted openly against the Emperor's backward-looking regime. The Viennese Secession (following in the wake of the Berlin and Munich Secessions) was a group and movement of artists, founded by painter Gustav Klimt and architect Otto Wagner among others, who responded critically to the conservative and traditionalist policies that had been imposed by the city's leading art schools and museums.

Unfortunately for Pum, his personal rebellion in the form of released anger comes too late and to no avail. His unhappy life as a passive conformist has led only to a damaging series of humiliations and injustices, and at the end of the movie he is compared in a momentary epiphany to the poor labouring donkey that had daily transported his heavy music box. Pum is a man whose regular and voluntary subordination to his repressive, antiquated society led him to deny the value and possibilities of his own innate freedom, most especially his freedom to change his life for the better, despite the circumstances that had constantly impinged upon him from the outside world. Just as Georges in *Hidden* chose a course of personal untruthfulness in dealing with the changing realities of his current life as well as the dramatic realities of his past, so too does Pum adopt a way of life in which he becomes untrue to his inner worth and potential.

The omission or denial of the truth may be related, then, to a repression of one's authentic self, and this type of self-denial is a negative use of freedom that excludes or rejects alternative life-possibilities that are more individualising or self-enhancing. Furthermore, repression and self-repression can lead at times to violence, including violence against oneself, once a person recognises not only the freedom to enact violence but also the dangerous resentment that has accumulated through habitual decisions to limit or negate one's true instincts and desires. For example, in Haneke's film *The Seventh Continent* (1989), a family is led to a horrifying act of self-destruction after apparently succumbing to the deadening effects of an overly routine and conventional existence. They are too weak or indifferent to forge a new way of life or set of values, and so the only 'rebellion' that they dare to undertake is total life-negation. Even the parents' process of preparing for their act of collective suicide becomes as methodical, robotic, and value-neutral as their previous lives appeared to be. And in *The Piano Teacher* (2001), the title character (Isabelle Huppert) commits acts of psychological sadism and physical self-mutilation after having devoted herself habitually and obsessively to her musical career and to a corresponding life of severe self-repression. In such movies the inherent autonomy of the human being is expressed in a negative and destructive fashion, in a way that indicates a misuse of this freedom and a lack of appreciation for the intrinsic value of self-realisation. Perhaps the clearest example of this connection between repression and violence in Haneke's oeuvre is his recent *The White Ribbon*, a film in which the collective, dogmatic order of a small community leads to negative acts of terrorism undertaken by those who seem, at first impression, the least likely to have committed such acts. In a sense, an indignant or inauthentic use of freedom, often a reaction against conformism and oppression, can lead to the 'killing' of genuine freedom – and especially the freedom of others.

Violence may therefore be viewed as an exercise of freedom but also as one possible consequence of the will to deny, omit, or conceal personal truth. Haneke makes violence, whether it is committed individually or collectively, a recurring theme.[7] Violence is presented in his films at times through the filter of the media (e.g., TV news) so that it becomes conventionalised and trivialised. At other times, violence is portrayed with the shocking and immediate suddenness of a gunshot on a quiet evening. In *Hidden*, two interrelated acts of past violence (the killing of young Majid's parents by the French police and the psychological violence committed against Majid by Georges' family when he was a boy) are swept under the carpet, so to speak, and this repression of truth results in the terrorism unleashed against Georges and Ann and also in Majid's sudden act of physical self-destruction that Georges eventually witnesses.

Violence against innocent others is an act of ignoring or rejecting the innate freedom and worth of the victim. Such violence is, in fact, a form of inauthenticity or 'bad faith', particularly given that a person who commits a violent act implicitly negates the very kind of autonomy that defines his own existence. According to Sartre, one should 'will' the safeguarding and enhancement of one's own freedom, since freedom *is* the fundamental condition of one's 'self' as an indeterminate subject. But this basic autonomy is the abstract condition of any and all subjectivity, whether it is one's own subjectivity or that of others. And so, in 'good faith' (as a form of 'strict consistency' and authenticity), we ought to 'will' both our own individual freedom as well as that of others. To do otherwise is to commit self-deception and implicit self-negation. As Sartre tells us:

> Obviously, freedom as the definition of man does not depend on others, but as soon as there is commitment, I am obliged to will the freedom of others at the same time as I will my own. I cannot set my own freedom as a goal without setting the freedom

of others as a goal. Consequently, when, operating on the level of complete authenticity, I have acknowledged that existence precedes essence, and that man is a free being who, under any circumstances, can only ever will his freedom, I have at the same time acknowledged that I must will the freedom of others. Therefore, in the name of this will to freedom, implied by freedom itself, I can pass judgment on those who seek to conceal from themselves the complete arbitrariness of their existence, and their total freedom.

(Sartre [1946] 2007: 48–49)

And thus, from a Sartrean perspective, the kind of physical violence done to others or even oneself in Haneke's films is an implicit extension of the 'violence' done to oneself when an individual denies his own radical freedom. According to Sartre's logic expressed in the above quotation, the act of destroying another person's life and autonomy derives from the aggressor's desire to repress or flee from, and therefore to negate, his or her own innate freedom.

Finally, there are some acts of violence that result from sheer irrationality and force us to question the very stability and intelligibility of our lives. These are not acts or decisions that can be easily reduced to conventional distinctions between good and evil. They are acts of violence, not merely against another's (or one's own) freedom, but against the value of life itself. Our experience of this kind of irrationality forces us to confront the 'horror of the void', since we immediately lose faith in the idea of any permanent foundations or unconditional guarantees: all is contingent, all is flux, nothing is secure. Haneke frequently evokes this type of nihilistic horror – our fear, not of some specific object or threat, but rather of the very emptiness or nothingness that pervades our existence and yet allows for our 'being-in-the-world'.[8] Haneke does this most effectively when he presents either the lightning-quick flash of violence that negates the value of life itself or the deadening numbness of life-denial, the very numbness that can occasion or result from acts of meaningless violence.

In Haneke's *Funny Games* (1997) and his American re-make of this film, *Funny Games U.S.* (2007), irrational violence becomes a horrifying game played for senseless kicks before a camera – as we learn later when the movie we have been watching begins to rewind and we realise that we have been watching the video recordings of two young thugs. Haneke tells us in an interview that *Funny Games* is chiefly about the way in which the media depicts violence, and he certainly makes the audience aware of his movie's self-reflexive commentary on its own presentation of violence (Haneke 1997). But ultimately the film's most provocative theme is that of the encounter between civilised rationality and savage irrationality, an encounter that is even more horrifying once we realise that its possibility always lurks within our own psyche.

The violence in Haneke's films is most terrifying, not merely when it is unexpected and almost casual, but when it reveals that human reason has been completely rejected – when the very attempt to rationalise or negotiate has provoked hatred, contempt, and ultimately destruction. Such violence is an act of indignation against the very value of human existence because it is an outright, unjustified rejection of the traditional idea of what allows humans to claim a right to life: the human power of thought and intelligence. One telling instance of this is in *The Time of the Wolf* (2003), when a family of hostile and hungry strangers has broken into another family's country house after some unexplained apocalyptic event. The victimised father (Daniel Duval) manages to convince his rifle-wielding counterpart to allow his two children to return to the family's car. When he then quietly suggests that they unload the car and eat, he is instantly shot dead and his wife (Isabelle Huppert), in a state of shock, can only respond by wiping the splattered blood from her face. Even the wife of the killer breaks down in a shocking fit of disbelief that her husband has actually pulled the trigger and killed a man in front of their own young son. Has he done so merely by accident, the mistaken impulse of his trigger finger? It does not appear so. Was he so embarrassed at watching his wife and children reduced to scavengers before the eyes of the house owners, his obvious superiors in social and economic status, that he can no longer stand the humiliation? Or is it an act of sheer irrationality? Since Haneke does not give us any further clue to the killer's motive, we might surmise that it was the very proposal made by the now dead father, an attempt at reasonable negotiation and further discourse (even in the face of a gun barrel), that prompted this man to fire unexpectedly. This act of violence is therefore an act of nihilistic terrorism, an assault upon the very value of rationality – and therefore upon the intrinsic value of humanity itself.

Nihilistic horror may be evoked when there is some attempt at rational dialogue but where that attempt is not only rejected, but rejected in a way that indicates no common ground or the least bit of desire for mutual understanding. This occurs also in *Funny Games*, for example, when the father (Ulrich Mühe) asks the young vandalisers (Arno Frisch and Frank Giering), 'Why are you doing this?' The reply is chilling: 'Why not?' When he later asks the same question, the response is a series of obvious lies about the other hoodlum's mother's incestuous wishes and their desire to obtain money for drugs. They make it conspicuous that these are arbitrary lies that are offered for entertainment purposes at best.

A traditional game has rules, however. These are funny 'games' because their players reject rational rules or goals that would otherwise allow one to win or lose. These games are there for sheer amusement, but with no clear scheme or standard for victory other than power over another for sadistic purposes. The 'fun' of the 'game' fades to indifference and then violence when the perpetrators of the game lose interest or decide simply that the game should end, for whatever reason – perhaps that of moving on to a new locale for the game to be continued with new participants. The funny games played here are even scarier when nihilistic indifference itself becomes parodied, as when one of the hoodlums tells the couple that his partner in crime suffers from 'world-weariness and ennui'. Here, human freedom is exercised at its most radically negative, as a complete negation of the worth of human life itself, and for no other apparent reason than a kind of monstrous pleasure in choosing to negate the very value of rational choice. Here again, life-negating freedom is used to destroy the possibilities of a life-affirming freedom.

It would be too easy, from an overly brief survey of Haneke's films, to label him as some type of cinematic nihilist, given his consistently dark subject matter and recurring themes. A director who chooses nihilistic subject matter is not necessarily one who maintains with consistent conviction that nothing matters or that human life has no intrinsic value. By his very will to make such films, Haneke is, it may be argued, a dedicated anti-nihilist. He exposes us to the darkness of modern times so as to reveal the dangers and to point beyond them. He presents us with our own tendencies toward untruthfulness, conformism, self-denial, numbness, detachment, and moral indifference – symptoms of various forms of pathological life-negation. The denial of the value of human individuality and rationality – and thus the rejection of the value of human life itself – must ultimately involve a rejection as well as an expression of our radical freedom. This basic truth is entailed by Sartre's fundamental proposition that the human subject is, at the end of the day, the locus and vehicle of true freedom.

Notes

1. Granted, Haneke does not give us direct evidence that the children are the instigators of the mysterious acts of violence occurring throughout the film, and part of this may be due to the director's penchant for ambiguity, especially as a way of capturing the enigmatic and indeterminate qualities of everyday human life. However, that said, the film's narrative makes the children's complicity in the violence quite apparent.
2. For Nietzsche's distinction between 'slave-morality' and 'master-morality', see Nietzsche ([1887] 1989), especially section 10 of the First Essay ('Good and Evil', 'Good and Bad').
3. For Heidegger's concept of 'thrownness' (*die Geworfenheit*), see his 1962 *Being and Time* (*Sein und Zeit*), especially section 38 ('Falling and Thrownness').
4. Nietzsche's distinction between a 'passive' or 'pathological' form of nihilism and a more 'active' or 'healthy' form of nihilism is spelled out most clearly in his collected unpublished writings *The Will to Power* ([1901] 1968), especially in Book One ('European Nihilism'). As he tells us there in a fragment: 'Nihilism. It is *ambiguous*: Nihilism as a sign of increased power of the spirit: as *active* nihilism. Nihilism as a decline and recession of the power of the spirit: as *passive* nihilism' (Fragment 22, p. 17). And as Nietzsche tells us in the fragment following that one, nihilism in its active form can be a 'sign of strength' in that 'the spirit may have grown so strong that previous goals ("convictions", articles of faith) have become incommensurate ...' He then refers in this fragment to 'passive' nihilism as 'the weary nihilism that no longer attacks ...' (Fragment 23, pp. 17–18). For an exploration of selected films and television series using Nietzsche's above-mentioned distinction between types of nihilism, see Kevin L. Stoehr (2006).
5. For an illuminating analysis of Haneke's use of fragmentation in terms of both narrative structure and visual stylisation – and most especially through his emphasis on multi-character, 'multistrain' narratives – see Roy Grundmann (2010: 371–419).
6. On Haneke's theme of truth-telling in relation to themes of perspectivism, repression, inauthenticity, violence, and nihilism, see Kevin L. Stoehr (2010).

7. For Haneke's own ruminations on the theme of violence in relation to the media, see his essay 'Violence and the Media', trans. Evan Torner (2010). For analyses of the theme of various forms of violence (ranging from personal to colonial) in Haneke's films – as expressed visually, narratively, or both – see Brigitte Puecker (2010); Eugenie Brinkema (2010); Jefferson Kline (2010); and Ipek Celik (2010).

8. For an existential analysis of the concept of nothingness (*das Nichts*) and the idea that 'nothingness' is inseparably interwoven with the 'worldhood' of human reality (*Dasein*), see Martin Heidegger's *Being and Time* ([1927] 1962), most especially section 40 ('The Basic State-of-Mind of Anxiety as a Distinctive Way in which *Dasein* is Disclosed'). For Heidegger's concept of 'Being-in-the-world' (*das In-der-Welt-sein*), see most especially section 12 ('A preliminary sketch of Being-in-the-world, in terms of an orientation towards Being-in as such') of *Being and Time*.

Bibliography

Brinkema, E. 2010. 'How to Do Things with Violences', in R. Grundmann (ed.), *A Companion to Michael Haneke*. Malden: Wiley-Blackwell, pp. 354–70.

Celik, I. A. 2010. '"I Wanted You to Be Present": Guilt and the History of Violence in Michael Haneke's *Caché*', *Cinema Journal: The Journal of the Society for Cinema and Media Studies* 50(1) Fall: 59–80.

Grundmann, R. (ed.). 2010. *A Companion to Michael Haneke*. Malden: Wiley-Blackwell.

———. 2010. 'Between Adorno and Lyotard: Michael Haneke's Aesthetic of Fragmentation', in R. Grundmann (ed.), *A Companion to Michael Haneke*. Malden: Wiley-Blackwell, pp. 371–419.

Haneke, M. 2005. Filmed interview. Special Features, Kino DVD version of *Caché*.

———. 1997. Filmed interview. Special Features, Kino DVD version of *Funny Games*.

———. 2010. 'Violence and the Media', in R. Grundmann (ed.), *A Companion to Michael Haneke*, trans. Evan Torner, pp. 575–79.

Heidegger, M. [1927] 1962. *Being and Time*, trans. John Macquarrie and Edward Robinson. New York: Harper & Row Publishers.

Kline, T.J. 2010. 'The Intertextual and Discursive Origins of Terror', in R. Grundmann (ed.), *A Companion to Michael Haneke*. Malden: Wiley-Blackwell, pp. 551–61.

Nietzsche, F. [1887] 1989. *On the Genealogy of Morals*, trans. W. Kaufmann and R.J. Hollingdale, in *On the Genealogy of Morals and Ecce Homo*. New York: Vintage Books.

———. [1901] 1968. *The Will to Power*, trans. W. Kaufmann and R.J. Hollingdale. New York: Vintage Books.

Puecker, B. 2010. 'Games Haneke Plays: Reality and Performance', in R. Grundmann (ed.), *A Companion to Michael Haneke*. Malden: Wiley-Blackwell, pp. 130–46.

Sartre, J.-P. [1946] 2007. *Existentialism Is a Humanism*, trans. C. Macomber. New Haven, CT: Yale University Press.

———. [1938] 2007. *Nausea*, trans. L. Alexander. New York: New Directions Books.

Stoehr, K.L. 2006. *Nihilism in Film and Television: A Critical Overview from Citizen Kane to The Sopranos*. Jefferson, NC: McFarland & Company.

———. 2010. 'Haneke's Secession: Perspectivism and Anti-Nihilism in *Code Unknown* and *Caché*', in R. Grundmann (ed.), *A Companion to Michael Haneke*. Malden: Wiley-Blackwell, pp. 477–94.

Filmography

Directed works with English titles (film and TV productions):
Haneke, M. (dir.). 1983. *Variation* (TV). SFB.
———. 1989. *The Seventh Continent* (*Der Siebente Continent*). Wega Film.
———. 1993. *The Rebellion* (*Die Rebellion*) (TV). ORF.
———. 1997. *Funny Games*. Austrian Film Institute.
———. 2001. *The Piano Teacher* (*La Pianiste*). Arte.
———. 2003. *The Time of the Wolf* (*Le Temps du Loup*). Bavaria Film.
———. 2005. *Hidden* (*Caché*). Les Films du Losange.
———. 2007. *Funny Games* (U.S.). Celluloid Dreams.
———. 2009. *The White Ribbon* (*Das weisse Band*). X-Filme Creative Pool, Wega Film, Les Films du Losange, Lucky Red.

3

NAKED, BAD FAITH AND MASCULINITY

Mark Stanton

Mike Leigh's film, *Naked,* won two awards at the Cannes Film Festival in May 1993: those for Best Actor and Best Director. It was the first major indication that Leigh had become a filmmaker of international importance and was arguably considered his most important film up to that point. The film's narrative centres on a character called Johnny (David Thewlis). He is first seen having rough sex with a woman in an alleyway who subsequently threatens him with death at the hands of '[her] Bernard'. This causes Johnny to flee his hometown of Manchester to London where he spends a night at his ex-girlfriend, Louise's (Lesley Sharp), rented house. He has sex with her needy housemate, Sophie (Katrin Cartlidge), but finally leaves to escape her. He then begins a nocturnal odyssey through the liminal spaces of London where he encounters a range of displaced and alienated characters, a philosophical security guard called Brian (Peter Wright), a depressed waitress, a violent bill sticker, and a homeless couple, each of whom he needles with a barrage of sarcasm, Socratic probing, rage and disjointed philosophical fragments. Johnny's story is intercut with that of Jeremy/Sebastian (Greg Cruttwell), a rapist and city boy who seems to represent Johnny's shadow. They meet briefly towards the end of the film as Johnny lies barely conscious on the landing of the rented house that is owned by Jeremy. *Naked* ends with a final tracking shot of Johnny limping away from the house along the centre of the road.

For many, the film captured the zeitgeist of the early post-Thatcher years but Leigh claimed to have broader ambitions: to address 'the apocalypse, the end of the century and impending doom' (Leigh quoted in Raphael 2008: 226). This end of millennium feel, along with the film's alienated central character, its discourses on the meaning of life and film noir leanings led to critics and commentators labelling it 'existential'.[1] The term, however, is often used negatively and juxtaposed with words such as 'dark', 'malaise', 'scepticism', or 'angst'. I believe that this indicates a fundamental misconception, or at least a limited understanding, of both *Naked* and existentialism.

The contention that existentialism focuses on the bleaker aspects of human life is not uncommon. Sartre addresses it in the opening paragraphs of his lecture, *Existentialism Is a Humanism*, where he defends existentialism from the charges of '... emphasizing what is despicable about humanity ... exposing all that is sordid, suspicious or base, while ignoring beauty and the brighter side of human nature' (Sartre [1946a] 2007: 17). Sartre went on to define it as 'a kind of "optimism," and a "doctrine of action"' (Cohen-Solal in Sartre 2007: 10), which shares some similarity with David Thewlis' perception of *Naked*: 'The film is made from a love of life and an anxiety about the future' (Thewlis quoted in Coveney 1996: 26). This chapter will examine the links between existential theory and *Naked* that lie beyond the superficial assumption that both deal with despair, anxiety, isolation and a world without objective moral values. Rather, it is established that certain existential concepts form a fundamental part of Leigh's oeuvre.

In his early years Leigh was influenced by existential ideas, either absorbed indirectly through various influences such as the plays of Harold Pinter and Samuel Beckett, whose *Endgame* Leigh watched fourteen times, or through Sartre's own writings. One Sartrean concept that serves a key function in Leigh's work is that of 'bad faith': Sartre's idea that people deny their essential freedom. Due to its centrality to many of Leigh's films and the interesting analysis of the concept that occurs in *Naked*, 'bad faith' will be the focus of this chapter. It will be approached from two perspectives: the bad faith of individuals towards themselves and the attitude of bad faith directed towards others. As *Naked* concentrates heavily on male characters and masculine perspectives, the study of masculinity, its representation in the film, and its relationship to bad faith will be at the forefront of this discussion.

Mike Leigh, Masks and Bad Faith

In an interview with Mark Lawson first broadcast on BBC4 on 19 April 2009, Leigh commented that his films are about the masks that people wear (Lawson 2009). This claim seems to hold true for all of Leigh's work to date. Whether you consider Keith from *Nuts in May* (1976), Beverley and Lawrence from *Abigail's Party* (1977), Aubrey from *Life is Sweet* (1990), or Jeremy from *Naked* itself you will find characters behaving in ways that indicate they have become identical with their social masks. As Ray Carney explains: 'Their stereotyped externals are only dramatic externalizations of their stereotypical internals. Their off-the-peg clothing only matters as evidence of their off-the-peg souls' (Carney and Quart 2000: 97). Central to Sartre's conception of bad faith is the commonly-held misapprehension that one's role is fixed and unchanging.

A famous passage from Sartre's key philosophical work, *Being and Nothingness*, 'made a big impression on Leigh as a young man ... It occurs in the discussion of "bad faith"' (Carney and Quart 2000: 108). In this passage Sartre describes a waiter working in a café:

> His movement is quick and forward, a little too precise, a little too rapid ... All his behaviour seems to us a game. He applies himself to chaining his movements as if they were mechanisms, the one regulating the other; his gestures and even his voice seem to be mechanisms ... he is playing at being a waiter in a café.
>
> (Sartre [1943] 1995: 59)

At the heart of Sartre's concept of bad faith is the idea that people convince themselves and others that they actually are, in their entirety, the social role that they perform: a waiter or a salesman, for example. It needs to be emphasised, however, that bad faith is not merely self-deception. Self-deception implies that you both know and don't know something simultaneously. For Sartre, who believed that conscious experience is a transparent unity, this contradiction is impossible. Bad faith is rather an ongoing project of self-distraction based on a false belief about the nature of conscious existence.[2] To put it succinctly, bad faith involves two fundamental types of false belief, which can be exhibited in many ways: the first is to be convinced that one is an object rather than a free individual and the second is to deny the physicality (or facticity)[3] of one's existence by assuming that one can entirely escape (or transcend) it. For instance, Jeremy from *Naked* clearly exhibits the traits of bad faith. He is an almost perfect stereotype, that of the young, upwardly mobile man of the eighties and early nineties, the yuppie. Jeremy adopts all the behaviours of this kind of man and is seriously committed to performing his aggressive, masculine role as if it were more than just a social mask but rather an essential trait from which his behaviours emanate. It is this serious belief about the concrete source of one's personality and behaviours which results in bad faith.[4]

Mike Leigh, as I have commented above, is particularly interested in the ways in which people become trapped by attitudes of bad faith towards their social roles and how this can lead to highly restricted perspectives. He contrasts characters who display rigid personalities with others who are more 'authentic': playful, inventive and unrestricted (Carney and Quart 2000: 73). This can be seen in films from *High Hopes* (1988) to *Happy Go Lucky* (2008) and is also apparent in *Naked*. It is clear that Leigh, like Sartre, is making a value judgement about which of these two modes of being is preferable.

Naked's title implies that we are being presented with a work that will show us life in the raw, or a soul left bare, unfettered by the usual masking behaviour that is so prevalent in Leigh's earlier films. This is partly, though by no means completely, the case. Johnny does not abide by the kinds of restricted rules that govern the behaviours of most of the lower-middle-class or upper-middle-class characters that Leigh explored previously, and he does demonstrate the playful, inventive and anarchic traits that are signs of a more 'authentic' character. There are aspects of Johnny's behaviour, however, that seem to preclude him from attaining authenticity. These are not necessarily related to the way in which he views himself but rather the way that he views others. In general terms the film exposes bad faith, in various forms, through the characters and narrative, and the techniques that are employed. This process can potentially illuminate bad faith in the members of the audience and encourage them to engage with ideas of bad faith and identity.

Masculine Identity as Bad Faith

A discussion of *Naked* and bad faith cannot ignore the film's representation and critique of masculine behaviour. Masculinity can be seen either from an essentialist perspective, as the innate, biological attributes of men, or as a culturally constructed identity. The cultural concept of masculine identity can itself be either broad or restricted in its definition depending on whether one considers that there are certain key traits that all men must share or that masculinity is far broader and more pluralistic. The male characters in *Naked* can be interpreted from either perspective. On one hand they appear to represent a broad range of masculine types: Jeremy may be seen as a violent hegemonic male, Johnny as a damaged male, and Brian as a voyeur. However, from an essentialist perspective they seem to share a number of traits that could be interpreted as part of their 'male nature': they are violent, aggressive and misogynistic.

For Sartre, the idea that male behaviour can be dictated by masculine traits, whether they are biological or cultural, would be an anathema. His philosophy is an argument against precisely this sort of essentialist attitude. As explained above, people are always free to choose, and as a consequence masculinity itself must be chosen by each individual. Where people believe in an essential form of masculinity they are in bad faith. It is possible, however, for bad faith to be shaken and the male characters in *Naked* exhibit differing reactions to the loss of a concrete sense of masculine identity: an exposure to freedom resulting in anguish.

Sartre claims that people want to deny their individual freedom because of 'anguish' or 'dread'. According to Matthew Eshleman, Sartre indicates in the preface to *Being and Nothingness* 'that anguish provides the motivation for many, if not all, varieties of bad faith, where anguish involves "the recognition of a possibility as my possibility"' (Eshleman 2008: 6). In order to fully understand this it is first necessary to know a little about Sartre's underlying ideas. He believed that the only essential characteristic of human existence is freedom, people are free to make any choice that they wish. This freedom, however, comes at a high price: it involves accepting personal responsibility for every act, accepting that there is no necessity to perform any particular act, and that resolutions made in the past and decisions made about the future cannot determine current behaviours.

Andrew Spicer identifies a general social trend associated with a 'pervasive sense of male insecurity and uncertain identity' precipitated by the loss of earlier myths of British masculinity such as the 'idealised gentleman' and the 'post-war ideal of the (white, heterosexual) common man' (Spicer 2003: 204). This insecurity of identity may also be related to a shift towards a relative 'feminisation' of social values where men, especially those tied to essentialist ideas of masculinity, do not know what form their identities should take. This instability can reveal the assumptions on which bad faith attitudes are based to be false. Men who consider themselves to be intrinsically stoical, emotionally controlled, the 'bread winners' and so on, may find that their beliefs are undermined and, as Eshleman contends in an article on bad faith, 'anxiety results from the confrontation with the possibility of significantly revising one's way of life (social identity)' (Eshleman 2008: 7). The loss of a sense of being a certain 'kind of man' causes a confrontation with the fact that one cannot be a certain 'kind of man' in the same way that one cannot be a 'waiter'. This confrontation with one's freedom may result in different reactions: the resulting anxiety (or anguish) can provoke the need to believe in an alternative determining identity so that anxiety can be avoided, or one can embrace the freedom that is revealed and attempt to live more authentically. I believe that Jeremy, Johnny and Brian each exhibit different reactions to the anxiety created by the possibility of freedom and an uncertain sense of their male identity. This claim will be investigated in relation to each of these characters.

Jeremy adopts all the behaviours of a 'yuppie' and is seriously committed to performing his aggressive, masculine role as if it were an essential trait from which his actions emanate. The yuppie persona provided a new form of identity where masculinity could be expressed through consumption. Identity became synonymous with the acquisition of tangible objects: Porsches, mobile telephones and so on. It was an ultimate material realisation of identity. This can be interpreted as an extreme form of bad faith where to give oneself an object-like nature one merely has to own a sufficient number of the right kinds of objects. Greg Crutwell, who played the part of Jeremy, was castigated by reviewers for delivering a clichéd, stereotypical performance.[5] Yet this is an almost inevitable risk when attempting to present a character in bad faith because the character's attitudes will often be based on a socially-accepted norm – they need to feel part of a collective. As Sartre says of the anti-Semite: 'He has made himself an anti-Semite because that is something one cannot be alone. The phrase, "I hate the Jews," is one uttered in a chorus' (Sartre [1946b] 1995: 22). For a misogynist, like Jeremy, his attitude towards women defines him as a man and forms his allegiance with other men. If women are weak then he is strong, if they are passive then he is active, if they are failures then he is a success.

There is clearly a problem here. Self-identity when incarnated through objects leaves the individual alienated. Jeremy cannot become the masculine role that he is enacting but neither can he relinquish it. He claims that he will 'commit suicide on … [his] fortieth birthday,' because he doesn't 'want to be old'. In fact, being old does not conform to the identity that he has created – he chooses death over the possibility of revising that identity. By rigidly defining his life, Jeremy is attempting to give it a sense of permanence. However, as Sartre writes: 'As soon as we posit ourselves as a certain being … we surpass this being – and that not towards another being but towards emptiness, towards nothing' (Sartre [1943] 1995: 62). Jeremy cannot exclude this nothingness, which is the key to his freedom and haunts every attempt to evade it.

Brian, the security guard, represents a contrast to Jeremy. Rather than possess objects he guards 'nothing', rather than live for the moment he lives only for the future and the past, rather than demand attention he lives in the twilight. His only interaction with another person, until he meets Johnny, seems to be voyeuristic: he watches a woman in an adjacent flat. Brian is defined by absences, and rather than accept his situation he chooses to believe in escapist notions such as metempsychosis, ghosts and fanciful ideas of a future life in rural Ireland. Brian's reaction to a loss of identity is to deny that he has one at all. As Sartre comments: 'There are even men (e.g., caretakers, overseers, gaolers) whose social reality is uniquely that of the Not, who live and die, having forever been only a Not upon the earth' (Sartre [1943] 1995: 47). For Brian, not only is his social role that of negation but also his life is all flight, he cannot accept his facticity and continually attempts to avoid it.

Brian only seems to consider what he will become or what he has been, not what he is in the moment: what his actions identify him as being. For Sartre what a person is, is defined by the actions that they take. Brian's actions are predetermined by his job; he has to walk a certain route around the disused office block and register his presence at certain locations. The route and the time of the walk are predetermined. For Brian, in the present, there is no sense that he has a freedom. He has a second form of bad faith: he denies his responsibilities by denying his actual situation in the world.

Johnny is presented as a mercurial character. He can be charming, vicious, charismatic, cruel, funny, violent, misogynistic and playful. He is in turmoil and someone who, like Antoine Roquentin in Sartre's *Nausea*, 'seeks to unmask the world by questioning the values that he has been taught to attribute to [it]' (Gordon and Gordon 1996: 235). Through an almost continual mocking harangue he targets ideas about progress, the validity of human projects, work, belief, aspirations and dreams. He uses these critiques in an attempt to force others to accept the absurdity of their own lives and in this respect he seems to be at the vanguard of exposing bad faith, of uncovering truths and revealing self-comforting beliefs: the very antithesis of the kind of person who attempts to avoid the anguish of his or her freedom.

Johnny is both victim and perpetrator, self-aggrandising and pathetic. He is depicted at one moment with a halo behind his head, another perhaps being mistaken as a rock star, another seeing himself as the rejected Christ and another as a crazed preacher, rapist or thief. His behaviour is in continual flux, and he passes through a series of parts that a man might play, but what Johnny is cannot easily be identified in the way that it can with Jeremy. We can focus on certain aspects of his behaviour and draw entirely different conclusions. Rather than being anguished by the fact that one can become a different sort of person by acting out of character, he appears to embrace it.

Sartre believed that individuals have a fundamental project which is part of a desire to overcome their sense of lack. Ultimately this project is aimed at becoming simultaneously conscious and complete. Sartre claimed that this kind of state could only be achieved by God but the aim of becoming whole can be directed towards any role that is the basis and coherent principle for further actions and aims to overcome any particular lack that the individual identifies within him or her self. This project can be initiated by an external event and I will argue in the following section on 'Bad Faith and the Audience' that this is the case for Johnny, for although Johnny's actions appear erratically free they do all seem to identify him with a certain kind of character: that of the outcast, the wanderer or condemned man. Yet he differs from Jeremy in that his behaviour evolves with each situation. He reacts to the world that he finds whereas Jeremy acts in a consistent manner regardless of the situation. Johnny is inventing his role as he lives it. He is playful in his approach to both his use of language and life. Sartre identifies this playful attitude as an indicator of authenticity.[6] Rather than the blinkered attitude of seriousness adopted by those in bad faith, the playful attitude highlights the individual's choice in their selection of rules and values, and encourages self-reflection. It brings freedom to the fore. For Sartre, each individual is free to choose and Johnny has chosen an ancient archetype. It may appear unacceptable to claim that Johnny has 'chosen' this pariah identity but it is fundamental to Sartre's perspective on the nature of human life that we always have this freedom, even when a certain course of action appears to originate in some external cause. Johnny could have reacted in a number of ways to the influences on his life but he chose to act in his own unique way. This choice gives Johnny a certain authenticity. Sartre's ideas about authenticity were expanded in his *Notebooks for an Ethics* but perhaps the most often quoted definition comes from his essay *Anti-Semite and Jew*:

> Authenticity, it is almost needless to say, consists in having a true and lucid consciousness of the situation, in assuming the responsibilities and risks that it involves, in accepting it in pride or humiliation, and sometimes in horror and hate.
> (Sartre [1946b] 1995: 90)

Although there are ongoing debates about the meaning of 'authenticity' it can reasonably be defined as a process, rather than a set state, whereby a person continually chooses authentically based upon a full acceptance of their basis in total freedom combined with an understanding of their facticity and responsibility for their choices. It has also been suggested that an authentic person must respect and recognise the freedom of others.[7]

Sartre, however, also argues that authenticity has to involve, to some extent, accepting one's role. This is illustrated in *Anti-Semite and Jew*:

> Jewish authenticity consists in choosing oneself *as Jew* ... he knows himself and wills himself into history as a historic and damned creature ... He knows that he stands apart, untouchable, scorned, proscribed – and it is *as such* that he asserts his being ... he derives his pride from his humiliation [italics in original].
>
> (Sartre [1946b] 1995: 136–37)

Something rather similar may be said of Johnny. Consequently, we can see authentic traits in Johnny from three perspectives: his playful self-invention, his choice of the 'outsider' role, and his use of his role to try and undermine the bad faith of others.

To conclude, these three male characters demonstrate different approaches to constructing masculine identity, two of which result in forms of bad faith. Jeremy wants to make himself as 'solid as a stone' to avoid confronting his freedom and the possibility of change and Brian attempts to make himself so light that he can be elevated above the miserable nature of his situation in the world. Johnny behaves in a way that implies he has a certain degree of authenticity. However, the position is not quite so clear because Johnny demonstrates attitudes of bad faith towards other people – especially women. This will be discussed in the following section.

An Attitude of Bad Faith towards the 'Other'

Masculinity is an 'inherently relational' concept and 'does not exist except in contrast with "femininity"' (Connell 2005: 68). Sartre developed the idea of such relational identities in *Anti-Semite and Jew* where he explains that the anti-Semite wishes to be 'French' completely and unchangingly in the way that only an object without consciousness, and therefore freedom, can be. Thus, the anti-Semite wants the Jew to incarnate all Evil: 'If all he has to do is to remove Evil, that means that the Good is already *given* ... The anti-Semite has cast his lot for Evil so as not to have to cast his lot for Good' (Sartre [1946b] 1995: 44). Similarly, '[t]he masculinity of the sexist male is, like the goodness of anti-Semites, established largely by contrast, what "women" are, "men" are not' (Bell 1999: 144). As with all instances of bad faith the male who wishes to identify himself completely with a certain form of masculinity, as if it is his 'nature', is seeking security away from the responsibilities of his freedom.

This is a common theme for all the male characters in *Naked*. Johnny, Jeremy and Brian all objectify women and Johnny and Jeremy are sadistic in their dealings with them. Johnny talks about his mother appearing in pornographic magazines and being dead and has violent sexual encounters with a woman in the opening scene and with Sophie. Jeremy treats women as if they are collections of body parts and rapes a waitress and Sophie; and Brian spies on the woman in the window and refers to women as 'whores and harlots'. They all use this process of objectification in futile attempts to define their masculine nature and reveal their own freedom.

The most extreme version of this objectification, expressed by both Johnny and Jeremy, is that of sadism – a bad faith attitude that, according to Martin, Sartre addresses directly in *Being and Nothingness*:

> The sadist attempts to appropriate the Other's freedom, thereby escaping the human condition: 'Sadism is a refusal to be incarnated and a flight from all facticity' (399). The sadist attempts this by *incarnating* the Other's freedom. This entails causing the Other's consciousness to become fascinated by his own body or, in other words, to have his body act as the pre-eminent object of his consciousness.
>
> (Martin 2002: 122)

Causing pain creates an absorption with the body which renders the Other 'thing like' to the sadist. This means that the sadist then feels justified in treating the Other as object and him/herself as transcendent. As Sartre says in *Saint Genet*: 'He seeks in submissive eyes the reflection of his infinite freedom' (Sartre [1952] 1963: 81). This attempt to realise a total freedom away from the objectifying gaze of another person is the aim of the sadist but it is ultimately futile: 'The Other's look in the world of the sadist causes the meaning and goal of sadism to collapse' (Sartre [1943] 1995: 406) and the Other is revealed as a free consciousness. Johnny's violent objectification of women demonstrates a deep-seated bad faith. He accepts little responsibility for his actions but it is this acceptance of responsibility that is a necessary precondition for authentic conversion and raises it above a merely playful attitude. Johnny demonstrates the playfulness but fails to accept the responsibility for the effects of his behaviour.

Bad Faith and the Audience

This final section will move beyond the depiction of the characters and their relationship to masculinity and bad faith by considering the ways in which *Naked* directs the audience's attention towards the problem of bad faith. The first scene provides an excellent example. It appears suddenly, after only one screen of credits, with a forward tracking shot in an enclosed, partially-lit alleyway. In the distance we see two figures having sex against a wall. At first it seems consensual but as we approach the mood changes. The male figure with his back towards us, enveloped in a black coat, pushes the woman's head back and she cries 'What are you doing!? You're hurting me!' Moments later she breaks away, runs a few metres, turns and shouts: 'I'm gonna tell my Bernard of you! You're fuckin' dead!' The man, his face still only partially visible to the audience, turns and runs in the opposite direction.

This scene is immersive and evokes a strong emotional reaction: the running camera, the enclosed alley, and the close proximity of the actors all involve the spectator. The horrible nature of the scene is likely to lead to reactions of revulsion resulting in aggression, which is subsequently directed at the character, film and perhaps even the filmmaker (Wheatley quoting Metz 2009: 85). The aggression directed at Johnny becomes accusation and condemnation; the 'death' that is promised is delivered by the accusatory gaze of the audience, and the passing of this sentence involves adopting an attitude of bad faith. It reduces Johnny's existence to one thing, 'rapist', and then moments later as he steals a car, 'thief'. The curse of Johnny's female victim is enacted with the solidity of a death. Johnny's perception of himself as a dead man is articulated later in the film when a homeless girl, Maggie (Susan Vidler), asks him whether he's ever seen a dead body and he replies, 'only my own'.[8]

Sartre discusses the effect of the accusatory gaze in his biography of Jean Genet. He identifies the act of being caught idly reaching into a drawer as a defining moment of Genet's life: 'Beneath this gaze the Child comes to himself. He who was not yet anyone suddenly becomes Jean Genet ... A voice declares publicly: "You're a thief"' (Sartre [1952] 1983: 17). Here Genet's identity is formed: 'Pinned by a look. A butterfly fixed to a cork, he is naked, everyone can see him and spit on him' (Sartre [1952] 1983: 43). The first scene in *Naked* recreates the moment of Johnny's condemnation, the genesis of his fundamental project: the role of outcast and thief. We are not told what happened in his past but it is hinted at, at various points in the film, specifically in a scene towards the end when Johnny, beaten and barely conscious, stares up with crazed eyes, at the monstrous Jeremy and splutters: 'I didn't do it ... Why didn't you ask her?' whilst Jeremy glares down at him with a mixture of accusation and disgust and snorts 'Aren't people pathetic'. Jeremy's look here mirrors that of the audience in the opening moments of the film, yet the most revolting character delivers it making it easier to see Johnny as its victim. As Jonathan Webber states: 'It is our bad faith that makes us see other people as having fixed natures, just as it makes us see ourselves in that way' (Webber 2009: 128). Here the bad faith of the audience, as well as that of the characters in the film, is being brought into question.

In a later scene Brian becomes the representative of the audience. He watches Johnny in the room of the woman that he has been spying on and interprets what he sees as Johnny attacking and having sex with her.[9] As in the opening scene, Johnny is condemned, but on this occasion he glances back out of the window to indicate to Brian that he himself is being watched. This reciprocal look reveals Brian and makes him an object. Sartre uses the example of a voyeur looking through a keyhole to explain how one's sense of self is altered by the appearance of another person – being observed causes a dramatic change in our being and we are overcome with shame as we are discovered: 'I am ashamed of what I am' (Sartre [1943] 1995: 221). Brian is no longer permitted to hide anonymously in the shadows, watching 'lost in the world'

(Sartre [1943] 1995: 259). Instead he is forced to recognise himself and his actions from the perspective of the Other. He continues to watch but the power of his look has evaporated. Johnny, already an object, cannot be objectified further and Brian's role as voyeur and his existence as object are revealed.

Christian Metz, in his 1975 essay, says of the cinema audience: 'All the viewer requires – but he requires it absolutely – is that the actor should behave as though he's not being seen, and so cannot see him, the voyeur' (Metz 1986: 229). Johnny's look to Brian must in turn reflect back on the cinema audience sitting anonymously in the darkness. The audience is often so immersed in the 'dream state' of the film that they 'cannot perceive that … [they] are participating in the act of spectatorship and thus cannot take responsibility for that participation' (Wheatley 2009: 45).[10] This is the intended effect of many mainstream films. The films of Mike Leigh are attempts to shake the audience out of their 'dream state' by creating a world that is challenging and enigmatic: 'You do not walk out of my films with a clear feeling about what is right and wrong. They're ambivalent. You walk away with work to do. My films are a sort of investigation. They ask questions …' (Mike Leigh quoted in Movshovitz 2000: 103–4).

For Sartre, to deny one's responsibility in situation is to deny one's authenticity: to fail to realise one's true nature. By attempting to push the audience into constructing a meaning for *Naked*, to decide for themselves what the moral position should be, Leigh encourages them to analyse and question what they have seen. Leigh is not criticising film per se, or the audience's contribution to the system, rather he is encouraging thought about the content of the film and society in general. Through the investigation of the role of other people in the creation of bad faith, *Naked* draws attention to the fact that this way of being is, in part, produced and sustained by society. By attributing an identity in the form of personality traits or a social role, the Other engenders a certain sense of self in the subject's consciousness. The subject is then in danger of erroneously interpreting it as something essential about him/herself. In an attempt to realise a state of completion and security they strive in vain to become this identity absolutely.

This raises the question of whether it is possible to accept a certain role but still avoid bad faith. Sartre clearly thought that it was as is indicated in his writing on Jewish identity and Jean Genet.[11] It is a mistake to think that authenticity can be realised through the expression of pure freedom alone. This can never be the case as we are born into a physical and social world. Rather, one must choose how one accepts and interprets one's facticity (sex, race, religion and so forth) by realising that the values of these categories are attributed by people and that one is free to interpret and use them in an idiosyncratic manner. The acceptance of facticity, as if it is a choice, represents a free decision to accept and live one's role rather than a passive acceptance of it as inevitable, restricting and beyond one's control. Johnny is allocated the role of outcast and he embraces it: he uses it as a way of being that is uniquely an expression of his freedom, and as a means of attacking the bad faith of others.

Conclusion

The influence of Sartre's concept of bad faith can be found throughout the work of Mike Leigh, as characters with closed senses of identity are contrasted with those who display inclinations towards freer, more playful and authentic behaviours. *Naked* is an attempt to investigate the possibility of expressing freedom in an alienating society that promotes attitudes of bad faith. It is for this reason that it deserves to be recognised as an existential film rather than for its more superficial similarities with clichéd interpretations of existential thought. The male characters in *Naked* are caught in different forms of bad faith: either denying their freedom or attempting to avoid their facticity. Even Johnny, who demonstrates some desire to expose bad faith, rejects personal responsibility for his actions and fails to acknowledge the freedom of others through his misogyny and sadistic attitudes towards women. The conflict that takes place within Johnny reflects that of the film as a whole: the conflict between the acceptance and realisation of one's freedom and the desire to be complete and the struggle between the transcendent experience of consciousness and the physically embodied state.

Although the subject matter of *Naked* is bleak it is an attempt to engage and challenge the audience. There can be no freedom and no ultimate redemption within the world of *Naked* but then this is not what the film seems intended to achieve. Rather, it highlights the flaws that exist in a society of bad faith; it encourages reflection on one's own bad faith attitudes; and it challenges engagement with a world of alienation, anxiety and desperation.

Notes

1. Existential philosophy is generally understood to be a study of the nature of free, individual, human existence in an absurd universe. Historically film noir has been seen as the most fertile film genre for the application of existential theory, an approach first demonstrated in essays such as Robert G. Porfirio's 'No Way Out: Existential Motifs in the Film Noir' (Porfirio 1976). It is unsurprising that *Naked* has similarly been classified in this way and likened to both the plays of Samuel Beckett and the sculptures of Giacometti (Carney and Quart 2000: 236).
2. Sartre believed that the only essence that people have is an intrinsic freedom, which he also referred to as 'ontological freedom': a nothingness that separates them from deterministic influences. Ultimately we always have a choice and are therefore personally responsible for all of our actions. For this reason, Sartre claimed that 'man is condemned to be free: condemned because he did not create himself, yet nonetheless free, because he is responsible for everything he does' (Sartre [1946a] 2007: 29).

3. By the term 'facticity' Sartre meant everything that is part of an individual's existence in the world. These include one's body, past history, and situation in the world: sex, race, social position, wealth and so on.

4. What is represented here is inevitably a simplified explanation of the phenomena of bad faith. The explanation of bad faith in its entirety is too complex to be discussed in full in this chapter. For a good introduction to bad faith I would recommend *Sartre: A Guide for the Perplexed* (2006), by Garry Cox. For a more comprehensive and detailed book length discussion refer to *Bad Faith, Good Faith and Authenticity in Sartre's Early Philosophy* (1995), by Ronald E. Santoni.

5. Leonard Quart contends that Leigh had constructed a set of truthful characters except for 'the one glaring exception, striking a thoroughly false note ... the character called both Jeremy and Sebastian' (Carney and Quart 2000: 232). Adam Mars-Jones in his review of the film for *The Independent* was more blunt: 'What's the point of a three-month rehearsal period when you can just go along Oxford Street and have a T-shirt printed with the words "SADISTIC YUPPIE" while you wait? Jeremy's character is no more rounded than that' (Mars-Jones 1993).

6. For a discussion on the connection between play and authenticity see Zheng (2002: 127–40).

7. The concept of authenticity is perhaps one of the most under-developed areas of Sartre's philosophy and is consequently open to further work and interpretation. The comments that he makes about it in *Anti-Semite and Jew* and *Notes for an Ethics* are still much debated. For an expansion on the argument that to be authentic one must respect the freedom of others see 'Authenticity and Others: Sartre's Ethics of Recognition', by T. Storm Heter (2006: 17–43).

8. The only way in which a person can become entirely object-like is to die but at this moment they cease being a person. To entertain the idea that one is already dead could be seen as a comforting conceit: to believe that one is dead is to have solidity. Yet Johnny's 'death' is manifest as outcast and wanderer: a purgatory where death does not bring completion. This living death is similar to the struggle with bad faith where a fixed identity is both a curse and a seductive security, the facticity of human life, and the vertiginous sensation of continual self-transcendence.

9. The male look is discussed by Laura Mulvey in her classic article 'Visual Pleasure and Narrative Cinema' (1975). Mulvey argues that women are the objects of the male subject's gaze in many mainstream films. Although there are many instances in *Naked* where women are subject to the male gaze, or are filmed from the male perspective, Leigh attempts to undermine these scenes by making them deliberately unpleasurable.

10. Sartre in *What is Literature* ([1948] 2001) acknowledged that readers should allow their imaginations to become enchanted by novels – to lend them enough of their freedom to permit them to be created but as Iris Murdoch comments: 'An excessive self-forgetfulness will break down its objective contours and blend it with private fantasy and dream. In the latter case novel-reading becomes a drug. (It is characteristic of the art of the cinema to encourage, by its very form, this extreme of self-forgetting.)' (Murdoch [1953] 1999: 97).

11. It is as an act of defiance that Genet embraces his pariah identity and chooses to become what society has made of him. Although this adoption of the role of 'thief' may appear to be an act of bad faith, 'Sartre is in fact describing a lifelong process of de-alienation whereby Genet recaptures his alienated freedom and turns it back onto those who had mutilated him' (Leak 2006: 98).

Bibliography

Bell, L.A. 1999. 'A Feminist Exploration of Anti-Semite and Jew', in J.S. Murphy (ed.), *Feminist Interpretations of Jean-Paul Sartre*. Pennsylvania: Penn State University Press, pp. 123–48.

Carney, R. and L. Quart. 2000. *The Films of Mike Leigh*. Cambridge: Cambridge University Press.

Cohen-Solal, A. 2007. 'Introduction', in J.-P. Sartre, *Existentialism Is a Humanism*, trans. C. Macomber. New Haven, CT: Yale University Press, pp. 3–15.

Connell, R.W. 2005. *Masculinities*. Cambridge: Polity Press.

Coveney, M. 1996. *The World According to Mike Leigh*. London: HarperCollins Publishers.

Cox, G. 2006. *Sartre: A Guide for the Perplexed*. London and New York: Continuum.

Eshleman, M.C. 2008. 'The Misplaced Chapter on Bad Faith, or Reading *Being and Nothingness* in Reverse', *Sartre Studies International* 14(2): 1–22.

Gordon, H. and R. Gordon. 1996. 'Sartre on Questioning Versus the Curse of Bad Faith: The Educational Challenge', *Studies in Philosophy and Education* 15(3): 235–43.

Lawson, M. 2009. *Mark Lawson Talks To*. First broadcast on BBC4 on 19 April.

Leak, A. 2006. *Jean-Paul Sartre*. (Critical Lives) London: Reaktion Books.

Mars-Jones, A. 1993. 'Stripped of the Bare Necessities: Life, Says Adam Mars-Jones, is Anything But Sweet in Mike Leigh's New Film, *Naked*', *The Independent*, 5 November. http://www.independent.co.uk/arts-entertainment/film--stripped-of-the-bare-necessities-life-says-adam-mars-jones-is-anything-but-sweet-in-mike-leighs-new-film-naked-1502225.html (accessed on 20 January 2011).

Martin, T. 2002. *Oppression and the Human Condition: An Introduction to Sartrean Existentialism*. Lanham, MD: Rowman and Littlefield.

Metz, C. 1986. 'History/Discourse: A Note on Two Voyeurisms', in J. Caughie (ed.), *Theories of Authorship: A Reader*. London: Routledge, pp. 225–31.

Movshovitz, H. (ed.). 2000. *Mike Leigh: Interviews*. Jackson: University Press of Mississippi.

Mulvey, L. 1975. 'Visual Pleasure and Narrative Cinema', *Screen* 16(3): 6–18.

Murdoch, I. [1953] 1999. *Sartre: Romantic Rationalist*. London: Vintage.

Porfirio, G. 1976. 'No Way Out', *Sight & Sound* 45(4): 212–17.

Raphael, A. (ed.). 2008. *Mike Leigh on Mike Leigh*. London: Faber and Faber.

Santoni, R.E. 1995. *Bad Faith, Good Faith and Authenticity in Sartre's Early Philosophy*. Philadelphia: Temple University Press.

Sartre, J.-P. [1938] 1965. *Nausea*, trans. R. Baldick. Harmondsworth: Penguin Books.

———. [1943] 1995. *Being and Nothingness: An Essay on Phenomenological Ontology*, trans. H.E. Barnes. London: Routledge.

———. [1946a] 2007. *Existentialism Is a Humanism*, trans. C. Macomber. New Haven, CT: Yale University Press.

———. [1946b] 1995. *Anti-Semite and Jew*, trans. G.J. Becker. New York: Schocken Books.

———. [1948] 2001. *What is Literature?*, trans. B. Frechtman. Intro. D. Caute. London: Routledge.

———. [1952] 1983. *Saint Genet*, trans. B. Frechtman. New York: Pantheon Books.

———. [1983] 1992. *Notebooks for an Ethics*, trans. D. Pellauer. Chicago and London: The University of Chicago Press.

Spicer, A. 2003. *Typical Men: The Representation of Masculinity in Popular British Cinema*. London: I.B. Tauris.

Storm Heter, T. 2006. 'Authenticity and Others: Sartre's Ethics of Recognition', *Sartre Studies International* 12(2): 17–43.

Webber, J. 2009. *The Existentialism of Jean-Paul Sartre*. (Routledge Studies in Twentieth Century Philosophy) New York and Abingdon: Routledge.

Wheatley, C. 2009. *Michael Haneke's Cinema: The Ethic of the Image*. Oxford and New York: Berghahn Books.

Zheng, Y. 2002. 'Sartre on Authenticity', *Sartre Studies International* 8(2): 127–40.

Filmography

Leigh, M. (dir.). 1976. *Nuts in May*. BBC TV.

———. 1977. *Abigail's Party*. BBC TV.

———. 1988. *High Hopes*. British Screen Productions/Channel 4 Films/Portman Productions.

———. 1990. *Life is Sweet*. Thin Man/Film Four International/British Screen.

———. 1993. *Naked*. Thin Man/Film Four International/British Screen.

———. 2008. *Happy Go Lucky*. Film4/Ingenious Film Partners/Summit Entertainment/Thin Man Films/UK Film Council.

4

PURSUITS OF TRANSCENDENCE IN
THE MAN WHO WASN'T THERE

Tom Martin

The Man Who Wasn't There is the tenth film to result from the prolific partnership of brothers Ethan and Joel Coen. Since its release, the film has received mixed responses. On the positive side, one reviewer judged that the film 'ranks with their [the Coens] most immaculately crafted work' (Sterritt 2001), while another stated, more effusively, that *The Man Who Wasn't There*

> is steadily engrossing and devilishly funny, and, o brother, does it look sharp. Shot in black and white by the great cinematographer Roger Deakins, *Man* hauntingly evokes such Forties film-noir classics as *Double Indemnity* and *the Postman Always Rings Twice*. Both those films were adapted from novels by James M. Cain, whose pulp style is a Coen inspiration, though Cain never imagined crime fiction that included a musical montage on haircuts and an alien visitation. Somehow, with the Coens, it all fits.
>
> (Travers 2001)

Perhaps most impressively, the film earned Joel Coen the award for Best Director at the 2001 Cannes Film Festival. Yet the film has also received its share of negative criticism. Stanley Kauffmann, for *The New Republic*, wrote that *The Man Who Wasn't There* has 'no integral reason for being' and that: '[T]he Coen brothers arouse no dram of sympathy, either for a small man whom a ruthless society brutalizes or for a frustrated underling who yearns to be a topling. We simply wonder why the brothers were interested in making a film about this dumb, blundering, unappealing nerd' (Kauffmann 2001). Meanwhile, Philip Kerr took a swipe not only at the film, but at those who might have enjoyed it:

> It's axiomatic that Coen-heads – the people who get off on 'getting it' – will like *The Man Who Wasn't There*. Coen-heads get off on the mechanics of film-making: the flashy stylistics, the look of the picture, the production design, the score, stuff like that. For them, style is all … and content nothing.
>
> (Kerr 2001)

In the present chapter, I provide a reading of *The Man Who Wasn't There* which draws into question at least some of the negative criticism noted above. According to this reading, *The Man Who Wasn't There* cinematically addresses a significant theme in the existentialist philosophy of Jean-Paul Sartre. This theme is the tempting, but misguided, project of escaping worldly existence through, what I will call, 'pursuits of transcendence'. If this reading is plausible, then it would seem that the film's protagonist should not be seen simply as 'a dumb, blundering and unappealing nerd', as Kauffmann claims. The protagonist may well be misguided, but in that case he is so in an interesting manner and with respect to a significant existential crisis.[1] It follows from this, further, that Kerr's claim that the film is without (significant?) content also misses the mark. On the contrary, the film addresses an important philosophical theme in a creative and evocative manner and, as such, has content enough for me and, I suspect, for many other viewers as well.

In conducting this reading, I want to avoid, as much as possible, the trap of imposing a philosophical framework on a film on the basis of only loose or tenuous parallels between cinematic content and theory. That is, I do not want to force the film into a philosophical mode. In an essay on the films of Terrence Malick, Simon Critchley offers the following warning to philosophers engaging with film:

> To read from cinematic language to some philosophical metalanguage is both to miss what is specific to the medium of film and usually to engage in some sort of cod-philosophy deliberately designed to intimidate the uninitiated. I think this move has to be avoided on philosophical grounds … Any philosophical reading of film has to be a reading *of* film, of what Heidegger would call *der Sache selbst*, the thing itself. A philosophical reading of a film should not be concerned with ideas about the thing, but with the thing itself, the cinematic *Sache*.
>
> (Critchley 2009: 17)

In what follows I will heed Critchley's advice, to the extent that I offer a philosophical reading of *The Man Who Wasn't There* which draws on peculiarities of this film's unique cinematic narrative, that is, on this film itself. I will, however, go beyond the film to ideas, drawn from the work of Sartre, about the 'things' (themes and motifs) contained in it, in order to provide an account of how those things might be seen to cohere.[2] Doing so is, I trust, not an exercise in cod-philosophy, and is certainly not intended to intimidate. Rather, the aim is to better appreciate and engage with the thing itself.

Outline of the Main Plot

Ed Crane (Billy Bob Thornton) is a quiet, chain-smoking barber who leads a so-called 'regular life' in the suburbs, in a modest house with his wife Doris (Francis McDormand), a bookkeeper at a local department store. Ed suspects

– rightly, as it turns out – that Doris is having an affair with her boss at Nirdlinger's department store, Big Dave Brewster (James Gandolfini). Things start to change for Ed when a stranger, Creighton Tolliver (Jon Polito), comes into the barber shop and tells him about the 'wave of the future': dry cleaning. He offers Ed the opportunity to join him in this revolutionary new business opportunity. All Ed has to do is invest $10,000 and he can be a 'silent partner' in the business. Ed is attracted to the idea of escaping his normal life and decides to go for it. The problem is that Ed does not have $10,000. He comes up with a plan to get the money by blackmailing Big Dave, threatening (in an anonymous letter) to expose to Ann Nirdlinger (Katherine Borowitz), Big Dave's wife and owner of the department store, the fact that Big Dave is having an affair; a revelation that would spell Big Dave's ruin. The plan works. Dave pays up (placing the money in a bin), Ed secretly collects the parcel of money, pays it over to Tolliver, and they sign a partnership agreement.

Unfortunately things start going bad. Coincidentally, Tolliver has been staying in the same hotel that Big Dave and Doris have been using to conduct their adulterous liaisons. Tolliver has approached Big Dave and runs the same spiel past him that he ran past Ed – asking for $10,000 to become a partner in the dry cleaning business. At the time, Big Dave had thought that Tolliver's proposal was just a load of rubbish and had promptly forgotten about it. But now, having received an extortion letter asking for the very same sum ($10,000) he starts to suspect that Tolliver may be the letter's author. He confronts Tolliver and, as he later puts it, 'roughs him up a little'. Eventually, Tolliver reveals that Ed had recently paid him $10,000 and so was, in all probability, the letter's author. Big Dave confronts Ed about this and a tussle ensues, during which Ed inadvertently kills Big Dave. This is bad, but it gets worse. The police investigating Big Dave's death discover that there is a discrepancy in the department store's books, a discrepancy to the tune of $10,000 (which we, the viewers, assume went to Big Dave to pay off the extortionist). As a result of this, Doris (the bookkeeper) is accused by the police of killing Big Dave, she is put on trial for murder, and commits suicide while in detention. Apart from losing his wife, who, despite her infidelities, he seems to continue to love, Ed now finds that he is unable to make further contact with Tolliver. The dry cleaning man seems to have disappeared without a trace. Ed takes it that he has been swindled and two people have died for nothing.

This, however, is not yet the end of the story. It turns out that when Big Dave had confronted Tolliver to find out about the $10,000, that Big Dave's 'roughing him up a little' was something of an understatement. In fact, Big Dave had beaten Tolliver to death and disposed of the body in a lake. The police find the body and, along with it, a brief-case containing the signed partnership agreement between Tolliver and Ed and paperwork indicating that Ed had paid $10,000 in cash over to Tolliver. The police surmise that Ed killed Tolliver to get back his money, Ed is falsely accused of having killed Tolliver, he is put on trial for murder, found guilty, sentenced to death, and executed. THE END.

If a viewer were to exercise an interpretation of the film, they may well turn to the possibility that it is some kind of morality play, in which immoral behaviours (such as sexual infidelity and extortion) and attitudes (such as greed) lead to ruin.[3] A reading of the film along these lines would not be without plausibility. There can be no doubt that Doris and Big Dave's infidelity, Tolliver's greed – possibly Ed's greed, too – are among the elements that drive the narrative. However, there are idiosyncratic elements or tropes of this film which would be either left out of such a reading altogether or, at least, rendered quite insignificant. Two of these have already appeared in the sketch of the main plot given above. These are, firstly, that Ed's 'regular life' is as a barber and, secondly, that the potential route of escape from his regular life that he pursues is dry cleaning. If we were just running the 'lust-and-greed-leads-to-ruin' interpretation – the possibility of a quick buck leads someone away from their mundane existence and in turn to their ruin – then it might not be of much importance that Ed is a barber (rather than some other kind of so-called 'working stiff' – such as a bus conductor, a post office worker, a sales assistant), nor that it is dry cleaning (rather than uranium mining, microwave ovens or digital watches) that is the revolutionary and prospective cash cow that enchants him. On the contrary, I suggest that we take very seriously the importance of these very factors, and find a way of reading the film that respects their standing.

Hair Cutting and Dry Cleaning

Let us begin by focusing on Ed's life as a barber. Q: What, in general terms, is a barber? A: Typically, it would be someone who cuts hair. And Ed, indeed, does cut hair. But we need to investigate further what Ed takes his being a barber to be all about. Early in the film, he tells us the following:

> There's not much to it, once you've learnt the basic moves. For the kids there's the 'Butch' or the 'Heinie', the 'Flat-Top', the 'Ivy', the 'Crew', the 'Vanguard', the 'Junior Contour', and, occasionally, the 'Executive Contour'.

As Ed narrates this account of his profession, the screen displays these 'moves', all of which, to me, at least, look somewhat similar to each other. As such, the film presents Ed's barbering activity as a matter of the imposition of order on a part of the world: namely, human hair. Furthermore, this imposition of order is to be achieved through the deployment of a fairly restricted set of norms regarding hair form, the imposition of one of a small number of acceptable 'styles'.

But this part of the world, hair, inexorably tends toward unruliness; it just keeps on growing. The fact that the object of Ed's labours is so recalcitrant, refusing to stay put, raises the question of the possibility of the absurdity or meaninglessness of barbering. With a gesture towards Camus, we might say that there is something Sisyphean about that task.

While this may be true, it would not, of course, be peculiar to barbering – the same could be said for any number of activities, such as street-sweeping or lawn-mowing, where the dust or grass just keeps coming back. However, barbering has a feature in addition to this 'never-ending' quality which sets it apart from street-sweeping and lawn-mowing. This feature is the ambiguous status of just what hair is, and the film draws our attention to it in the following exchange between Ed and his fellow barber, Frank (Michael Badalucco):

> Ed: Frank? This hair ... do you ever wonder about it?
> Frank: What do you mean?
> Ed: I don't know ... how it keeps on coming. It just keeps growing.
> Frank: Yeah. Lucky for us, huh pal?
> Ed: No, I mean ... it keeps on growing. It's a part of us, and we cut it off and throw it away.

Thus it appears that, for Ed, hair is not just a simple material object like Sisyphus's Stone, or the dirt on the streets that needs to be swept up. Rather there is something quite intimate (and possibly abject) about human hair. Hair, which it is Ed's business to deal with, work on, and maintain, is both a part of us and external to us.

While there is still more to be said about the nature of barbering, let us turn now to the other key activity that we are dealing with in this section: namely, dry cleaning. From its first appearance in the narrative, dry cleaning is something that the film invites us to compare with barbering. It is in a barbershop that the idea is introduced to Ed (and the viewer) by Tolliver, a man with a toupee (and, so, a man whose hair does not keep growing). But what relationship might there exist between barbering and dry cleaning? In the initial sales pitch that he delivers to Ed, Tolliver describes dry cleaning as follows:

> It's called 'dry cleaning'. You heard me right, Brother. *Dry* cleaning. Wash without water. No suds. No tumble. No stress on the clothes. It's all done with chemicals, Friend.

Even from this brief description, we can conclude the following about barbering and dry cleaning; while they are the same general kind of activity, both being exercises in 'world maintenance', the former involves ambiguities or messiness in a way that the latter does not. We have already seen that the object of concern in barbering, hair, is presented as having an ambiguous status, being both a part of us and not a part of us. In the case of dry cleaning, however, there are no concerns we could have about what it is that is being removed from the clothes. It is, presumably, 'just dirt', and so there is nothing ambiguous about it in the conceptual economy of cleaning.

In addition, there is a further comparison that the film draws between barbering and dry cleaning, one which focuses on the 'hands-on' nature of the former activity in contrast to the 'hands-off' nature of the latter. Barbering has a tactile quality to it that dry cleaning, at least as it is presented in the film, does not. Cutting hair involves being in close proximity to that of which one is cleansing the world. Ed touches the hair he cuts, and the debris produced by his labour surrounds his feet. He remains in contact with it even after his job (at least the hair-cutting that is the essence of his job) is done. Dry cleaning, however, is a process that involves little if any contact with the object of labour and the waste that that labour aims to extract. Apart from, presumably, being carried out by a machine rather than human hands, dry cleaning is, as Tolliver stresses, 'all done with chemicals' as opposed to with suds and water. In the following, memorable scene, the film focuses the viewer's attention on both the tactile nature of employing 'suds and water' and dry cleaning's status as an activity antithetical to this. Ed is standing in the hallway just outside the open bathroom door through which the viewer can see, in the background, Doris taking a bubble bath. Ed is reminiscing about his recent, initial encounter with Tolliver and deliberating over the offer Tolliver has made him:

> Ed [voice-over]: *Dry* cleaning. Was I crazy to be thinking about it? Was he [Tolliver] a huckster, or an opportunity, the real McCoy? My first instinct was 'No, the whole idea was nuts'. But maybe that was the instinct that kept me locked up in the barber's shop, nose against the exit, afraid to try turning the knob.
>
> Doris [calling out to Ed from the bathroom]: Honey? Shave my legs, will you?
>
> *The viewer now sees Ed shaving Doris's leg. The camera focuses on the soap he rubs on her calf and the hair washing out of the razor into the bath water.*
>
> Ed [voice-over]: It was clean. No water. Chemicals.

It is in this scene that the film first signals to the viewer that Ed is indeed going to pursue dry cleaning as a way of getting him out of the barber's shop. But what this scene also captures, through a combination of Ed's voice-over and the camera's focus, is that it is particular features of dry cleaning – features opposed to those of barbering – that attract him to the plan. Ed is not pursuing just any alternative to being a barber. He is pursuing an alternative that gets him away from tactile, suds-and-water-type labour.

Furthermore, Ed's pursuit of dry cleaning is presented as being one that is, at least in part, related to his desire to escape the ambiguous status of hair as something that is both self (a part of us) and other (cut off and thrown away). The crucial scene, in this respect, occurs immediately after the viewer has witnessed Ed typing the extortion letter to Big Dave, thereby indicating that Ed has not only made the decision to follow Tolliver's plan, but is now acting upon it. The scene takes place in the barber's shop. Ed has just expressed to Frank his thoughts about hair being 'a part of us, and we cut it off and throw it away', and then continues:

Ed: I'm going to take this hair and throw it out in the dirt.
Frank: What?
Ed: I'm going to mingle it with common house-dirt.
Frank: What the hell are you talking about?
Ed: I don't know. Skip it.

Rather than confining the viewer to a position in which they must follow Ed's advice and just 'skip it', the film does provide the viewer with resources to answer Frank's question. Given the scene's location in the narrative – such that at this moment, Ed surely has his move toward dry cleaning on his mind – in addition to his immediately preceding claim regarding the ontologically ambiguous status of hair, Ed's statement about taking hair and 'mingl[ing] it with common house-dirt' becomes open to a straightforward interpretation; it indicates Ed's resolve to disambiguate his worldly concerns. Rather than resting with hair being both a part of us, yet something that we cut off and throw away, such that its status hovers ambiguously between being dirt and not dirt, by saying that he is going to 'mingle it with common house dirt' Ed is performing a disambiguation of hair. Hair for him now just is dirt, pure (or impure) and simple. With these words he is proclaiming that he will no longer have truck with that kind of ambiguity. Dry cleaning, should it ever be realised, may stand as a profession that facilitates the escape from interactions with ambiguous parts of the world. But, in the meantime, even while he is still a barber, Ed is signalling the change in his life that he thinks dry cleaning will bring about. Though, for the time being, Ed may have to continue dealing with hair, he can be closer to the kind of life he wants if he can treat hair simply as dirt.

Sartre on Human Existence and the Temptations of Transcendence

The themes that emerged from the preceding section – engagements with the world that have the character of ambiguity and the seductive possibility of escaping such engagements – are themes that loom large in the philosophy of Jean-Paul Sartre. In this section, I turn to a brief examination of some of this philosophy, not in order to impose it upon *The Man Who Wasn't There* but, rather, with a view to illuminating some of the points I have already drawn from the film.

Sartre claims, throughout his early philosophical works, that the human 'may be defined as a being having freedom within the limits of a situation' (Sartre [1946] 1995: 90). That we are free, radically free, and that this freedom is the central feature of human existence, is perhaps the best-known proposition to emerge from Sartre's existentialism. 'Man is', Sartre claims, 'condemned to be free: condemned, because he did not create himself, yet nonetheless free, because once cast into the world, he is responsible for everything he does' (Sartre [1946] 2007: 29). However, while Sartre claims that we are radically free and responsible for all of our actions, this does not mean that we can do just anything. As indicated in the definition above, whatever freedom we have is confined to the situation we are in. No matter what our circumstances we always have choices and we are responsible for the choices we make. Nevertheless, the range of choices we have is limited by our situation. So, for example, sitting in my office I am faced with a vast range of options of what to do next: I could read a book, play solitaire on the computer, sing a song, dismantle the desk, etc. I could do any of these things and, if I did, it would be a matter of my freely choosing to do so. However, I cannot order a beer from the bar or walk straight out of the door to take a look at the Eiffel Tower. This is because there is no bar in my office, and my office is in South Africa. In other words, my present situation – being in my office – is such that there are options that are not available to me and so cannot be chosen by me. These limitations, however, do not detract from the fact that my pursuit of whichever of the options my situation *does* make available to me is a function of my radical freedom. That I am *radically* free means that I am always free, not that I am free to do just anything.

In casting the human condition as having two key features – freedom and situation – we must be careful not to misconstrue Sartre as claiming that there are two (potentially) independent parts of which we are a combination. Sartre is no dualist.[4] Our freedom to transcend determination and the situation within which we live depend upon each other. Sartre insists that we understand freedom and situation as dialectically related:

> This dialectic goes as follows: the original project [i.e., that which freedom has chosen to pursue] illuminates the surroundings of the situation. But already the surroundings lay siege to and color the original project. What is more, the situation defines itself insofar as it is surpassed by the project and the project has no signification except as the project of changing *this* disposition of the world; therefore it gets defined by the situation. Situation and project are inseparable, each is abstract without the other and it is the totality 'project and situation' that defines the person.
> (Sartre [1983] 1992: 463)

On the one hand, it is only by virtue of our status as freely choosing subjects that our surroundings can exist as a situation, a sphere of potential action, rather than just 'stuff'. So situation relies on freedom. On the other hand, it is only because we are immersed in a situation, a world of options that we could choose between, that we have the possibility of being free. So freedom, in turn, relies on situation. It is not that freedom and situation are, in fact, the same thing – they are not. While they rely on each other, there is something of a tension that exists between them. Freedom is all about transcending the given, while situation is all about providing the given. While they are, as Sartre says, 'inseparable', unable to exist apart from each other, freedom and situation cannot be reduced to each other.

The human condition, according to Sartre, consists of these two inseparable features – freedom and situation – which, nevertheless, exist in a relationship of tension. As such, human existence is far from straightforward, and is characterised by a number of ambiguities. One such ambiguity concerns the nature of our bodies (Sartre [1943] 1998: 303–59). With his emphasis on action, Sartre insists that our bodies are integral to us as non-determined, free subjects. We are embodied agents. Yet, at the same time, our bodies are material objects, subject to cause and effect, and they are crucial aspects of our situations, through their provision of both opportunities and limitations to action. If we were to ask 'Are our bodies part of our free subjectivity or our situation?', the correct answer would be 'Both'. Our bodies have an ambiguous status with respect to freedom and situation. A further ambiguity concerns our engagement with the world. As seen in the above-quoted passage about the dialectical relation between freedom and situation, as a free subject I have a role in constituting the world I experience by 'illuminating' it, ordering and giving significance to its contents in the light of my projects. At the same time, however, the world impresses itself on me and my projects. This ambiguous relation between subject and world is seen most clearly when we consider objects that have the character of 'stickiness' or 'sliminess'. Unlike interactions with objects such as stones and pens, which we could – understandably, though incorrectly – view as things we can, in our capacity as embodied subjects, touch, use and then be done with without them affecting us, 'slimy' things do not let us get away so easily. They, quite literally, stick to us, possibly long after we are done with them. 'Slime is', as Sartre puts it, 'the revenge of the In-itself' (the world of objects) on the for-itself (subjectivity) (Sartre [1943] 1998: 609). It is important to stress that slime is not unique in putting the subject in a 'messy' relationship to the world – in all of our interactions with the world, the world affects us and leaves its impression on us regardless of our wishes – but slime does make more evident this otherwise potentially overlooked aspect of our condition.

It is precisely the negotiation of ambiguities such as these (and there are many others that can be drawn from Sartre's work) that is the wonderfully difficult challenge of human existence. For Sartre, an authentic person, one who lives the fullness of their complex condition, has 'a true and lucid consciousness of [their] situation, in assuming the responsibilities and risks that it involves' (Sartre [1946] 1995: 90). In other words, an authentic person, as much as possible, sees their circumstances and their roles in them as they are and acts with that awareness. Authenticity demands meeting the ambiguities, difficulties and messiness of human existence head on and acting in terms of them. But this is no easy task and the temptations to pursue a simpler, easier existence are powerful. For example, Sartre tells me that I am radically free and responsible for all I do, and yet at the same time I am limited by external circumstances. Would it not be easier to just 'go with the flow', to be determined by worldly and social circumstances, to not have the continual burden of choice and responsibility? Alternatively, if I am to be free, would it not be easier to not have so many limitations placed on me by my situation, to not have the world forcing itself upon me? Tempting as these possibilities might be, Sartre holds that the complex human condition cannot be simplified. Any attempt to simplify it in the ways described will require a person to deny, ignore, or wish away an aspect of their existence which simply cannot be escaped. It will require precisely *not* having 'a true and lucid consciousness of the situation, in assuming the responsibilities and risks that it involves'. Instead it will require that we lie to ourselves, and such self-deception with respect to our condition, Sartre calls 'bad faith' (Sartre [1943] 1998: 47–70). As bad faith requires self-deception with respect to an unavoidable condition, bad faith can never actually succeed. One cannot escape the condition of being both radically free and embroiled in the world. In fact, precisely in the attempt to *escape* an aspect of our existence, we are (covertly at least) *faced* with that aspect. Nonetheless, a person can live in bad faith by repeatedly avoiding troublesome aspects of their condition, trying as best they can to not notice them, and act as if they were not there (Sartre [1943] 1998: 50).

Sartre considers bad faith to be both common and important.[5] While he provides numerous examples of bad faith throughout his philosophical and literary works, they can all be interpreted as taking one or other of two general forms, which have already been gestured toward above.[6] The first involves attempts to escape or lessen one's sense of freedom and responsibility in favour of a more determined existence.[7] These we could term 'pursuits of immanence'. The second is to escape or lessen one's sense of embroilment in the world in favour of a less limited freedom.[8] Bad faith of this latter type involves an attempted distancing from situation, a transcending (in the sense of 'standing apart from') situation and, in virtue of this general feature, bad faith projects of this type can be termed 'pursuits of transcendence'. It must be stressed that, for Sartre, transcendence per se is not a problem. On the contrary, as free beings we necessarily are not confined to the world in the manner that pursuits of immanence would have it. It is as transcendent beings that we author our lives. But this authorship is conducted by making our way *through* the world – that is, *engaging* with the world – and not through *escaping* the world. It is this latter attempted use of transcendence that Sartre considers inauthentic, and it is 'transcendence as escape' that is referred to in the term 'pursuit of transcendence' as I shall use it for the remainder of this chapter.

Ed Crane's Pursuits of Transcendence

Having considered some aspects of Sartre's account of the human condition and the temptation to attempt to escape it or simplify it through (ultimately futile) pursuits of immanence or transcendence, let us turn back to the analysis of Ed's attractions to dry cleaning. Dry cleaning, for Ed, as we saw, stands as an alternative to being a barber, an alternative that offers him the possibility of escaping 'hands-on' engagements with ambiguous, worldly objects. Casting this in terms discussed in the previous section, we can see Ed's pursuit of dry cleaning as a pursuit of transcendence. Dry cleaning is not just the possibility of ceasing to be the barber in the sense that he no longer has to work for a salary, but in that Ed can stop being 'the barber' in a figurative sense too – dry cleaning offers the possibility of a quite 'hands-off' relationship to the world and others. Also, and in accordance with the notion of 'pursuits of transcendence' developed above, Ed's project is doomed to fail. Sartre, as we saw, holds that bad faith attempts to attain escape from the messiness of human life through transcendence are inevitably thwarted by the ineradicable intrusion of just such messiness, even in the throes of pursuing transcendence. In Ed's case, it is not simply that his project to escape normal life fails through, say, bad luck, but it fails precisely because his pursuit of dry cleaning involves him in messy affairs (such as violence and dishonesty). If this reading of the film, in terms of an examination of a pursuit of transcendence, is sound, then we are in a position to view the story of 'Ed the barber who wants to be a dry cleaner' neither in terms of a banal morality play in which greed-leads-to-ruin, nor as pointless and contentless, as Kauffmann and Kerr suggest in their reviews. Rather, this admittedly quirky tale engages with a deep and rich philosophical theme.

Furthermore, viewing Ed as engaging in a project characterisable in terms of escape from grimy, worldly engagement in favour of transcendence gives sense not only to his particular situation regarding being a barber and his attraction to dry cleaning (and in particular his distaste for 'suds and water' – something 'slimy', which, as we saw for Sartre, was paradigmatic of complicated, ambiguous worldly engagement), but can also help to draw into the narrative two other memorable features of the film which have yet to be mentioned; Ed's relationship with Birdy Abundas and the repeated appearance of flying saucers. It is to these two elements that I now turn.

Birdy Abundas

Running alongside and, at times, intersecting the main plot that I outlined earlier is the sub-plot of Ed's relationship with Birdy Abundas (Scarlett Johansson). Birdy is the teenage daughter of Walter Abundas (Richard Jenkins), a lawyer and acquaintance of Ed's. Ed is enthralled by Birdy's abilities as a pianist and, following Doris's imprisonment, he spends much of his spare time visiting her. He encourages her to pursue a career in music and dreams of the possibility of touring with her as her manager. Their relationship ends when they are involved in a car accident, following which Ed awakens to find himself in hospital and under arrest for the murder of Tolliver. As with the possibility of dry cleaning, a viewer could try to provide a fairly straightforward interpretation of this narrative in terms of Ed trying to escape his regular life in a misguided or foolhardy fashion, motivated by mundane concerns of greed or the attractions of an easier or more exciting life. But again, as with the case of dry cleaning, I suggest that greater attention to the details of this narrative will lead the viewer to a richer and more nuanced reading. Furthermore, I argue, doing so reveals another of Ed's pursuits of transcendence.

The scene in the film in which Birdy first appears occurs immediately after Ed, at a department store party with Doris, has just slipped away and advised Big Dave to pay the demands of the blackmailer (whom the viewer knows to be Ed); a crucial moment in the narrative, as it is at this point that the viewer sees that Ed's plan might just work. Ed is now alone, walking along a dimly lit corridor, mulling over to himself (in a voice-over) the details of the blackmail and the affair between Doris and Big Dave. In other words, he is going over what would count as the grimy and sordid nature of his worldly encounters with others. He hears a piano playing in the distance, follows the music, and meets the beautiful, youthful Birdy, seated at a grand piano, playing the adagio from Beethoven's Piano Sonata No. 8. The contrast between the crass dance music from the party Ed has just left and the sublime simplicity of the piano sonata he is now hearing is striking. So too is the contrast between the apparently angelic, pure, virginal Birdy and the lying, cheating, lascivious Doris and Big Dave. Birdy and her music are the antitheses of what Ed has just walked away from. But they are not simply antitheses; they are antitheses with a theme. Birdy is not simply other to Doris and Big Dave; she is purer, less worldly than them. Similarly, her music is not just different to the dance music from the party; it is different in being heavenly and unfamiliar.[9] Both of these contrasts, experienced by Ed, cast Birdy as a somewhat transcendent character, far removed from the messiness of Ed's everyday life. It is on these grounds that I suggest that we see Ed's attempts to be close to Birdy and to, in some way, share in her music, as another pursuit of transcendence.

As with dry cleaning, the pursuit of transcendence through Birdy is misguided and doomed to fail. Ed's dreams of her illustrious musical career are dashed when he is told by an expert piano teacher that Birdy has little musical talent (though she could make a 'very good typist'). What is more, she is in no way disappointed by this news, revealing on the drive home from the meeting with the expert that she would much rather be a veterinarian (a very down-to-earth occupation) anyway. If that were not enough to shatter Ed's illusions about her, grateful that he has taken such an interest in her career, she offers to perform oral sex on him. Not only has Ed misunderstood Birdy to have ethereal musical talents, he has also mistaken her for a pure and virginal, transcendent being.[10] She is, after all, just a regular person, and in no way some kind of portal to a different mode of existence.

Flying Saucers

The final element of the film I wish to draw into my reading is the flying saucer motif. Flying saucers appear throughout the film, both explicitly in the narrative and implicitly through flying saucer imagery. On my reading of the film, flying saucers are symbolic not just of transcendence (being, quite literally, about 'otherworldliness') but of the futility of pursuits of transcendence. The first explicit reference to flying saucers is in a scene in which Anne Nirdlinger comes to Ed's house to tell him that she and Big Dave had had, some years before, a close encounter with a flying saucer. Ed clearly thinks that she is crazy. However, the film situates this moment just after Dave's death, Doris's subsequent arrest and Tolliver's disappearance. In other words, Anne's visit coincides with Ed's pursuit of transcendence through dry cleaning starting to go horribly wrong. In this way, the film juxtaposes Ed's pursuits of transcendence (through dry cleaning and Birdy) to Anne's 'crazy' transcendence. At this point, the observant viewer might notice that, in fact, flying saucers have already been alluded to earlier in the film. In both the scene in which Ed is convincing Big Dave to pay over the money and in the scene in which Ed first meets Birdy, the viewer can clearly see in the background, almost hovering over Ed's shoulder, flying saucer-shaped light fittings. If I am right about flying saucers being symbolic of the futility of pursuits of transcendence, then we may view these early appearances of flying saucers as bad omens regarding the success of the projects that Ed is embarking on in each of these scenes. A further connection between flying saucers and Ed's pursuits of transcendence is clearly made at the moment of, and just following, the car crash which spells the end of his pursuits. Taken aback by Birdy's offer of oral sex, Ed loses control of the car. The camera shifts attention from the car to a single hubcap (shaped like the light-fittings mentioned earlier) rolling down a hill. The hubcap morphs into a flying saucer, and the flying saucer then morphs into a doctor's head-mirror. The doctor is flanked by detectives who reveal that Ed is under arrest for Tolliver's murder. So, it is the image of a flying saucer that links the failures of Ed's two pursuits of transcendence – dry cleaning and Birdy. The two points in which the film clearly juxtaposes the elements of dry cleaning, Birdy and flying saucers are like bookends, between which lie Ed's pursuits of transcendence from their promising beginnings, to their eventual demise.

Concluding Remarks

I have attempted to show, through closely examining features of *The Man Who Wasn't There*, that the film confronts us with the theme of attempts to escape mundane existence toward something purer, simpler, and perhaps even otherworldly. With the help of Sartre, I have framed these attempts as 'pursuits of transcendence', which, Sartre would claim, are aimed at inauthentically and futilely dealing with ambiguities that inevitably arise in human–world interactions. The three activities in the film that I claim gesture toward transcendence are dry cleaning, Birdy and engaging with flying saucers. It needs to be stressed that the futility attached to these activities does not necessarily reside in the impossibility of their objects per se – in fact, in one scene, the viewer sees Ed reading in a magazine an article about dry cleaning now being a reality, and then another about confirmed sightings of UFOs – but, rather, the impossibility of escaping ambiguous, worldly existence through them. It is in their capacity as 'solutions' to existential crisis that these projects are doomed.

The film's ending suggests that Ed realises both the futility of his pursuits of transcendence, and the necessity for him to face his life as it really is. In the dream sequence that takes place on the night before his execution, Ed claims to have found peace with respect to his life, bids farewell to the flying saucer in the prison yard – as if to say that he is done with dreams of transcendence – and walks back into the prison building to face his fate. The film's final scene, on my reading, signals Ed's (exceedingly brief) return to, acceptance, and, as Sartre might say, 'lucid awareness' of his human condition. He walks to the electric chair, past the witness gallery which is a line-up of haircuts; strongly reminiscent of the line-up seen in his barbershop when he was explaining what being a barber is all about. He takes his seat, is strapped in, and has a patch of hair shaved off his calf. The camera closes in on the sudsy water in a bucket, in which the warden rinses the hair from the razor, just as Ed had rinsed the razor while shaving Doris's legs in the bath earlier in the film. The film thus signals that Ed has come full circle, back to where he was prior to embarking on his pursuits of transcendence. Although his life is about to end, Ed has, in some ways, returned to the condition that was truly his, and he does so with remarkable acceptance. While his final thoughts are of the possibility of going to a realm 'beyond the earth and sky', these thoughts do not stand as hankerings to achieve transcendence in *this* life. Rather, they are speculations regarding transcendence in another life. In terms of *this human* life (what little remains of it) Ed is no longer trying to avoid his condition and has, to that extent, achieved something along the lines of what Sartre would deem authenticity. Seen in this light, Ed is not simply a 'dumb, blundering, unappealing nerd'. If anything he is, in his own, quiet way, an existentialist hero.

Notes

1. I have no comment to make with respect to whether or not the protagonist is 'unappealing', other than to say that it is far from clear to me what significance character 'appeal' (whatever that is, exactly) has to do with the value of film.
2. It may seem odd that in a contribution to a volume devoted to Sartrean perspectives on cinema there is no direct engagement with Sartrean thought until roughly half way through the essay. This is a consequence of the method I have adopted here of examining, initially, at least, only the film itself, drawing from *the film* its key content, rather than

extracting that content through the use of philosophy. This approach should not be seen to diminish the value of bringing Sartrean philosophy to bear in an engagement with the film. As the second half of the essay demonstrates, Sartrean philosophy can indeed be usefully employed to draw together what may otherwise be disparate threads of the filmic narrative.

3. It was, perhaps, with such a reading in mind that a reviewer for *Time* (3 September 2001: 80) wrote that 'the Coen film serves up a lovely, lurid brew of greed, murder and twisted identities'.

4. The most famous example of dualism in philosophy would be that of René Descartes, who held that mind and body (which includes the whole material world, including the human body) are completely different entities. While they may contingently interact, they are, in principle, utterly independent of each other.

5. Bad faith is not simply a personal matter, but can promote disastrous relations with others. Examples of these would include anti-Semitism (Sartre [1946] 1995) and slavery (Sartre [1983] 1992), both of which are diagnosed by Sartre as being promoted and made possible through bad faith.

6. For a more detailed account of the typologies of bad faith than can be offered here, see Martin (2002: 29–43).

7. See, for example, Sartre's discussion of the café waiter (Sartre [1943] 1998: 59, 60).

8. See, for example, Sartre's discussion of the woman in the café (Sartre [1943] 1998: 55, 56).

9. The viewer will note further that this music is quite new to Ed – 'Did you make that up?' he asks her. This adds a further layer to the 'otherworldliness' of Birdy and her music, at least as Ed experiences them.

10. In his review of *The Man Who Wasn't There*, David Sterritt (2001) writes that 'they [the filmmakers] make occasional missteps – a sexual moment near the end is wildly out of sync with the movie's overall tone'. On the reading of the film I am offering here, this moment clearly stands as the 'last straw' for Ed's misconceptions about Birdy's purity. It is, in some ways, jarring; but events that shatter illusions tend to be, by their nature, jarring.

Bibliography

Critchley, S. 2009. 'Calm – On Terrence Malick's *The Thin Red Line*', in D. Davies (ed.), *The Thin Red Line*. London and New York: Routledge, pp. 11–27.

Kauffmann, S. 2001. 'Odd Leading Men', *The New Republic*, 19 November, 30.

Kerr, P. 'A Coen-trick', *New Statesman*, 22 October, 46.

Martin, T. 2002. *Oppression and the Human Condition: An Introduction to Sartrean Existentialism*. Lanham, MD: Rowman and Littlefield.

Sartre, J.-P. [1943] 1998. *Being and Nothingness: An Essay on Phenomenological Ontology*, trans. H.E. Barnes. London: Routledge.

———. [1946] 1995. *Anti-Semite and Jew*, trans. G.J. Becker. New York: Schocken Books.

———. [1946] 2007. *Existentialism Is a Humanism*, trans. C. Macomber. New Haven, CT: Yale University Press.

———. [1983] 1992. *Notebooks for an Ethics*, trans. D. Pellauer. Chicago: University of Chicago Press.

Sterritt, D. 2001. 'Coen Brothers Revisit Shadowy Tale in *Man*', *Christian Science Monitor*, 11 February, 15.

Travers, P. 2001. 'Movies: *The Man Who Wasn't There*', *Rolling Stone*, 22 November, 95.

Filmography

Coen, J. (dir.). 2001. *The Man Who Wasn't There*. Good Machine.

5

LORNA'S SILENCE:
SARTRE AND THE DARDENNE BROTHERS

Sarah Cooper

When Pascal writes: the eternal silence of these infinite spaces terrifies me, he speaks as an unbeliever, not as a believer. For if God exists, there is no silence, there is a harmony of the spheres. But if God does not exist, then, yes, this silence is terrifying, for it is neither the nothingness of being nor Being illuminated by a look. It is the appeal of Being to man; and already Pascal takes himself to be a passion caught up *alone* into these spaces in order to integrate them into the world.

(Sartre [1983] 1992: 494)

In his diary notes on their filmmaking practice, *Au dos de nos images*, Luc Dardenne makes numerous references to Western philosophers, in addition to literary writers and other filmmakers, all of whose work informs his and his brother Jean-Pierre's desire radically to rethink cinema. While numerous commentators on their work, myself included, have noted that the Dardenne brothers' most explicit philosophical debt is to the ethics of Emmanuel Levinas, two fleeting mentions of Jean-Paul Sartre in Luc Dardenne's diary underline an ongoing, and more tacit, interest in this latter philosopher too. It is this more tangential but nonetheless significant interest in Sartre on the part of these two directors that will be addressed here. In an entry on 22 August 1996, Luc Dardenne cites a passage from *What is Literature?* on the status of the artwork, and in an entry on 27 April 2000 he quotes an extract from *Notebooks for an Ethics*, part of which is cited in the epigraph above, concerning the death of God and man's inheritance of his infinite mission (Dardenne 2005: 60, 111). Following the trajectory of these brief but important references, my reading of their most recent film, *Lorna's Silence* (2008), will begin by addressing a Sartrean – as differentiated from a Levinasian – perspective on the aesthetic dimension to which their films belong, and will reflect subsequently on the frightening silence that Sartre opposes to the harmony of the spheres in his atheistic reading of Pascal. Lorna's silence is articulated in a manner that emphasises the cinematic specificity of its incarnation, while indicating a relationship to Sartre's views on art and his broader philosophy. Most fundamentally, Sartre's existentialism will be seen to resonate through the Dardennes' humanism, which conjures forth a godless world in which existence precedes essence and human beings are called upon to take responsibility for their actions.

The Dardenne brothers first won international acclaim in the late 1990s, but began their career in documentary making two decades earlier. They founded the 'Dérives' production company in 1975 and then the 'Films du fleuve' in 1994. Their early social documentaries and first forays into fiction testify to their intense productivity from the 1970s onwards. However, it was not until the release of *The Promise* (1996) that they were to establish the innovative style that makes their work immediately recognisable and for which critical praise has as yet been unceasing. To date, they have made four further fictions, all of which have been singled out at the Cannes Film Festival: *Rosetta* (1999) and *The Child* (2005) were awarded the prestigious Golden Palm; Olivier Gourmet won best actor award for *The Son* (2002), as did Emilie Dequenne for her role as the eponymous Rosetta; and *Lorna's Silence* won the prize for best screenplay in 2008. Each of the five low-budget features is written and directed by the two brothers, who also play a central role in their production. Documentary qualities are discernible in the post-1996 films, which, at the outset, placed seasoned actors alongside non-professionals, used mainly handheld camerawork, and privileged direct sound. Set principally in or around Seraing, an industrial region in decline just outside of Liège, the films probe the stark realities of immigration, people trafficking, unemployment, and existence on the margins of society. The handheld camera that frequently tracks the actors and follows them at close proximity gives the sense of being with them but being led by them, avoiding judgement of the choices they make. Attention to the physicality of the actors' bodies, along with their gestures and activities, confirms that this cinema is not concerned with psychology, or with the revelation of inner or hidden depths. Thus, and in tune with the humanist drive of Sartrean existentialism, access to any essential core of their being is denied, as we watch what they do and remain on the surface of the many acts that define who they are and what they can become (Sartre [1946] 2007: 22).

Lorna's Silence suggests continuity with, as well as difference from, the other features made since 1996. The most recent film shifts location from Seraing to Liège, features a musical soundtrack briefly at the end, rather than using direct sound throughout, and is less frenetic with its handheld camerawork. The brothers made a choice to work with 35 mm stock for this film, and the change of camera technology with its heavier equipment slowed the pace and reaction times slightly, and caused the cinematographer to take more of a distance from the figures that were tracked restlessly in works such as *Rosetta* and *The Son* (Renzi 2008: 30). Furthermore, the brothers' desire to team up with people they trust has led them, over the years, to return to crew and actors they have already worked with. In *Lorna's Silence*, familiar actors from earlier films form the main cast, with the exception of Lorna (Arta Dobroshi) and Sokol (Alban

Ukaj). The familiar Dardenne actors have now accrued associations from the other parts that they have played, but *Lorna's Silence* re-casts them into new roles, thereby affording them the possibility of a fresh start, which is future-directed – in Sartrean terms, which 'projects itself into a future, and is conscious of doing so' (Sartre [1946] 2007: 23) – rather than backward-looking, even though the trace of earlier filmic associations remains. Although different from the human trafficking that formed the basis of *The Promise*, the concern with an illegal marriage racket that breaches conventional international border controls on citizenship suggests a connection with the intrigue of the earlier film. Yet *Lorna's Silence* is still the most plot-driven of the Dardennes' films to date, and, as Jacqueline Aubanas suggests, with its little crooks, pitiful crimes and moral anaesthesia, it also shares an affiliation with film noir (Aubanas 2008: 231).

Lorna, a young Albanian woman, is a central player in the illegal marriage scam, run principally by Fabio (Fabrizio Rongione) with his sidekick Spirou (Morgan Marinne). The scam serves first of all, through her marriage with a drug addict, Claudy (Jérémie Renier), to give her Belgian citizenship. Ignoring her wishes for a speedy divorce, the gang she works with kills Claudy instead, in order to set her up quickly with another husband, a Russian this time, who will pay a high price to gain Belgian nationality. Lorna keeps silent about Claudy's murder and confirms the belief of the investigating police officer (Olivier Gourmet) that he could have taken an overdose on hearing that their divorce had come through. Yet a malaise when making plans with Sokol, her boyfriend, to purchase a snack bar with their ill-gotten gains, suggests that her body carries with it the unresolved relation with Claudy, and she creates a belief in a pregnancy that even medical evidence to the contrary will not dispel. Her belief that she is pregnant is the catalyst for the Russian to pull out of the marriage deal, and for all of the men she works with, including her boyfriend, to break their ties with her and to send her back to Albania. However, en route, and possibly fearing that Spirou is going to kill her, she asks him to stop the car so that she can go to the toilet. When she returns, she hits him twice over the head with a rock, before running back into the woods, talking all the while to the child that she believes to be in her womb, and reassuring it that while she let them kill its father, she will not let the same thing happen again. She finds a cabin and says that they will rest there for the night before setting out the next day to find food and drink. Collecting twigs for firewood with only the sound of birdsong audible, she has faith in the possibility that they will find someone to help them. As she lies in the cabin and the screen goes black, we hear a Beethoven Arietta, from the Piano Sonata in C Minor, Op. III, which is light but retains the tension and uncertainty of her still precarious situation. For the Dardennes, her ultimate abandonment is not a cause for despair but is the very condition of possibility for a fresh start. It is this connection between bleakness and optimism that brings their vision close to that of Sartre, and it is by broaching questions of aesthetics and then ethics that we can chart this film's Sartrean path towards freedom.

Aesthetics from Levinas to Sartre

The fact that Luc Dardenne draws on a range of philosophical texts for filmic inspiration suggests the openness of their films to a Sartrean reading that can be made without contradicting the debt to Levinas that I have already observed at some length when writing on their work (see Cooper 2007). It is worth signalling briefly where the two philosophers converge and differ on the question of aesthetics in order to suggest why Sartre is the more relevant to this particular filmic analysis. The most palpable difference between Levinas and Sartre in the early years emerges in response to the publication of Levinas's 'Reality and its Shadow' (1948) in the existentialist journal *Les Temps Modernes*. In this piece, Levinas privileges philosophical exegesis and criticism over the idolatry of art. This controversial early article on aesthetics drove a wedge between the artwork and the opening to a future-directed temporality that was fundamental to his emergent ethics. For Levinas, art is the shadow of life, and its time is that of the interval: it neither corresponds to the time of life, nor does it allow for an encounter with death. This *entretemps* of the artwork is a time that never advances. The objection brought to bear on the essay on the part of the Sartrean editorial board was that Levinas omits what Sartre had written on the image in *The Imaginary* in 1940 and also neglects how painting and poetry are understood to operate on a lower level than the concept in Sartre's *What is Literature?* Levinas's views towards the aesthetic dimension mellowed over the years and he was ultimately to appreciate – in the poetry of Paul Celan, for example – that the literary dimension was not fully incompatible with the ethical. Yet he never explicitly revoked his early views. From the outset, Sartre's views on the artwork were different and, thus, unlike the justificatory moves that some Levinas scholars, myself included, feel they need to make when discussing his philosophy within film studies, the shift into the aesthetic dimension, albeit at the expense of as extended a development of an ethics, is easier to make when dealing with Sartre's work.

Sartre's reflections on the aesthetic dimension privileged literature, and he is well known as a playwright and novelist. He works through his philosophy within the aesthetic dimension, rather than separating the two, and his characters play out existentialist dilemmas, sometimes exposing thorny issues that the philosophy cannot resolve. Significantly for my discussion here, and unlike Levinas, Sartre wrote about and for cinema. His screenplay for *The Chips are Down* (*Les Jeux sont faits*) was filmed by Jean Delannoy and screened at the Cannes Film Festival in 1947, and through his early criticism, most notably on Orson Welles's *Citizen Kane* (1941), he gained notoriety. Dudley Andrew tells of how Sartre saw *Citizen Kane* in New York and did not like its fatalism, which he thought was supported by its flashback structure. Andrew explains how, analysing the tenses of the work, Sartre argues that the editing is akin to narrative techniques fit for literature only, and that the film promotes a false romantic attitude towards the world rather than the engaged position he was aiming to bring out. As Andrew also suggests, cinema for Sartre was the art of the present tense (Andrew [1978] 1990: 121–24). A key film critic of the time, whose own work was informed by Sartre's broader philosophy, but who took a more positive view of *Citizen Kane*, was André Bazin. Bazin was especially influenced by Sartre's view in *The Imaginary* that art was an activity in which human beings attempt to reshape the world and their own situation in it. Although the Dardennes are closer to asking the Bazinian ontological question, *What is Cinema?*, rather than the Sartrean question, *What is Literature?*, it is to the latter that they turn when reflecting on the ontology of the artwork in relation to their own film-making practice.

Luc Dardenne quotes the following passage from *What is Literature?* to mark out a fundamental difference between the work of art and the idea:

> the work of art is not reducible to an idea; first, because it is a production or a reproduction of a *being*, that is of something which never quite allows itself to be *thought*; then, because this being is totally penetrated by an *existence*, that is, by a freedom which decides on the very fate and value of thought. That is also why the artist has always had a special understanding of Evil, which is not the temporary and remediable isolation of an idea, but the irreducibility of man and the world of Thought.
>
> (Sartre [1948] 2001: 88)

The understanding of evil on the part of the artist is something that preoccupies the Dardenne brothers throughout their work, yet this interest is coupled with another that lies in the constant possibility of a character's transformation. Indeed, Luc Dardenne remarks in interview after the release of *Lorna's Silence* that evil is interesting to them precisely because it presents them with the possibility to explore change (cited in Renzi 2008: 30).

While it would be untrue to say that the characters of *Lorna's Silence* do not have a past, it is true that they exist in the present with one eye directed towards their future gains, and although their deeds can re-cement a relation to what has served hitherto to put them beyond the bounds of social and moral acceptability, there is also scope for transformation. Badness or evil are not innate: they are the product of a character's upbringing and social surroundings. Whether the Dardennes' characters work illegally, or work legally but live below the poverty line, they are all fighting to survive financially and socially on the margins, and to do things that in some cases enable them to be someone different. There are decisive moments in all of the films when characters have a choice of whether they will carry on in the way that they have been living, or whether they will change. Elsewhere, I have read this potential for change – which usually represents a break from repeating the most violent of reactions to others – in relation to the Levinasian ethical injunction not to kill: to choose not to reiterate the past and not to kill, whether symbolically or literally (see Cooper 2007). Here, and without contradiction, such a choice can be read in Sartrean terms as the very act that could set the Dardennes' characters on the existentialist road to freedom and responsibility. And given that most of the characters who make these choices are young, they correspond to the existentialist hero who has a lifetime ahead of him/her in order to remake the future. These figures include Igor in *The Promise* who confesses the secret he has been keeping from Assita about the death of her husband; Rosetta whose final gaze of the film suggests a desire for contact and help that will save her from killing herself and her mother; Olivier in *The Son* who chooses not to kill his son's killer; and Bruno in *The Child* who takes responsibility for his actions towards the end of the film. Lorna can be added to this list but her refusal to reiterate the act of killing takes a different turn, one that resonates more consistently with a Sartrean, rather than a Levinasian, position. The key to this reading lies in the film's creation of an ethics of silence and the relation it establishes between the choices Lorna makes and a belief in the unborn, as opposed to a sole concern with the repetition of killing that turns the living into the dead. The move towards Lorna's transformation, and her Sartrean drive towards freedom that still preserves a bond with an other who is both loved and lost as well as yet to be, involves a withdrawal from the different circulatory systems on which the film depends. This removal happens gradually but is hinted at from the opening of the film onwards.

Towards a Sartrean Ethics of Silence

As in the so-called respectable world of legality and order that is nonetheless responsible for engendering its flip side of iniquity, it is money that makes this criminal underworld go round. Jacqueline Aubanas observes more generally across the films of the Dardennes that bodies are either to be bought or sold, and this is nowhere more apparent than in *Lorna's Silence* (Aubanas 2008: 229). The first image we see is a handheld sequence shot of a wad of euro notes being passed under the protective glass of a bank teller's counter, which connects Lorna seamlessly to the circulation of currency that defines her existence throughout the film. Lorna is paying in her cash earned on the borders of criminal and legal activity: she works at a laundry in addition to working for Fabio. She confirms to the teller that she will soon have Belgian identity. Unbeknown to her, the price of her citizenship will be a Belgian citizen's life. Claudy has entered into the marriage with a view to getting money to feed his habit, but it is clear that he wants to change. Fabio and the others he works with refer to Claudy derogatorily throughout as a junkie, and need to keep him in this state, fixed in this category, in order to deny him the relative freedom of defining himself in a new way. His death means more to them than his life, since it precipitates Lorna into a further moneymaking venture and prevents them from having to pay Claudy for his services. In turn, Lorna's body becomes their possession – Fabio dictates that she must have an abortion when she says she is pregnant, orders her about in other ways, and also says that the Russian can have her examined to verify that she is not pregnant when they marry. She works for Fabio, and her life and body are in his hands, as were Claudy's. Claudy's desire to give up drugs eventually draws Lorna to him in spite of herself. Although neither Claudy's nor Lorna's acts are always Sartrean acts made in good faith, their separate desires to do something in order to be different signify a search for freedom as such.

In keeping with the focus on the circulation of money, and in spite of the negativity of the deals and the high cost in terms of human life, Jean-Michel Frodon reads *Lorna's Silence* aptly in relation to the work of Robert Bresson, as 'a kind of voluntarily optimistic response to *L'Argent*' (Frodon 2008: 28 [my translation]). The Dardennes' debt to Bresson is one that they speak of frequently, and is clearly apparent in their earlier film *Rosetta*, which looks back to Bresson's *Mouchette* (1967) and recalls some of its key scenes with a more positive vision at the end. *L'Argent* (*Money*, 1983) begins with the handing over of a counterfeit bank note that sets off an inexorable chain of events that ruins the life of a young mechanic and his family, and positions him as both victim and perpetrator of crimes. Bresson's subtle and pared down filming, which gives a central place to materiality and objects, is discernible in the Dardennes' work. Yet there is a further connection between Bresson and *Lorna's Silence* that emerges in Bresson's *Notes on the Cinematographer*. Bresson writes: 'THE SOUNDTRACK INVENTED SILENCE' (Bresson [1975] 1986: 38 [emphasis in the original]). While the initial image of *Lorna's Silence* refers us to Bresson through the subject matter of money, it is the soundtrack that actually opens the film over a black screen. My interest here is in how sound or its absence is portrayed visually, since it is the visible articulation of silence that connects this film to the Dardennes' reading of Sartre.

Lorna's Silence contains the most dialogue since *The Promise* and is their most loquacious film to date. Over the black screen at the start, we hear the noises of a road – vehicle engines, hooting – and the sound of someone's shoes, presumably Lorna's, walking along a pavement. This initial focus on sound, its priority over vision in the first twenty seconds of the film, prior to a richly spoken scenario, works the better to highlight both the moments of silence, and the moments where the extra-linguistic dimension breaks through to trouble the circulation of words. The literal reading of the film's title pertains to Lorna keeping her silence when she could have spoken up prior to, or after, Claudy's death, to expose the scam of which she was part. Yet Luc Dardenne's reference to, and commentary on, a passage from Sartre's *Notebooks for an Ethics* suggests a more complex reading of this film's silence.

Luc Dardenne cites a lengthy extract from *Notebooks for an Ethics*, part of which is quoted in epigraph to this chapter, and which concludes with Sartre's words: 'Consequently *to see* is to pull Being back from its collapsing' (Sartre [1983] 1992: 494). Luc Dardenne's gloss on the exorbitant responsibility for the filmmaker reads as follows:

Infinite mission for the film-maker: to bring the world into being, to bring man into being through vision, by making him visible. His solitude is greater than in Pascal's time, his fear too, for the silence of the infinite spaces now lies in the human gaze.

(Dardenne 2005: 112 [my translation])

Remarking on the solitude of man in the transition from the time of Pascal to that of the twenty-first century, Luc Dardenne is at one with the Sartrean existentialist shift towards a secular world in which responsibility rests firmly on human shoulders. The fright of which Luc Dardenne speaks is also registered in Sartre's *Existentialism Is a Humanism*.

In his defence of existentialism against attacks from Christians and Marxists, Sartre was keen to emphasise the optimism of a philosophy in which everything lies in our hands and cannot be deferred to a higher authority. Yet it is precisely this optimistic thrust that he suggests scares people. Indeed, he asks: 'For when all is said and done, could it be that what frightens them about the doctrine that I shall try to present to you here is that it offers man the possibility of individual choice?' (Sartre [1946] 2007: 19–20). The fright of optimism in *Existentialism Is a Humanism* looks forward to *Notebooks for an Ethics*. Sartre's attempt to make a connection between the individual and the collective in the earlier text – insofar as the choices we make affect everyone – gestures towards the ethics that he never completed in his lifetime: 'I am therefore responsible for myself and for everyone else, and I am fashioning a certain image of man as I choose him to be. In choosing myself I choose man' (Sartre [1946] 2007: 24–25). What Luc Dardenne emphasises in his reflection on Sartre's *Notebooks* and, specifically, on how frightening the infinite post-Pascalian space is to us today, is not only its silence, but also its presence in the human gaze. *Lorna's Silence* works slowly to palliate the fright of silence within the human gaze.

In the first instance, and in keeping with the start of *Lorna's Silence* in which sound precedes vision, any possibility of silence is invaded by imploring cries. Claudy cries out for help as Lorna tries to go to sleep towards the start of the film, but she is angry and resistant. In a long sequence shot, we see Lorna in bed, sitting up at first, with her back against the wall, drinking tea. She hears his music, shouts for him to turn it down, and when this gets no response, she goes to the door and shouts again. As she tries to go to sleep, Claudy calls out to her from off-screen space. She is cold to his dependence on her at this stage, and this is reinforced by the separation of their spaces, both visually and aurally. She answers back to him, telling him to go away and thereby creates a barrier against his desire to come off heroin with her help. Slowly, however, she becomes more compassionate. Another day, and after refusing and arguing with him for a while, she agrees to get him some replacement medicine for his addiction from the chemist. She also starts to talk to Fabio about alternatives to the planned overdose that will kill him – she has the idea that if Claudy is seen to beat her, she will get a quick divorce, and she offers to pay Fabio the money that Claudy is owed for participating in the fake marriage. While filmed with Fabio in his taxi, Lorna and Fabio are shot separately, the cut of the edit serving to reinforce her separation from him from the start. In contrast, after her initial separation from Claudy in her room, their subsequent encounters, although confrontational, bring them closer together.

They have two encounters in the hallway of their flat that strengthen their relation, both of which unite them in sequence shots: the first is when Claudy throws himself at her feet to persuade her to buy medication to help him give up drugs; the second is when she strips off her clothes and has sex with him, partly in an effort to prevent him from buying more drugs, but also confirming an initially unconscious attraction to him. The second encounter is wordless, intuitive, and follows an altercation after she asks a drug dealer to leave. After their sexual encounter, and presumably the next day, they are filmed briefly in a two-shot, suggesting togetherness: in a shop he purchases a bike and they share the cost of the broken door lock. The hallway encounters are sealed by one final one, after Claudy's death, between Lorna and the police officers who ask her questions about the overdose. She keeps her silence but cannot contain her emotions as the associations of the space itself serve to reinforce her bond with Claudy's post mortem. Her silence, fleshed out in this space, has more to do with her previous connection to Claudy and to what it will engender within her, than to protecting the men for whom she works. Her choice to keep quiet places her on the borders of morality – to confess would be to abide by the system of law and order, but would be to do the wrong thing by all of the people she has been involved with thus far for her survival in the illegal racket. Furthermore, doing the right thing by Claudy after his death is presented as a tacit ethical decision that has to be kept secret. While she is not portrayed as going through a Sartrean series of responsible questions about what could happen if everyone did as she did, her actions do implicate and reach out to a broader humanity.

A main turning point in Lorna's attitude towards Claudy, and towards whether she does something or nothing to help him occurs in the hospital when she visits him with a change of clothes. She virtually carries him on her back down the stairs of their block of flats when he is almost crippled by cramps from attempting to withdraw from drugs. When she visits the hospital later she wants to just leave his things with a nurse, but the nurse says twice that she can go and see him, and after objecting initially, Lorna takes his things to him herself. Once in his room, all we see of Claudy is a bundle wrapped up in white linen, but his regular breathing assures us that he is still a living presence. In a sequence shot we see Lorna place his things, then walk around the bed and watch him silently, lingering far longer than her earlier oscillation between hostility and indifference suggested that she would. Such silences, as with the bereaved father Olivier's taciturnity in *The Son*, bring with them a sense of foreboding, since they block access to what the character is thinking, and heighten tension and ambiguity. Yet Lorna's subsequent desire to arrange for a quick divorce, rather than an overdose, suggests that she is already on the side of wanting to keep Claudy alive, and a second pensive silence in a later scene confirms what she has resolved to do.

After a brief clandestine meeting with Sokol, her Albanian boyfriend with whom she speaks her mother tongue, we see her alone in the flat she shares with Claudy. She perches against the radiator in her living room, drinking from a mug, and is focused on her inner thoughts. She then paces the room, before sitting on the coffee table, and pacing the room again. After a couple of minutes, she puts the mug down, walks towards the door of the lounge and hits her arms against the door frame so violently that it causes her to bend double with pain. This is the starting point of her attempt to free Claudy from the clutches of the gang. While the filmic construction of her silence in the two scenes outlined above comprises a vision of internal contemplation and a literal absence of speech, it occurs in the absence of another human gaze: in the first scene, Claudy sleeps; in the second scene, she is alone. Indeed, the entire film works towards bringing Lorna's silent solitude into being in order to distance her from the human gaze and to enable her to be free to start again.

Re-orienting the Gaze: Towards Sartrean Responsibility and Freedom

After buying the bike, Claudy cycles away, having arranged to meet Lorna at lunchtime. Lorna walks away with a smile on her face. The next shot we see is of her folding his clothes in the flat, seemingly a continuation of the previous connection established between them, now within the domestic space. We then see her in a men's clothes shop, purchasing something new, presumably for him. In the next shot, in a clinical environment, however, she hands over the clothes to a male orderly and we learn that Claudy is dead: the clothes are for him to be buried in. The ellipsis of Claudy's death is enhanced by the fact that we never see his body or coffin, even though Lorna gets to see him a second time. She also goes to meet his family outside the funeral parlour to return his money to them – a gesture that the family refuses. Although we know that he is gone, the fact that this departure and the sight of a dead body are denied us are the first indications that his loss will never be final, even though it is never disavowed. The circulation of the money continues beyond his death, but while his brother refuses it, Lorna buries it first in the soil of the garden outside her workplace before digging it up again at a later stage to deposit it in an account for her future child. The money is the material connection between the living and the dead here that harks back to their sexual bond, fantasises Claudy's siring a child, and thus creates a belief in a new life beyond his death. As with Olivier's anguished chase of Francis in *The Son*, shouting 'reviens!' ('come back!'), with the sense that he is calling out to his dead son through the living, Lorna's phantom child connects her to Claudy. The baby is a felt and imagined presence through which Lorna is able to gesture towards reparation for the past without being defined by it: she was unable to save the father, but will fight to save the child.

In some respects, and although their nationalities differ at the start, Lorna is a grown-up Rosetta. Different in build, their haircuts are nonetheless similar, as are the stomach cramps Lorna suffers from, which connect her back to Rosetta's unexplained pains. While hope for Rosetta is glimpsed in her acknowledgement of Fabio's gaze in the final shot of the film, Lorna breaks away from all of her former relationships with the living. Indeed, unlike Rosetta and the other characters whose gaze is returned in the final shots of the Dardennes' films from *The Promise* onwards, Lorna has no such external point of reflection. But this isolation is precisely what is necessary for her finally to make a change. The visual and material absence of the child does not prevent Lorna from believing in him/her and talking to him/her. While her self-definition from this moment is still relational in the sense that she fantasises a child, and this may strike us as part of the cumulative formation of an identity, there is, in fact, denudation, rather than accumulation, in the progression of Lorna's life story: each event, each act serves to take her to a fresh starting point at the end of the film. The men in her life are taken away one by one, and even though there is no other person implicated visually in the frame with her at the end, Claudy remains with her in a profoundly Sartrean sense.

In his reading of *The Chips are Down*, in which the dead are part of the world of the living but remain invisible to them, Colin Davis draws on Sartre's *Being and Nothingness* to explain the attitude on the part of the living to the dead (Davis 2007: 43–65). As is also evident in the closed off space of the play *No Exit (Huis clos)*, the dead here no longer have the capacity to change or to have an active impact on the world of the living. Yet, as their fleshed out existence in both play and film suggests, rather than just live on in memory or consciousness, the dead continue to form part of the world in the way that they did before they departed and, thus, never really leave us. It is the living who choose whether or not to see the dead all around them; the living have to take responsibility for the dead and this is non-negotiable. As Sartre writes in *Being and Nothingness*, 'we choose our own attitude toward the dead, but it is not possible for us not to choose an attitude' (Sartre [1943] 2003: 563). In *Lorna's Silence* the female protagonist's choices are based on her response not only to the dead, but also to the unborn. Her belief in a figure that medical science has told her is non-existent is precisely what is necessary for her to make a defining break, to do something that orients her life in a different way from this moment onwards. While on one level, her belief structure mimics a quasi-religious faith in the invisible and the intangible, it is clear that there is no higher being here to guarantee her fate or that of her imagined child. Acknowledging this, Lorna says to her child that she is sure that someone will help them in the morning. The terrifying silence of Lorna's solitude may never be exchanged for the harmony of the spheres, but is soothed, for us at least, by the tones of the Beethoven Sonata that plays at the end.

Incomplete and on-going, Lorna's transformation is as open-ended as a Sartrean project waiting for a more fully developed ethical conclusion. Her only opportunity for re-entry into the mainstream of social respectability and responsibility is by breaking free of the gang's clutches. If viewed with the key Sartrean question of responsibility in mind from *Existentialism Is a Humanism* – what would happen if everyone did as I do? – then while such extreme acts as hitting Spirou with a rock, even though in the service of self-preservation, have no place in society, she is trying to break free from a closed society that operates on the edge of systems of law and order, and her actions are therefore more difficult to judge. Enabling her to hold on to her connection with Claudy without allowing this bond to drag her back to her past, Lorna's imagined child suggests that she has moved beyond melancholic incorporation of her lost love object, and is working through any guilt she feels for his loss by investing in the future. The primordial woodland where she finds herself in conclusion (with soil and foliage akin to where she buried Claudy's money before depositing it in a bank for their child) is distant enough from the surrounding human world for her to rethink her relation to that world differently from this point on. Stripped of all her worldly goods, the creation of the imagined body of their unborn child whom she will care for is all that is necessary for her to start again with her human relationships. Lorna's true testing journey begins as the film ends, as the absent figures of Claudy and their phantom child condition the more concrete possibility of her continuation along the existentialist road to responsibility and freedom.

Bibliography

Andrew, J.D. [1978] 1990. *André Bazin*. New York: Columbia University Press.

Aubanas, J. (ed.). 2008. *Jean-Pierre & Luc Dardenne*. Brussels: Editions Luc Pire.

Bresson, R. [1975] 1986. *Notes on the Cinematographer*. London: Quartet Books.

Cooper, S. 2007. 'Mortal Ethics: Reading Levinas with the Dardenne Brothers', *Film-Philosophy* 11(2): 66–87.

Dardenne L. and J.-P. 2005. *Au dos de nos images 1991–2005*. Paris: Seuil.

Davis, C. 1996. *Levinas: An Introduction*. Cambridge: Polity Press.

———. 2007. *Haunted Subjects: Deconstruction, Psychoanalysis and the Return of the Dead*. Basingstoke: Palgrave Macmillan.

Frodon, J.-M. 2008. 'Décrochage', *Les Cahiers du cinéma* 636: 26–28.

Levinas, E. 1948. 'Reality and its Shadow', in S. Hand (ed.) (1989), *The Levinas Reader*. Oxford: Blackwell, pp.129–43.

Renzi, E. 2008. 'Conversation avec les frères Dardenne', *Les Cahiers du cinéma* 636: 29–30.

Sartre, J.-P. [1940] 2004. *The Imaginary: A Phenomenological Psychology of the Imagination*, trans. J. Webber. London: Routledge.

———. [1943] 2003. *Being and Nothingness: An Essay on Phenomenological Ontology*, trans. H.E. Barnes. London: Routledge.

———. [1944] 2000. *Huis clos and Other Plays*, trans. K. Black and S. Gilbert. London: Penguin.

———. [1946] 2007. *Existentialism Is a Humanism*, trans. C. Macomber. Intro. A. Cohen-Solal. Notes and preface by A. Elkaim-Sartre, J. Kulka (ed.). New Haven, CT: Yale University Press.

———. [1948] 2001. *What is Literature?*, trans. B. Frechtman. Intro. D. Caute. London: Routledge.

———. [1983] 1992. *Notebooks for an Ethics*, trans. D. Pellauer. Chicago and London: The University of Chicago Press.

Filmography

Bresson, R. (dir.). 1967. *Mouchette*. Argos Films.

———. 1983. *L'Argent (Money)*. France 3 Cinéma. Eôs Films.

Dardenne, L. and J.-P. (dirs.). 1996. *The Promise (La Promesse)*. Eurimages. Les Films du Fleuve.

———. 1999. *Rosetta*. ARP Sélection. Canal +.

———. 2002. *The Son (Le Fils)*. Archipel 35. Les Films du Fleuve.

———. 2005. *The Child (L'Enfant)*. Les Films du Fleuve. Archipel 33.

———. 2008. *Lorna's Silence (Le Silence de Lorna)*. Archipel 35. Les Films du Fleuve.

Delannoy, J. (dir.). 1947. *The Chips are Down (Les Jeux sont faits)*. Les Films Gibé.

Welles, O. (dir.). 1941. *Citizen Kane*. Mercury Productions.

PART II

FILMS OF SITUATION

6

BEING – *LOST IN TRANSLATION*

Michelle R. Darnell

Sartre was a prolific author, and each of his many writings focuses on the
freedom of the human person, and the subsequent ambiguity of the universal
human situation. Still, despite his many attempts at communicating his
conclusion to a wide audience, much of Sartre's philosophy is rejected by those
who clearly do not understand what Sartre was intending to communicate.
Consideration of why Sartre's attempt at communication with others about the
human situation was, and continues to be, so difficult is provided below, with
special emphasis on the role of language. Sartre's insistence that words are
freely interpreted as signifying a reality that is not contained in a word itself
ultimately establishes the importance of focusing on the situation within which
words are chosen, which is exemplified by Sartre's use of 'theatre of situations'
as a means of communicating his own findings about the human situation to
others. Interestingly, Sartre's views on film are themselves rather ambiguous,
but it is argued here that a 'film of situations' is not only possible, but is
exemplified by Sofia Coppola's 2003 film *Lost in Translation*. Indeed, *Lost in
Translation* addresses some of the primary aspects of the human situation that
Sartre addresses in his lecture *Existentialism Is a Humanism*, but, by virtue of
being a film, is able to contextualise the words Sartre relies on by situating
them within the projection of the complexity and ambiguity of the world, and
the requirement of individuals making choices within the world. Ultimately it
is suggested that consideration of the potential role for 'films of situations' by
screenwriters and directors will assist in the continued development of film as
a critical inquiry into the freedom of the human person, and less as a means of
escapism. Subsequently, film can be considered a medium through which a
continuation of the Sartrean project is enabled.

Lost in Translation

Existentialism, as a form of philosophy, begins with, and thereby is fundamentally about, the human individual. Accordingly, it is reasonable to assert that each individual person can contribute to, and learn from, contemplation of existential literature. Indeed, it would seem that each individual is being addressed in Sartre's existential writings, especially given Sartre's own words that 'the exigency of the writer is, as a rule, addressed to *all* [persons]' (Sartre [1948] 2007: 50), and that each person needs to rediscover him- or her- self (Sartre [1945] 2007: 53). Nonetheless, in Sartre's famous lecture *Existentialism Is a Humanism*, he claims that existential philosophy, as a doctrine, 'is strictly intended for specialists and philosophers' (Sartre [1945] 2007: 20). If existentialism is pertinent to every person, prima facie it seems quite odd, if not outright contradictory, for Sartre to acknowledge an audience that is limited to a seemingly elite few. The reason for Sartre's limitation on the appropriate audience for philosophical doctrines begins to become clear if focus is given to the limitation of writing, and language more generally.[1] Sartre himself notes that writing for the universal reader is only an ideal (Sartre [1948] 2007: 50), because there is no given 'reconciliation between the writer and his public' (Sartre [1948] 2007: 97). The author, who in the case of *Existentialism Is a Humanism* is Sartre himself, is often misunderstood by his audience because 'a work of the mind is by nature allusive' and thereby the author 'knows far more than he tells. This is so because language is elliptical' (Sartre [1948] 2007: 51). In an author's rendering of his or her beliefs into language there will always be an excess of some manner that is not fully expressed in the translation from a work of the mind to objective language, which is to say that something is lost in translation. Consequently, understanding of words becomes possible only with interpretation, for example, when the *context* within which Sartre writes is understood by his reader (Sartre [1948] 2007: 51). For this reason, Sartre relies on an 'audience of specialists' who have made an effort to understand the context within which Sartre's individual writings exist (Sartre [1948] 2007: 97).

While we may understand Sartre's claim that his existential writings are intended for specialists, such understanding is not sufficient reason for maintaining that the content of Sartre's writings cannot, or should not, be addressed to a wider audience. Indeed, Sartre's philosophy as a whole makes it clear that he recognises his freedom is intertwined with the freedom of others.[2] This suggests that part of Sartre's project is to be successful in revealing his finding on the human situation to everyone, a suggestion that is confirmed by Sartre's views on his own dramatic writings (for example, Sartre [1959] 1976: 65). Subsequently, those who have picked up Sartre's project and made it their own, or those who have drawn the same or similar conclusions within the ontology of the human person as Sartre, have the task of finding a way to effectively reveal the human situation to others. As suggested above, however, such a task must be undertaken within the limitations of language. Specifically, an author is not able to provide the meaning and value of a situation in a given word itself, since words are mere signs that require the other, to whom the words are directed, to recognise and disclose the meaning signified by the words (see Sartre [1948] 2007: 34–35). Meaning is precisely what is not written or spoken, but remains in the silence of the contextual whole (see Sartre [1948] 2007: 31–32). The author must freely and carefully choose a word to offer his or her audience as a sign of an experienced reality,[3] and the audience member must interpret the sign, and perceive the reality that the author was signifying with the use of the word, if the task of language is to be achieved. The choosing and interpretation of a sign, however, is ultimately an act of freedom, such that each person 'bears the full responsibility for his (or her) interpretation of the sign' (Sartre [1945] 2007: 34); for this reason, language is fundamentally a 'calling forth of freedom' (Sartre [1948] 2007: 35). In that the end of language is communication, that is, language is social, the meaning of a word is contingently established within the existing tension between the intentions of the writer and the audience member (Sartre [1948] 2007: 31). Fundamentally, it is the above mentioned struggle of freedom(s) that Sartre wants his audience to rediscover about and within themselves, though to accomplish this calling forth of freedom within a social enterprise of communication, meaning must be projected in language even though it is not simply given (see Sartre [1948] 2007: 31–32).

The concept of *projecting* meaning in language involves the idea of *distance* from meaning. An author may choose to use language with which the audience is familiar, yet is also distanced from, in order to encourage the audience member to recognise her or his own role of interpreting a language of signs:

> Sartre sees distance as a means to provoke thought which leads to the taking up of a position … For the dramatic language has to be both familiar … and distant (a speech that has undergone a process of 'distancing' so that he perceives it as though from 'outside'): 'You give an audience its everyday language' says Sartre, 'but with a sort of distance, and that makes a witness of it'. This distancing of ordinary speech, experienced from the 'outward' viewpoint from which we look at the most basic component of our consciousness, gives to the distance from language, as presented by Sartre, a reflective character of self-criticism.
>
> (Milman 1991: 155)

Such distance in language is not designed to bring about a lack of interest by the audience, rather it is designed to enable the audience member to take a position from which the contingency of language is acknowledged and the responsibility each person has in choosing the meaning of the words/signs is recognised. It is not only the audience member that can experience distance in language, for this approach to language impacts awareness of the reality of choice, action, and freedom of the author as well. To successfully apply the technique of distancing an audience member from the language he or she is presented with, the writer must also experience a form of distancing, which is described in Sartre's account of the 'prosaic' attitude towards language, within which the word 'tears the writer of prose away from himself' and throws the writer 'into the midst of the world' (Sartre [1948] 2007: 8).

The attempt by an author, such as Sartre, to encourage reflection on, and responsibility for, one's own freedom through a process of distancing in language impacts not only what words are chosen, but perhaps more importantly how those words are organised into a synthetic whole that contributes to the context within which meaning is established. For example, the human situation cannot simply be narrated or explained, for with an explanation

> one reduces the entire effect to the entire cause, the unforeseen to the expected and the new to the old. The narrator brings the same workmanship to bear upon the human event as ... the nineteenth century scientist brought to bear upon the scientific fact. He reduces the diverse to the identical.
>
> (Sartre [1948] 2007: 109)

The establishing of a context of determination, necessity, and given-ness works counter to a calling forth of freedom. For this reason, Sartre's use of, and approach to, theatre in order to communicate the human situation becomes more significant. Sartre's dramatic works were designed to establish a 'theatre of situations', in which actions are not explained according to the isolated past of a single individual, as in theatre of character, but become meaningful only when the changing social complexity of situations in terms of the past, present, and future is considered. In a Sartrean approach to theatre, 'free choice must be shown ... by placing undefined characters in restrictive circumstances (the situation) where they have to choose for themselves' (Milman 1991: 149) such that 'the topic that will stand in the centre of the drama will not be the "soul" of the participants, but a struggle ... (between) opposing ideological and moral issues' (Milman 1991: 150).

We may justifiably assert that Sartre, and his contemporary 'young French playwrights', created a new fictional technique with their theatre of situations (Sartre [1946] 1976: 35), and also that additional new techniques are to be pursued by others who are continuing a Sartrean project of utilising language to reveal the human situation (see Sartre [1948] 2007: 112). One technique with which Sartre obviously saw potential was film. In 1931, Sartre conveyed the status of art on cinema in a speech delivered at a secondary school in Le Havre, and suggested that cinema is not a 'bad school' (Contat and Rybalka 1970: 546–52), at a time when cinema was viewed largely with suspicion by the French bourgeois, and well before the popular recognition of film as a subject for serious criticism, which may be dated as only beginning in the 1950s with the development of the journal *Cahiers du cinéma*, and the beginnings of a popular recognition of film as a legitimate academic field, which may be dated as beginning in the late 1960s. Similarly, in *The Words*, Sartre references the role cinema had on his own childhood, and describes it as a 'new art, the art of the common man' (Sartre [1964] 1981: 118), which he noted as also still in its 'childhood' ([1964] 1981: 122).

Despite this early recognition of the potential of cinema by Sartre, and his own authorship of several screenplays, he appears to have struggled with the role cinema could play in his project of communicating the possibility of self rediscovery, and reinvention, even sometimes explicitly citing the strengths of theatre over cinema. In a 1958 lecture, Sartre enumerates a number of differentiating factors between theatre and film,[4] one of which is that film involves 'actors and action ready-canned' while theatre is described as 'a true event' (Sartre [1958] 1976: 59), a description that is a more meaningful criticism given that he also notes that 'appearance merges with reality' in film while comparatively he describes actions in theatre as gestures, i.e. acts which have no purpose in themselves, but are intended to show something else (Sartre [1960] 1976a: 90). These descriptions of film and theatre may be applied to the role of language in these mediums; Sartre insists 'that there is a language peculiar to theater and that this language must never be descriptive ... language is a moment in action, and it is there ... for an active purpose' (Sartre [1960] 1976a: 105), which tells us that, for Sartre, language in theatre can, and should, be gestural. Words in theatre point to something else, a reality that is not simply given but must be perceived through an act of freedom. However, if in film 'appearance merges with reality', language will cease to be gestural, and the Sartrean emphasis on using language to reveal the freedom essential for interpretation and possibility will be lost.

Whether film does or does not promote a merging of appearance and reality, and with such promotion whether or not a prosaic attitude towards language is possible, is debatable. Cinema has grown out of the 'childhood' stage that Sartre recognised, and the possibility of film as a technique for the continuation of a Sartrean project of revealing the human situation to a wide audience must be reconsidered. With respect to the charge that, in film, actions are 'canned', while in theatre there are occurrences of 'true events', when it comes to the development of projected individual characters, there is reason to suggest that swapping these descriptions might be more appropriate. Sartre himself noted that exploration of the depth of a character is best undertaken in film (Sartre [1960] 1976b: 282), though it appears that Sartre associated this deepening of a character with his critique of 'theatre of character', which essentially begins with an assumption of humans as determined. This is to say that Sartre's recognition that film is the medium for probing deepest into the individual character is an assertion that film is more equipped than theatre to analyse the totality of a person's essential psychological traits in order to *explain* the human situation. 'Character', however, need not be understood in the sense of an individual's 'essence'; instead the term 'character' may be used to reference a particular individual qua free being, 'a naked will, a pure free choice' (Sartre [1946] 1976: 34).

Sartre's statement that film allows a deeper probe into the individual than theatre may still hold true even if the term 'character' signifies the projection of a free will. With this interpretation, it is worth considering that film theorist Stanley Cavell suggests an actor is enabled to more truthfully lend his or her own being to a fictional character in film than theatre:

> for the stage, an actor works himself into a role; for the screen, a performer takes the role onto himself ... In this respect, a role in a play is like a position in a game ... various people can play it ... The screen performer explores his role like an attic and takes stock of his physical and temperamental endowment; he lends his being to the role and accepts only what fits.
>
> (Cavell [1971] 1979: 27–28)

In this way, Cavell notes that 'the screen performer is essentially not an actor at all: he is the subject of study, and a study not his own ... On a screen the *study* is projected; on a stage the actor is the projector' (Cavell [1971] 1979: 28) (my italics). The 'subject of study' in a film is thereby a human who we would say, from a Sartrean perspective, is free to make his or her own choices, but who must choose within a situation that has 'limits which enclose him on all sides' (Sartre [1946] 1976: 35), and it is precisely the activity of choosing, of living, that is projected.

Increased depth in character, or subject, development, conceived as revealing the fact of human freedom, the showing of 'a character creating himself, the moment of choice, of the free decision which commits him to ... a whole way of life' (Sartre [1947] 1976: 4) is intimately connected to the provision of greater insight into the character's situation, a connection that is explicitly drawn by Sartre who notes that freedom is always situated freedom. Willingness to embrace the complexity of a character, the freedom of the 'subject of the study', is willingness to accept the complexity of the individual's situation, an acknowledgment of 'the ontological fact that actions move within a dark and shifting circle of intention and consequence' (Cavell [1971] 1979: 153). It also may be argued that, because an audience member has greater insight into the complexity of the subject's existence, distancing within language is possible in film. Additional evidence of a distancing in language via purposefully, and economically, writing dialogue that 'emphasizes the point that ... behaviour and setting', understood as action and situation, 'really can be the most important elements for telling the story' in films (Batty 2005: 37). Cavell writes that

> movies, unlike performances in a theater, will contain long stretches without dialogue, in which the characters can be present without having to say anything (not: without having anything to say). We can observe the activities that involve them at points that precede or succeed the words surrounding them – their fights or their struggles with objects and places ...
>
> (Cavell [1971] 1979: 150–51)

Accordingly, a suggestion is made that means are provided for action, including the use of language, to be gestural in film, such that films are capable of 'conveying the unsayable by showing experiences beyond the reach of words' (Cavell [1971] 1979: 152–53). Indeed, others have confirmed that 'movies address matters of intimacy and do so in a language of indirectness and silence' (Rothman and Keane 2000: 17), whereby the meanings of words, objects, or the lived world more generally, are not simply provided but must be interpreted, such that 'the film spectator's observer status is never passive' (Shaw 2008: 39).

The above suggests that a 'film of situations', akin to Sartre's 'theatre of situations', approach to cinema is possible. If it is adopted, then, because of its ability to display in more complexity the situation of persons, film may be well suited to show the 'true event' of human existence. In this way, the fundamental human condition that Sartre tries to reveal in his philosophical writings may be revealed more truthfully to an audience beyond that of specialists. In the remaining portion of this chapter it will be argued that Sofia Coppola's film, *Lost in Translation*, is an example of how a film of situations may be viewed as a successful continuation of a Sartrean project of making the universal human condition better understood.

Lost in Translation

Sofia Coppola's second feature film, *Lost in Translation*, was, among other acclamations, nominated for the best picture Oscar, and earned Ms. Coppola Academy Awards for best writing, best original screenplay, as well as an Academy Award nomination for best director. The film centres on Bob Harris (Bill Murray), a middle-aged American actor who is in Tokyo to film a whisky commercial, and Charlotte (Scarlett Johansson), a young American woman who recently graduated with a degree in philosophy and is in Tokyo because she 'wasn't doing anything' and thereby is accompanying her husband who has travelled to Japan for his work as a photographer. Bob and Charlotte encounter each other in the hotel they are sharing, primarily as a result of both being unable to sleep, and develop a relationship with each other over the course of the few days they share in Japan. Both individuals reveal that they travelled to Tokyo as an attempt to escape the situations they previously found themselves in, Bob attempting to escape his unhappy marriage and strained relationship with his children, and Charlotte attempting to escape the uncertainty of her future. Despite Bob's hopes for a future that is different from his past, which is partially demonstrated in his affair with the hotel's lounge singer, and Charlotte's hope for guidance in her future, shown in part by her exploration of rituals that are grounded in the rich history of Japan,[5] both individuals come to realise that escape is not possible and struggle, together, to accept the fact that meaning comes from their actions and they each must choose a response to their present situations, and take full responsibility for that choice.

If we may appropriately describe a 'film of situations' as a film which takes as its subject matter the universal situation of humans, namely that each human is a 'free being, entirely indeterminate who must choose his own being when confronted with certain necessities' (Sartre [1946] 1976: 35), *Lost in Translation* is an example of a 'film of situations'. Indeed, *Lost in Translation* actually includes a playful attack on what may be called 'film of character', in which actors and actions are 'canned', appearance is conflated with reality, and language is accepted as descriptive. One of the most memorable scenes in *Lost in Translation* is 'Suntory Times', in which Bob is filming a whiskey commercial. In this commercial filming, Bob is directed to evoke the 'essence' of a fictional character, to accept that the stage is his den and to drink a glass of 'whiskey' which is in reality tea,[6] and to act with passion despite the fact that he feels none. The ridiculousness of such an approach reaches a climax when the director of the commercial makes it clear that the vision he has in his mind can be perfectly translated not only into Japanese, but then further translated from Japanese to English, such that complete understanding is expected:

> Director (in Japanese)[7]: Translator, it is very important to translate this.
> Mr. Bob, you are sitting in your den silently and comfortably.
> In front of you, there is a glass of Suntory whiskey.
> Do you understand this so far?
> Then, with intense emotion, look into the camera slowly.
> Say this kindly as if you are talking to an old friend who you have not seen for a long time.
> Say this as if you are Bogie in *Casablanca*.
> 'Here's looking at you kid. Suntory times.'
> Translator: Um, he wants you to turn, look in the camera. Okay?
> Bob: That's all he said?
> Translator: Yes. Turn to the camera.
> Bob: All right. Does he want me to turn from the right or turn from the left?
> Translator (in Japanese): Well, he is ready. Oh, he has one question, though.
> He is wondering whether he should turn from the right or the left after the director says action.
> How should I advise him?
> Director (in Japanese): I don't care. It doesn't matter. We don't have much time. Mr. Bob. Hurry up, and don't forget your emotional intensity. Look into the camera. Don't look at anything other than the camera. Slowly. Don't forget the passion. Show your passion in your eyes. Do you understand?
> Translator: Right side, and uh, with intensity. Okay?
> Bob: Is that everything? I mean it seems like he said quite a bit more than that.
> Director (in Japanese): What you are saying is not just about whiskey. Remember you are talking to an old friend whom you haven't seen for a long time. Say it tenderly. Don't forget the passionate intensity that comes from the bottom of your heart.
> Translator: Like an old friend, and into the camera.

The situation being filmed is forged or neglected entirely, the individual (Bob) is not to engage in any action except to repeat a slogan that was written for him, and he is asked to work himself into a role, an object, and deny his own personality.[8] It must be acknowledged that the event being filmed was a commercial, which is certainly distinct from feature-length films in a variety of ways. Still, the approach to, and display of, an individual in the commercial is a prime example of what Sartre critiques as focus on character. This approach to an individual is shown again in Bob's participation in the filming of a variety show, in which his participation is perceived by others as successful, despite the fact that what we see of his participation largely consisted of mimicking the words and actions of the show's host, which for Bob were meaningless.

That many feature films do fit what Sartre describes as focus on character is playfully acknowledged in *Lost in Translation* through the presence of Kelly (Anna Faris), an American actress who is also in Tokyo, staying at the same hotel as Bob and Charlotte, to promote her latest 'action' film. During a press conference she reveals that during filming she apparently never learned anything other than superficial qualities of her co-star, for example she claims that she is only able to note that she and her co-star share such qualities as liking martial arts and Mexican food, which suggests that the characters in the film were completely dissociated with the individuals playing the film. Kelly also assumes a pseudonym while staying at the hotel, and chooses, apparently unknowingly, a male fictional character's name as her own, which again suggests that she does not meaningfully relate to the characters she portrays. Kelly's acting is suggestive of what Cavell describes as playing a role that anyone can play, because it is an objective role devoid of individuality that is portrayed, and what Sartre describes as 'canned'. The history of films objectifying humans and exploiting the notion of a human nature, as well as the common role of films as enabling the type of escapism that Charlotte and Bob are attempting in Tokyo, is humorously suggested as Bob watches a replay of one of his older films on the television, a film which has him conversing with a monkey. The suggestion that a monkey has the language skills of a human functions to place humans and animals as equals, which is counter to the approach Sartre describes within a theatre, or we may say film, of situations, in which 'man is not to be defined as a "reasoning animal", or a "social" one, but as a free being' (Sartre [1946] 1976: 35). Unlike Kelly's response to her film, which is a perpetuation of escapism, Bob admits to Charlotte that he would be happier if he were 'doing a play somewhere' rather than continue to film projects that are canned. Bob's response is suggestive of Sartre's distinction between film and theatre, and indicates that film can be, and has been, used to perpetuate a denial of the view that humans are free. That a character within *Lost in Translation* offers this subtle criticism of film indicates that *Lost in Translation* is intended to be distinct from such films. Indeed, in sharp contrast to many other films, *Lost in Translation* projects a study of the ambiguity and complexity of the human situation in part by exaggerating how frequently humans attempt to ignore, or lie to themselves about, their situation and showing how such attempts are futile.[9]

As *Lost in Translation* shows, the attempt to deny the human situation is manifested in attempts at communication. Batty describes *Lost in Translation* as filled with 'false communication' (Batty 2005: 38): Bob communicates with his wife almost exclusively via a fax machine; Kelly seems to never stop talking but her attempts at communication remain at a very superficial level; Charlotte's friend accepts that everything is 'great' with Charlotte, despite Charlotte's obviously troubled state of mind .... Unlike the other (minor) characters in the film, Bob and Charlotte both recognise the limitations of words and repeatedly show frustration when words are not intended, as Sartre would say, to call forth their freedom. For example, Bob and Charlotte excuse themselves from conversations in which the purpose of the conversation is simply to converse; they both, to the surprise of their conversation partners, admit to lack of understanding in conversations; and Bob and Charlotte always use minimal words with each other.

With the recognition that meaning can be lost in translation, that meaning is found in something other than what is objectively given, *Lost in Translation* also enables insight that meaning of and in our own lives is also not objectively given, but that we must interpret our own lives and choose meaning for ourselves. This point is raised directly to the film's audience in the movie's last scene, in which the words Bob whispers to Charlotte are left entirely inaudible to anyone other than Charlotte. By raising the audience member's awareness of his/her own freedom to make meaning out of the situation, to freely interpret the scene and subsequently take responsibility for such an act, *Lost in Translation* is again shown to be a film of situations. Consequently, *Lost in Translation* is able to further communicate some of the central insights Sartre had within his ontology of the human person to a potentially wide audience.

The fundamental truth Sartre attempts to reveal in all of his writings is that the human subject is free: for humans, existence precedes essence (Sartre [1945] 2007: 20), humans are not formulaic (Sartre [1945] 2007: 21), or 'man is nothing other than what he makes of himself' (Sartre [1945] 2007: 22). In *Existentialism Is a Humanism*, among other texts, this freedom is described by Sartre in such terms as abandonment, anguish, action, despair, and dignity. The complex and ambiguous situation that is projected in *Lost in Translation*, and the response individuals within the film choose to that situation, address these elements of freedom by offering a connection between Sartre's words and the choices, actions and responsibility taken by Bob, Charlotte, and others, by projecting a situation in which each human being is 'a free being, entirely indeterminate, who must choose his [or her] own being when confronted with certain necessities, such as being already committed in a world full of both threatening and favourable factors among other [persons] who have made their choices' (Sartre [1946] 1976: 35). Accordingly, Sartre's words are like signs that help to point out that certain choices are being made and actions are taken, while the film is able to project the choices and actions out of which Sartre's words can have meaning. Examples of this connection between Sartre's words and the film's projected action are provided below.

Abandonment: 'Charlotte Can't Sleep'

Sartre describes the human situation as one of abandonment, and it is clear that Charlotte, who accompanies her husband on a business trip to Tokyo, only to be left alone in the city while her husband continues his travels in an attempt to complete his work, is abandoned in a number of obvious ways. However, consideration of the complexity of Charlotte's situation, and her actions within that situation, provide an opportunity for increased insight into the reality that is signified by Sartre's term 'abandonment'. Sartre most generally describes abandonment, for example, as the fact that 'it is we, ourselves, who decide who we are to be' (Sartre [1945] 2007: 34), which stems from Sartre's ontological claim that 'we can never explain our actions by reference to a given and immutable human nature' (Sartre [1945] 2007: 29). While Charlotte has, most superficially, been left alone in Tokyo, a place that she is not particularly familiar with (as evidenced by her need to check maps, for example), Charlotte does make and have friends in Tokyo, and her husband does remain in contact. Charlotte's experience of abandonment is not projected in such an exaggerated, and unlikely, situation as being left alone on an uninhabited island; rather, Charlotte finds herself in a place where she is forced to realise the contingency of all the sources from which she previously found all meaning and value, including language, art, food, entertainment, and social roles.

It is telling that, in the scene 'Charlotte Can't Sleep', Charlotte calls her friend in the United States, who is within a culture from which Charlotte presumably accepts as being able to give her meaning, in an apparent attempt to make sense out of her experience of 'not feeling anything' when she listened to chanting monks. At the end of the conversation, which is brought about quickly by Charlotte's friend, Charlotte recognises that her friend is not able to give the meaning of the rituals she observed, or Charlotte's (lack of) reaction to these rituals, and Charlotte is forced to decide for herself the meaning she will attribute to the experience. Charlotte's response to this situation is an indication that she is beginning to realise that the objective world does not give her meaning, rather it is she that must give meaning to the world.

Anguish: 'The Jazz Singer'

Sartre writes that abandonment is anguish, such that 'a man who commits himself, and who realizes that he is not only the individual that he chooses to be, but also a legislator choosing at the same time what humanity as a whole should be, cannot help but be aware of his own full and profound responsibility' (Sartre [1945] 2007: 25). With this statement, Sartre commits himself to accepting the ultimately subjective source of meaning and value while simultaneously denying ethical relativism, a commitment that is not easily comprehensible by those unfamiliar with Sartre's wider philosophical views. However, the particular relationship between Charlotte and Bob provides a context within which Sartre's position can be understood. For example, Bob and Charlotte have had many conversations about marriage, with Charlotte, a newlywed, at one point explicitly asking Bob, who has been married for several years and has children with his wife, if marriage 'gets easier' with time. Bob responds to Charlotte's question with the acknowledgement that 'marriage is hard', though Bob ultimately tries to tell Charlotte that life does become 'easier' over time. Bob's actions come to show Bob is lying when he says that life becomes easier over time, lying both to himself and Charlotte. Bob has an affair with a jazz singer at the hotel, an act which Bob unsuccessfully tries to hide from Charlotte. When Charlotte discovers Bob's affair, considerable tension builds in the relationship between Charlotte and Bob, while Charlotte is forced to realise that, although she looks to others for values, 'it is still I myself who must decide', and she must approach her marriage as a unique opportunity within which *she* must choose her actions and be responsible for such choices. In a parallel movement, Bob also comes to realise that when he chooses to have an extramarital affair, he is responsible for creating a standard for Charlotte, for all humans, of value and meaning, including the meaning and value of marriage; accordingly Bob is forced to realise that 'I am therefore responsible for myself and for everyone else, and I am fashioning a certain image of man as I choose him to be. In choosing myself, I choose man' (Sartre [1945] 2007: 24–25).

Action: 'Are You Awake?'

According to Sartre, 'reality exists only in action ... "Man is nothing other than his own project. He exists only to the extent that he realizes himself, therefore he is nothing more than the sum of his actions, nothing more than his life"' (Sartre [1945] 2007: 37). While staying in Tokyo, both Charlotte and Bob, despite their desires to, are unable to sleep, and thus while they are subsequently nearly continuously 'active' in the world, their actions are not purposeful in the sense of fulfilling a larger project that either has adopted for him- or herself, and Charlotte explicitly notes that she feels 'stuck' in life. In the scene that shows both Charlotte and Bob finally being able to sleep, which is suggestive of an opportunity to put an end to their acting without purpose, Charlotte tells Bob 'I just don't know what I want to be'. Up to this scene Charlotte has given several indications that she believes that her value will be bestowed by others only upon the completion of a project (for example, she asks her husband if the scarf she has been knitting is 'done' yet). Bob's advice is for her to just 'keep writing', an activity about which Charlotte acknowledges she feels passionate. Charlotte begins to learn that she 'is' the life that she lives, the actions that she engages in, and that the activity does not have value merely in its completion, but value is given by engaging in the activity itself; Charlotte's struggle is with what Sartre acknowledges as realisation that 'life is nothing until it is lived; it is we who give it meaning, and value is nothing more than the meaning we give it' (Sartre [1945] 2007: 51).

Despair: 'Calling Home'

Despair is rather cryptically described by Sartre as the realisation that 'we must limit ourselves to reckoning only with those things that depend on our wills, or on the set of probabilities that enable action' (Sartre [1945] 2007: 34). Sartre offers one's choices in relationships with others as a more specific example of the experience of despair: 'in confronting any real situation, for example that I am capable of having sexual intercourse with a member of the opposite sex and of having children, I am obliged to choose an attitude to the situation' (Sartre [1945] 2007: 44). Within a situation, future possibilities are recognisable only insofar as our choices and actions render them as real possibilities. Accordingly, in a relationship, 'there is no love apart from the deeds of love; no potential for love other than that which is manifested in loving' (Sartre [1945] 2007: 37), and if an individual questions the possibility of a future involving love within a present relationship, that future is in question as a possibility only because of one's own choices. This Sartrean example of despair is projected through Bob, who desires a future relationship with his family that is different from his present relationship with them. In the scene 'Calling Home', Bob calls his wife and makes an effort to show he values his relationship with his wife. It is clear, however, that conflict is at the centre of their relationship. Bob is forced to realise that his relationship with his wife and children will not change simply because he wants a change, but that he must choose his actions in light of the situation he is responsible for creating in the first place in order to make a change possible. The scene ends with Bob telling his wife that he loves her, but his wife has already terminated the phone call and his declaration of love is responded to with a dial tone. Bob's evaluation of the phone call is that it was 'a stupid idea', though it remains unclear why Bob believes calling his wife was 'stupid'. More specifically, it is unclear whether he recognises that 'he has no recourse to excuses or outside aid' (Sartre [1945] 2007: 47) for the state of his marriage and that his words are meaningless unless his actions manifest a reality 'I love you' signifies.

Film as a Continuation of the Sartrean Project

The above consideration of specific scenes within *Lost in Translation* as connecting action to such Sartrean words as anguish and despair serves as an example of the tension that exists between intentions of different persons, in this case between Sartre's intentions with his word choices in such texts as *Existentialism Is a Humanism* and the fact of the human situation that Coppola intends to express through her writing and direction of *Lost in Translation*. This is to say that it is entirely inappropriate to conflate Coppola's project with Sartre's project, and yet a keen audience member can perceive the tension between these two intentions, such that there is the recognition of the ambiguity and possibility of meaning in both Sartre's texts and Coppola's film(s). Sartre writes 'there is universality in every project, inasmuch as any [person] is capable of understanding any human project' (Sartre [1945] 2007: 43). Others can pick up Sartre's project and make it their own, though this is not to say that the exact project is perpetuated; i.e. Sartre's project is not continued beyond his death, but a Sartrean approach to the project of contributing to the creation of a situation in which humans freely rediscover themselves is possible by anyone who shares Sartre's views on the freedom of the human person. What has been suggested above is that film is a legitimate method for engaging in a Sartrean project, a suggestion that is evidenced by *Lost in Translation*, so long as film is approached in terms of situation, and not character.

Sartre states 'I cannot discover any truth whatsoever about myself except through the mediation of another' (Sartre [1945] 2007: 41). Accordingly, we do need to interact with others to learn about ourselves. Still, these interactions will be most fruitful if they provide an opportunity for critical consideration of life, of the human situation, and if critical consideration is translated into action. Critical consideration within social interactions is itself dependent on not only my own understanding of the human situation, but others' understanding as well. Accordingly, abstract philosophical reasoning is valuable, but such reasoning is not by itself sufficient for increasing existential awareness or living a life with the recognition of the freedom, i.e. the dignity, of the human person and the responsibility this entails. Such reasoning must be shared with others in a meaningful way, and creative techniques for revealing the complex and ambiguous human situation to others, so that others may also embrace their own freedom, must be sought. Despite the more recent consideration of film as valuable in terms of more than mere escapism, particularly relative to the millennia long history of philosophy, the two disciplines have the potential of working well together, particularly with respect to recognition of one's own situation:

> Movies exercise a hold on us, a hold that, drawing on our innermost desires and fears, we participate in creating. To know films objectively, we have to know the hold they have upon us. To know the hold films have on us, we have to know ourselves

objectively. And to know ourselves objectively, we have to know the impact of films on our lives. No study of film can claim intellectual authority if it is not rooted in self-knowledge, our knowledge of our own subjectivity. In the serious study of film, in other words, criticism must work hand in hand with the perspective of self-reflection that only philosophy is capable of providing.

(Rothman and Keane 2000: 17–18)

Considering this perspective on film that is provided by Rothman and Keane, film seems to be a medium for the continuation of the project of realising the human situation that has not received proper attention, from both those within the field of philosophy and those within film studies. Indeed, using *Lost in Translation* as a case study, it becomes clear that a 'film of situations' is different from a 'film of character', which in turn allows for clarity of a perhaps under-developed approach to film criticism, a perspective that can also be a guide for those writers and directors whose projects are intended as a critical inquiry into the human situation.

Notes

1. The term 'author' will be used generally also to refer not only to an individual who communicates his or her thoughts to others via written communication, but also, for example, oral communication.
2. See Sartre's account of 'Being-for-Others' (Sartre [1943] 2008: 243–452).
3. According to Sartre, the author has a responsibility to uphold a 'rigorous economy of words' (Sartre [1946] 1976: 42).
4. Differences also include: theatre as allowing more freedom than film on the grounds that (1) actors dominate the audience in that they are above the audience, while the 'superman' sensation of the actors' size and weight does not exist in theatre, (2) film directs the audience members' perceptions while in theatre one can look at whomever one wants to, and (3) film depicts humans who are conditioned by the world in which they live while theatre shows that the world itself is only revealed through the actors' actions.
5. Coppola establishes the parallel between Bob's and Charlotte's attempt at escapism in part by showing that every day Bob agrees to work in Tokyo is also a day in which Charlotte explores a Japanese ritual.
6. It is made explicit that Bob is drinking tea, not whiskey, when he is completing the still photography aspect of the marketing conducted for the whiskey.
7. Translation of dialogue from Japanese to English by Naoki Shikimachi and Karra Shikimachi.
8. This is an example of what Sartre describes as 'bad faith' (see Sartre [1943] 2008: 78–90).
9. It is worthwhile to note that Coppola has stated she had Bill Murray in mind when writing the screenplay, which suggests Coppola intended for the actors to bring themselves to the film, and did not intend the characters to be canned (see Hurd 2007: 132).

Bibliography

Batty, C. 2005. 'Subtext, Symbolism and Metaphor in Lost in Translation', *Script Writer* May: 37–9.

Cavell, S. [1971] 1979. *The World Viewed: Reflections on the Ontology of Film (Enlarged Edition)*. Cambridge, MA: Harvard University Press.

Contat, M. and M. Rybalka (eds). 1970. *Les Ecrits de Sartre*. Paris: Gallimard.

Hurd, M.G. 2007. *Women Directors & Their Films*. Westport: Praeger Publishers.

Milman, Y. 1991. 'Aesthetic Distance and the Moral Value of Drama in the Dramaturgy of Jean-Paul Sartre', *Journal of the British Society for Phenomenology* 22(3): 148–57.

Rothman, W. and M. Keane. 2000. *Reading Cavell's 'The World Viewed': A Philosophical Perspective on Film*. Detroit: Wayne State University Press.

Sartre, J.-P. [1943] 2008. *Being and Nothingness*, trans. H.E. Barnes. London: Routledge.

———. [1945] 2007. *Existentialism Is a Humanism*, trans. C. Macomber. New Haven, CT: Yale University Press.

———. [1946] 1976. 'Forgers of Myth', in M. Contat and M. Rybalka (eds), *Sartre on Theater*, trans. F. Jellinek. New York: Pantheon Books, pp. 33–43.

———. [1947] 1976. 'For a Theater of Situations', in M. Contat and M. Rybalka (eds), *Sartre on Theater*, trans. F. Jellinek. New York: Pantheon Books, pp. 3–5.

———. [1948] 2007. *What is Literature?*, trans. B. Frechtman. London: Routledge.

———. [1958] 1976. 'Theater and Cinema', in M. Contat and M. Rybalka (eds), *Sartre on Theater*, trans. F. Jellinek. New York: Pantheon Books, pp. 59–63.

———. [1959] 1976. 'The Author, the Play, and the Audience', in M. Contat and M. Rybalka (eds), *Sartre on Theater*, trans. F. Jellinek. New York: Pantheon Books, pp. 64–76.

———. [1960] 1976a. 'Epic Theater and Dramatic Theater', in M. Contat and M. Rybalka (eds), *Sartre on Theater*, trans. F. Jellinek. New York: Pantheon Books, pp. 77–120.

———. [1960] 1976b. 'The Condemned of Altona', in M. Contat and M. Rybalka (eds), *Sartre on Theater*, trans. F. Jellinek. New York: Pantheon Books, pp. 253–308.

———. [1964] 1981. *The Words*, trans. B. Frechtman. New York: Random House.

Shaw, S. 2008. *Film Consciousness*. Jefferson: McFarland & Company, Inc.

Filmography

Coppola, S. (dir.). 2003. *Lost in Translation*. Universal Studios.

7

IF I SHOULD WAKE BEFORE I DIE: EXISTENTIALISM AS A POLITICAL CALL TO ARMS IN *THE CRYING GAME*

Tracey Nicholls

In a world devastated by war and terrorism, there is, I submit, a special relevance to an analysis that pairs Neil Jordan's 1992 film *The Crying Game* with Jean-Paul Sartre's existentialist philosophy. Juxtaposing the two challenges us to consider the extent to which our lives really are the product of our own complex choices, and to acknowledge latent possibilities for dramatic transformation of what we all too often take to be our immutable characters. In my opinion, the driving force of this film is the existential anguish that Sartre describes as being triggered by the profound sense of responsibility we feel when we become aware that our own personal choices may be taken up as a model for others to follow. However, while Sartrean anguish drives the film's narrative, Sartrean abandonment – the aloneness we experience in a world without God – gives the central character of Fergus (played by actor Stephen Rea) his psychological complexity and gives the film its tragic drama. The story told in this film resonates because of its clear-eyed, unromantic treatment of the desperation and misery that are fostered by occupation and insurgency. Far from being a minor film of a past decade, I argue that *The Crying Game* offers important insights into political decolonisation.

For reasons I can no longer clearly remember, I became fascinated during my early adolescence with the tangled and conflict-ridden history of Ireland. In the course of trying to read my way to an understanding of the politics behind Bobby Sands' hunger strike, I came across a photograph of a piece of graffiti which posed the stark question 'is there life before death?' That question struck a chord within me, in no small part because of the ease with which my youthful heartstrings could be manipulated. But also, I think, it touched the same part of me that leapt headlong into existentialist philosophy when I encountered it in college. To my mind, there is an echo of the finitude and fragility of existentialist humanism in that question, a hint of why we should care so much about the view of freedom, choice, and responsibility that Sartre's writings impart to us. It is because our lives are so easily lost to us, denied by us, and alienated from us that we need existentialism's lessons of conscious agency. This, implicitly, is the constant, haunting reminder that runs through *The Crying Game*.

The Story Told in *The Crying Game*

This is a film structured around absence and loss. Jody (Forest Whitaker), the British soldier whose shocking death occurs about forty minutes in, casts a long shadow over the entire rest of the film, which is largely dedicated to showing us how Fergus, the Irish Republican Army (IRA) 'soldier' who is responsible for his death, tries to put a new life together after the foundational beliefs structuring his old life have become untenable.

The film opens with Jody's capture by the IRA cell to which Fergus belongs. We and the prisoner are told that the cell intends to exchange him for a man of theirs who is currently being interrogated by the British Army, and that Jody will be shot if the British do not agree to the exchange within three days. Thus begins an odd dance between Jody and Fergus, who has been tasked with guarding him, in which the captured soldier tries desperately to humanise himself to his captor in a faint hope that he will be kept alive long enough to make his escape, and the guard comes reluctantly to an awareness of his enemy's basic likeability and likeness to himself. For the first time, Fergus encounters an individual human being who breaks down the monolithic image of 'the British invaders' he is at war with; Jody is a man who joined the army because he needed a job and then got sent to Northern Ireland, 'the one place in the world where they call you "nigger" to your face', he remarks. Fergus is increasingly revealed as a man with fairly stereotypical Irish Catholic beliefs: the British have no right to be in his country and should get the hell out (by force, if necessary) and women are the appropriate yet subordinate companions of men. (The only female member of the cell, Jude (Miranda Richardson), is used quite cynically as bait to lure Jody and is tasked with making tea and meals, but is also the woman Fergus is shown kissing and talking to intimately.)

Jody shares with Fergus his theory that the world is made up of two types of people – givers and takers – and illustrates his point through a story of a scorpion, unable to swim, who asks a frog to take him across a river on his back. The scorpion reassures the hesitant frog that there is no danger in this transaction as he, the scorpion, is equally at risk of drowning if he harms the frog. Halfway across the river, however, the scorpion stings the frog to death and as they both drown, the frog demands to know why the scorpion betrayed his promise to abstain from harm. 'I can't help it,' replies the scorpion; 'it's in my nature.' The point of this story, for Jody, is to convince Fergus that kindness and compassion are in his, Fergus's, nature, that he will prioritise his personal friendship over his ideological commitments. This possibility that Fergus will betray his IRA cell members is Jody's only hope of survival, but Fergus is already starting to experience the destabilising effect of calling his foundational beliefs into question, and is no longer willing to say with any certainty what his nature is.

Towards the end of his captivity, as Jody starts to accept the inevitability that he will be shot, he makes a final request of Fergus, that he seek out Dil (Jaye Davidson), Jody's girlfriend and tell her that Jody was thinking about her in his last moments. On the third day, Fergus takes him outside into the woods to kill him. Jody makes a desperate dash, gambling that Fergus has too much honour to shoot him in the back, and runs, tragically, out of the woods, onto a road and into the path of a British army convoy sent to destroy the cell (and possibly rescue him). Fergus survives the attack by the British, and seeks the help of an old friend to get himself out of Northern Ireland until the heat dies down.

In England, calling himself Jimmy, working on a construction site, and living in a small rented room, Fergus keeps the promise he made to find Dil. While he initially wants only to fulfil Jody's request and assuage his own guilt, he drifts into a relationship with Dil that amounts to an attempt to place himself in the role that Jody had previously occupied in her life. He repeatedly questions her about feelings for 'her man' and how Jody treated her, all the while holding back any mention that he himself had ever met Jody. 'Jimmy' reacts violently to the discovery that Dil, despite her flamboyant performance of feminine identity, is biologically male but he is forced to admit – to her and himself – that he has already developed an emotional attachment to her that transcends his beliefs about sexual propriety and normality, just as his feelings of friendship for Jody transcended his political animosity. Just as Fergus resigns himself to an uneasy romance, pretending Dil is a 'real' girl and keeping their relationship at the level of foreplay, his IRA past reasserts itself in the form of Jude, his sometime girlfriend and former fellow cell member, who shows up unexpectedly in his room one evening and demands an account of his actions during the British attack (from which only she, Fergus, and Peter (Adrian Dunbar), the cell leader, escaped). Jude brushes aside Fergus's declaration that he is out of the IRA and uses threats of harm against Dil to get his grudging cooperation in a hit that she and Peter are planning against a local judge.

Finally, on the evening before he is to fulfil the certain death mission of assassinating the British judge, Fergus confesses to a drunken, barely conscious Dil that he knew Jody. He awakes the next morning to find himself tied to her bed, with his own gun held on him. Frantically, he struggles to convince Dil to release him, believing they will both die if he fails to kill the judge. Instead, when Jude appears, seeking revenge, Dil kills her with Fergus's gun. Fergus then convinces Dil to disappear and let him take responsibility for the crime. The final scene of the film shows us a now short-haired but again-hyper feminine Dil visiting Fergus in prison. When she asks him why he is serving the prison sentence that should rightfully be hers, Fergus responds that it is in his nature, repeating the story that Jody told him about the frog and the scorpion, to the closing strains of the country and western song 'Stand by your Man'.

The Crying Game's Existentialist Commitments

I spoke in my prefatory comments about the sense in which I think this film exemplifies Sartrean anguish and Sartrean abandonment. Together with despair, of which there is also plenty in the film, these emotional responses are presented by Sartre as definitive of the consciously-lived existentialist's existence, and so one might take *The Crying Game* to illustrate Sartre's philosophy simply through the portrayal of these responses. But I think that existentialism permeates the film both more broadly and more deeply, providing a narrative through which to draw out whole strands of argument that Sartre marshals in the defence of his philosophy in *Existentialism Is a Humanism,* and providing small, perhaps seemingly insignificant, moments of human existence that, on further inspection, we can see as drenched in the respect for life existentialism demands of us. Existentialism is, after all, 'a philosophy of lived experience', as Annie Cohen-Solal notes in her introduction to the 2007 republication of Sartre's 1946 essay (Sartre [1946] 2007: 14).

In the lecture that was later published as *Existentialism Is a Humanism,* Sartre claims 'the first effect of existentialism is to make every man conscious of what he is, and to make him solely responsible for his own existence' (Sartre [1946] 2007: 23). This responsibility is not a simple isolationism; in making one's choices, one's life becomes a possible path for others – an (implicit) invitation to 'follow my lead'. That is what makes responsibility profound enough to trigger anguish: if one's actions only made an impact on one's own life, one could perhaps cultivate a stoicism or a blasé 'qué será, será' attitude towards the world, but when one considers the way that any chance action or careless word might be taken up by someone else, the awesome power each of us has to change others' futures settles like a heavy weight on one's shoulders. This is why Fergus is so tortured by Jody's death. In refusing to shoot the soldier in the back as he ran for freedom, Fergus was clearly hoping that Jody might survive. Instead, Jody's dash through the woods resulted in his death, and the weight of responsibility on Fergus turns into an unspeakable guilt when Fergus is confronted by Dil's raw grief for Jody.

Sartre's account of responsibility is married to his account of human freedom. 'Man is condemned to be free,' he tells us; 'condemned, because he did not create himself, yet nonetheless free, because once cast into the world, he is responsible for everything he does' (Sartre [1946] 2007: 29). The abandonment he theorises derives from this awareness that we are alone in the world, that we lack anything (that is, a God) which could underpin objective values and a fixed human nature, or essence (Sartre [1946] 2007: 27, 29). In the film, Fergus never appears to depend on, or be troubled by the absence of, a

God, but he is portrayed by Stephen Rea as a man cast adrift by the crumbling of his foundational beliefs. As a result of Jody's death and his growing attachment to Dil, Fergus must relinquish the two articles of faith at the base of his belief system: the conviction given to him by the IRA that there can be no rapprochement between British soldiers and Irish citizens, and the sexual morality given to him by the Catholic Church. The major part of the film involves his struggle to rebuild himself without that sense of certainty that had previously grounded his existence. Watching someone trying to put his life back together without his previously secure foundations dramatises for us what has been described elsewhere as 'an epistemology of loss' (De Curtis 1989).[1] In this sense, then, the film itself can be viewed as embodying Sartrean responsibility: Fergus's reaction to his loss of certain foundations becomes one possible model for each of us, should we lose our epistemological bearings.

The crisis of freedom and responsibility is one that each of us must wrestle with in the course of developing ourselves as human beings, and it cannot be solved by an appeal to external authorities or belief systems. 'Even if God were to exist,' Sartre tells us, 'it would make no difference. The real problem is not one of [God's] existence; what man needs is to rediscover himself and to comprehend that nothing can save him from himself" (Sartre [1946] 2007: 53). This central assertion of Sartre's existentialism, that there are no principles to guide our choices beyond those we devise for ourselves, is woven into the narrative of *The Crying Game*. Sartre observes that even our emotions cannot guide us because they develop as they do only through our actions (Sartre [1946] 2007: 32–33). As an illustration of this point, we might consider the love Fergus develops for Dil: it cannot motivate him to push past his sexual conservatism because his love has grown only through the very willingness to take care of her that presupposes his turn away from Catholic moral teachings. Even after he realises that she is not the girl he thought she was, Fergus still tries to make amends for hurting her feelings (and her face), still tries to protect her from harm, and still tries to prove to her that there is someone in the world she can rely on. 'For existentialists there is no love other than the deeds of love; no potential for love other than that which is manifested in loving,' according to Sartre (Sartre [1946] 2007: 37). This, he argues, is existentialism's virtue; it is a philosophy of human action, one that can give us real insight into how human beings do, and should, encounter themselves, their worlds, and each other.

To Sartre's consternation, the truth about existentialism has been distorted by its most vocal critics, the Christians and the Communists. He claims that Christians denounce existentialism for ignoring the (objective) values that discipline humanity and thereby licensing a moral relativism that justifies an animalistic self-absorption (Sartre [1946] 2007: 18). Communists also object to what they see as an inward-looking stance on the part of the existentialist, but they understand this preoccupation with the self as an impotent isolationism rather than a hedonism (Sartre [1946] 2007: 18). They charge that the existentialist is overly concerned with individual subjectivity, and this forecloses any philosophical articulation of human solidarity (Sartre [1946] 2007: 18). I think the character of Jude, Fergus's sometime, sort-of girlfriend, articulates both of these criticisms of Fergus, the unwitting existentialist, at different points in the film. During the early stages of his captivity, Jude calls Jody an animal and berates Fergus for his moral concern with the unworthy. This is a denial of humanity born of Jody's enemy status as dictated by the ideology of Irish republicanism, the objective 'God' of Jude's (and, initially, Fergus's) world. Later, when Jude tracks Fergus down in England, she employs an appeal to solidarity reminiscent of the objection Sartre attributes to the Communist, dismissing Fergus's desire to be done with the IRA as a decision he has no freedom to make. He is part of the collective, in her view, regardless of his change of heart and circumstance. Sartre's denial of objective values is not a relativism, nor is his concern with subjectivity insular, and his defence of his philosophy can be seen as the insight that Fergus struggles towards for the entire length of the film. 'The other is essential to my existence, as well as to the knowledge I have of myself,' Sartre argues, and

> under these conditions, my intimate discovery of myself is at the same time a revelation of the other as a freedom that confronts my own and that cannot think or will without doing so for or against me. We are thus immediately thrust into a world that we may call 'intersubjectivity'. It is in this world that man decides what he is and what others are.
>
> (Sartre [1946] 2007: 41–42)

This is the world that Fergus is living in, in sharp contrast to his IRA cell members who have no intention of confronting the other as a free and responsible being 'for himself'. One of the small moments of the film that is particularly revealing of Sartre's existentialist thought is the debate within the group about whether their prisoner should remain hooded. Jody repeatedly claims to have difficulty breathing when wearing the thick black hood that Peter, the cell leader, insists on. Fergus intercedes with Peter for permission to take the hood off, and Peter allows it only when Fergus is on guard duty. The rationale given for keeping Jody hooded – so he won't recognise their faces – is an instance of what Sartre theorises in *Being and Nothingness* as 'bad faith' (Sartre [1943] 2003: 70ff). It provides a respectable reason for their actions that conceals their true motive, even from themselves, thus allowing them to avoid confronting their own characters. As Lt. Col. Dave Grossman observes in *On Killing*, his scholarly account of how soldiers are trained to be killers, 'not having to look at the face of the victim provides a form of psychological distance that enables ... acceptance of having killed a fellow human being' (Grossman 1996: 128). Grossman cites Miron and Goldstein's 1979 research 'that the risk of death for a kidnap victim is much greater if the victim is hooded' (1996: 128). In the repeating moments concerning Jody's hoodedness – Jody asking to have the hood removed, Fergus taking it off, the other cell members insisting it be put back on and berating Fergus for his 'softness' towards the prisoner – we see precisely this dynamic in play: the psychological distance between Fergus and Jody is broken down, and they recognise each other as fellow human beings in ways that complicate Fergus's effort to execute Jody. For the others, locked in their bad faith, Jody never becomes a real person; he remains a symbol of the British occupation they are resisting.

Perhaps the most obviously existentialist challenge in the film, though, comes in the closing moments. Here, however, it appears as a possible contestation rather than an endorsement. Sartre explains that the catchphrase of existentialism – 'existence precedes essence' – means simply that all of our philosophical analyses must begin with subjectivity, moving outwards to the identity that is constructed, over time and through that subjectivity's interaction with its environment (Sartre [1946] 2007: 20). Existentialism diverges from traditional Western philosophy in that individual human beings are not seen, in existentialist thought, as merely particular instantiations of a universal human nature (Sartre [1946] 2007: 21–22). We see the essentialism of the Western philosophical tradition, its belief in the fixedness of human nature, in the story that Jody tells of the frog and the scorpion, and existentialism's contestation of the tradition in Fergus's reluctance to commit himself to saying what his nature is. This is what makes Fergus's decision to retell the story to Dil at the film's end so curious, especially as it is presumably meant to explain why he is serving a prison sentence for her. Perhaps there is bad faith in Fergus's apparent sacrifice for Dil? In prison, Fergus doesn't have to confront the reality of her challenge to his heterosexism, so we might speculate that this particular foundational belief of his requires more 'replacement work' than the anti-occupation commitment that drove his involvement in the IRA. If this is so, then the bad faith here would lie in the extent to which Fergus is fully committed to the kind of relationship Dil wants: he does love her, but he is most comfortable with her as his girlfriend when no one knows what she 'really' is by looking at her and he does not have to deal with the mechanics of a non-platonic relationship involving two penises. And again, if this is right, the decision to end the film to the tune 'Stand by your Man' plays us out on an amusingly ironic note.

However, we may equally argue that, at the film's end, Fergus is still in the late stages of his epistemological transition: in the 'Special Features' segment of *The Crying Game* DVD, the actor who plays Fergus, Stephen Rea, observes that, 'the characters in the movie survive because they change, because they accept change'.[2] And in an interview he did with film theorist Carole Zucker, he says:

> The emotional journey is that Fergus realises that you can love anyone. He goes from being a man who's got a very rigid code about who you can offer love to, and it doesn't include British soldiers, it doesn't include the British, it doesn't include loving other men, and it probably doesn't include black men, or black people. So by

the end of the movie, he knows, and we all know and feel it, you can love anyone – race, gender, nationality are all meaningless.

(Rea, quoted in Zucker 1999: 115)

This marks as existentialist Fergus's new conception of himself, an essence that is consciously and always in the process of being constructed from experience – as Zucker puts it, 'the notion of identity as performance' (Zucker 2008: 51).

Existentialism in the Film's Broader Context

An apparently existentialist commitment to the radical freedom of subjectivity and the consequent fluidity of personal identity marks many Neil Jordan films. 'Transmutation in … identity is a trope articulated throughout Jordan's work,' Zucker tells us, citing *Angel* (1982), *The Crying Game*, *In Dreams* (1999), *Breakfast on Pluto* (2005) and *The Brave One* (2007) as examples (Zucker 2008: 178). Further coherence with existentialist attitudes can be found in Jordan's filmmaking style; Rea, the actor who is a perennial feature of many Jordan films, describes his directing as process-driven, an almost improvisatory style of filmmaking that was evident from his very first film, *Angel* (Rea 2007: ix–xi).

Framing her sustained analysis of Jordan's body of work to date, Zucker asserts that 'his films continually embrace the deepest question one can ask: what does it mean to be human?' (Zucker 2008: 1–2). 'It is really the experiential component that most interests the filmmaker,' she argues; his characters interact in ways that produce insight into our shared humanity (Zucker 2008: 2). Another commentator on Jordan's work, Maria Pramaggiore is correct when she analyses Fergus as another instance of the 'men in crisis' that frequently appear in Neil Jordan films (she cites the central characters of *Angel* and *Mona Lisa* (1986) as similar instances). Fergus is indeed someone 'whose experiences assault [his] ideas about who [he is]' and about the world he lives in (Pramaggiore 2008: 79). But to see these characters only as traditional men confused by the racial, sexual, and nationalist destabilisations of identity is to miss a powerful (albeit arguably unintended) existential message of Jordan's films: the point is not just to depict a man whose identity has melted away from him, but to encourage us to identify with the overwhelming disorientation that a destabilised identity confers. Pramaggiore observes of his first film, *Angel*, that it too 'emphasizes a fluidity of identity that undermines the essentialist notions of sectarianism' (Pramaggiore 2008: 88). The performance of the iconic protest song 'Strange Fruit' is, she thinks, significant in this regard: it 'expresses the view that the Troubles are rooted in the same deep-seated racism associated with lynching in the United States' (Pramaggiore 2008: 88).[3] Likewise, she says, *The Crying Game*

is subversive mainly to the extent that it exposes identities as fictions. The film refuses to endorse an oppositional political rubric, a refusal that suggests that positions defined in opposition to the status quo are all too often based on the same dangerous adherence to essentialist notions of 'us and them' that characterize the status quo.

(Pramaggiore 2008: 93)

A conscious decision to emphasise universality over identity politics would seem to explain why *The Crying Game*'s racial politics, which seem so crucial to a North American audience, are largely unaddressed.[4]

Jordan's films are not concerned only with casting personal identity as problematic; they also call into question beliefs about essentialised national identities. Citing *High Spirits* (1988) and *Michael Collins* (1996) as the clearest examples, Pramaggiore argues that a significant aspect of Jordan's work is his recurrent meditation on Irishness as a contested identity (Pramaggiore 2008: 47, 49). Both Pramaggiore and Zucker note the controversy that *Michael Collins*, the mythico-biographical saga of the man who negotiated freedom from the British for the counties that became the Republic of Ireland, elicited within Ireland (Pramaggiore 2008: 64–66; Zucker 2008: 9–12). But the cultural impact of Jordan's films extends beyond Ireland's borders, beyond even the fractious relations of the United Kingdom and the Irish Republic. Pramaggiore speaks of Jordan as being in the vanguard of 'the commodification of Irish ethnicity that took place during the 1990s, when "the lifestyling of Irishness [became] a *bona fide* cultural phenomenon in the U.S."' (2008: 52, quoting Negra 2004: 54).

American essayist Eula Biss dissects this phenomenon through a relentlessly romanticising feature article in the March 2006 issue of *National Geographic* titled 'Celt Appeal'. The author, Tom O'Neill, writes about travelling through Ireland, the British Isles, and northern France, encountering everywhere people whom he dubs 'Celtic' with an utter lack of concern for cultural complexity and – although he records grievances articulated by 'the blood Celts' and 'the Celts of the spirit' – a cavalier disregard of historical national divisions. Biss quotes his description of these so-called Celts, who 'are commanding attention as one of the new century's seductive identities: free-spirited, rebellious, poetic, nature-worshipping, magical, self-sufficient', and remarks on how curious it seems to her that O'Neill 'does not seem to feel the need to explain the new century's shopping spree for identities, particularly white identities that have remained untainted by colonialism' (Biss 2009: 180).[5] There is, I think, no sense in which Jordan's portrayal of Irishness enacts the same uncritical trivialisation that O'Neill passes off as cultural commentary, but each of them does contribute to this unexpected valorisation of Irish identity.[6]

Jordan's preoccupation with questions of Irish identity is no side issue, but rather an integral aspect of his contributions to the world of film. 'It is important to underscore that a work on Neil Jordan would be impossible without contextualising him as a filmmaker who came to adulthood just as "the Troubles" resurfaced in Ireland in the late 1960s', Zucker argues in her analysis of his films (Zucker 2008: 2). His recurrent attention to the raging political conflict of his place and time is what fuels observations that, for instance, his first film, *Angel*, was a 'dry run' for *The Crying Game* (Burr 1993). Jordan's work in *Angel* 'is engaged with history in a concrete way', observes Rea; 'but the action takes place on an intangible, highly ambiguous level of experience that was to become increasingly recognisable … as his directing career progressed' such that one was aware of watching 'a Neil Jordan film' (Rea 2007: ix). This once again points us to a broader existentialist context: whether consciously or not, Jordan has taken up Sartre's dictum that any war which forms part of his situation is his to take responsibility for (Sartre [1943] 2003: 574–75). But Jordan's attention to the ambiguity of experience also recalls Sartre's characterisation of the radically free subjectivity as 'being for itself' (Sartre [1943] 2003: 118).

Zucker asserts that 'the central question [for Jordan] is: what happens to a human being once he becomes enmeshed in violence?' (Zucker 2008: 3). She makes this assertion with respect to *Angel* but I think the question can stand as a guiding and unifying theme to all of the Jordan films that have the Irish political conflicts as their backdrop. To support her assertion, Zucker quotes Richard Kearney's observation that, in *Angel*, Jordan explores 'the psychic roots of violence [by] cutting through ideological conventions' (Zucker 2008: 24, quoting Kearney 1988: 179). Through the violence depicted in the film, she thinks 'the director shows how the refusal of ethical decision-making can lead to destructive fanaticism' (Zucker 2008: 25). While *Angel* was not widely released in North America, the 'Irish conflict' films that were – *Michael Collins* and *The Crying Game* – had very different receptions in the United States than they did in the United Kingdom and Ireland (Pramaggiore 2008: 51). Both films attracted considerable controversy in Britain because of their representations of a history that continues to drive current political realities, whereas American audiences appeared largely oblivious to questions of whether IRA terrorism was being romanticised (Pramaggiore 2008: 51; Rea interview [DVD special features], 2005). Zucker argues that *Michael Collins* in particular can be understood, by those audiences who are fully cognisant of the historical and political realities, 'as a "shadow text" of the Troubles, regarding the inability of post-colonial societies to produce coherent narratives' (Zucker 2008: 13).

The Call to Political Action

If consensus among oppressors and the oppressed is the mark of a coherent narrative, the inability revealed by *Michael Collins* may be all we are left with, but both this criterion of coherence and its impossibility are disputed by the comments Cohen-Solal makes about Sartre's anti-colonial commitments in her introduction to *Existentialism Is a Humanism*.

Recounting the high-profile friendship and subsequent falling-out between Sartre and Albert Camus, Cohen-Solal characterises their political rift as a disagreement over the appropriate ethical stance to take concerning the independence movements that emerged in Europe's former colonies (Cohen-Solal 2007: 9). 'Camus, the Algerian, withdrew into an attitude of consensus-seeking', she notes, whereas 'Sartre, the writer from metropolitan France, became the apostle of anticolonialism and took a radical, global position as prophet of every third-world cause' (Cohen-Solal 2007: 9).

> Sartre would follow the path of cultural inter-relations, foresee the change in the balance of world power, predict the end of European imperialist legitimacy, and discern the emergence of postcolonial politics in a prophetic world vision that was radically different from that of the pre-war era.
>
> (Cohen-Solal 2007: 12)

Cohen-Solal attributes to Sartre a commitment to the notion of a 'universal project', the view that anyone, including 'the European of 1945, though his situation is different ... can reinvent within himself the project undertaken by the Chinese, Indian, or black African' (Sartre [1946] 2007: 43). This amounts to a preview of the declaration of solidarity with the emerging decolonisation movements of the 1950s and 1960s that Sartre made in his preface to Frantz Fanon's *Wretched of the Earth* (Sartre [1961] 2004).

The possibility of a deliberately chosen alternative to passive acceptance of postcolonial stalemates is the very thing that existentialism can contribute to our existence, and we can see this suggested in *The Crying Game*. Zucker pessimistically concludes that 'the tale [of the frog and the scorpion] indicates the impossibility of solutions for a situation of suffering and misrecognition' (Zucker 2008: 59). Indeed it might, if one were to take it as a description of a non-negotiable reality, but if we take it as a representation of one choice we might make about the world, the possibility of making a different choice opens up to us. The conscious choice to change our belief systems, to adopt new lives and new types of relations with people who had previously only represented enemies or unknowable 'Others', is, on a deeply personal level, the model of reconciliation that Fergus offers us. *The Crying Game*'s commentary on global postcolonial situations is that the world goes on and we must go on with it. We can lurch forward while looking backwards, tangled up in our pasts and growing increasingly bitter that the world we once knew how to live in has melted away from us, or we can remake our identities so they function more productively in transformed communities. At our most transformative, we can awaken into the ethical consciousness and engagement with the world that both Sartre and *The Crying Game* urge upon us, and live fully human lives before our inevitable deaths.

Notes

1. See Anthony De Curtis's liner notes for the 1989 Verve release of 'The Best of the Velvet Underground'. This is his description of what is going on in the song 'Pale Blue Eyes'. I find this term appropriate for Jordan's film also because of the observation Carole Zucker makes in her analysis of his films. 'While the sense of enchantment that often accompanies ruptures in identity and narrative allows for rearrangements of the real', she writes, 'for Jordan, it frequently entails a fundamental loss, the impossibility of healing what really hurts' (Zucker 2008: 4). Given our common human need to construct belief systems that make sense of our hurts and losses, I would argue that speaking of an epistemology is particularly apt.

2. Rea offers this very existentialist analysis without ever using the label or terminology of existentialism as such.

3. This, I believe, is quite right but I wonder if perhaps it is not equally a bit too obvious. As an example, reports of recent hate crimes against Romanian immigrants in Belfast were accompanied by a rather facile commentary that 'racism is the new sectarianism' (Ann MacMillan, *Roma seek shelter after racist attacks in Northern Ireland* (17 June 2009). [Television]. Canada Broadcasting Corporation). This formulation is objectionable because it is so clear that that the two terms have always been coextensive in their essentialism and their hostile exclusionism. In my view, racism is not the new sectarianism at all; it is simply another word for the same old sectarianism.

4. For instance, except for his own remarks about the racism he encounters in Belfast, nothing ever seems to be made of Jody's blackness, or of Dil's, despite the obvious possibility that skin colour is a visual trigger allowing Fergus to separate them in his own mind from the white Anglo Saxons he has been taught to hate.

5. 'There is,' Biss contends, 'something disingenuous about European Americans – particularly those whom it might be fair to call the "winners", in terms of economic power and freedom in America – adopting the identity of Europe's "losers" because we recognize belatedly how much we lost in the transaction that made us white in this country' (2009: 180–81). Her reference to the Irish as 'losers' is borrowed from O'Neill's article, which quotes without attribution a description of them as 'Europe's beautiful losers', hence is not intended by Biss to be pejorative. Rather, the notion of the Irish as the losers of Europe's colonial history highlights how deviant this contemporary American romanticisation really is. In the essay from which this discussion is taken, 'Nobody Knows Your Name', Biss traces the history of how the Irish in America (she means the United States, of course, but a similar argument could be made in the Canadian context) became white. She notes that 'poor whites', including working-class immigrants, 'have always had more in common with poor blacks than with anyone else' (Biss 2009: 174). Despite sharing a common class position, however, 'these Irish immigrants not only refused to align themselves with black Americans in solidarity, they locked blacks out of their jobs and neighbourhoods. And so, over the course of a hundred or so complicated years, years punctuated with race riots and bloody beatings, the Irish became white' (Biss 2009: 176). In essence, they became white by aligning themselves with 'the winners', against the blacks who were demonised and marginalised as 'savages'. Ironically, as Biss observes in the beginning of her essay, 'the Irish themselves were the first people the English called savages' (2009: 171). This dehumanisation common to the Africans and the Irish is a history that seems to have been lost to the American identity-shoppers who attempt to culturally rehabilitate, even glamorise, a group widely acknowledged in history as powerless and unsuccessful (until they sided with their oppressors and against the group one might think of as their 'natural' allies). Given the overt and persistent cultural imperative to succeed that dominates life in the United States, this 'lifestyling of Irishness', as Pramaggiore terms it (2008: 52), can perhaps only be made sense of through an analysis like the one Pierre Bourdieu offers of the bohemianism adopted by the

'dominated fractions' of the dominant class, those members of the upper classes who have 'cultural capital' (such trappings of high social status as having read 'the right books', travelled widely, and been exposed to fine cuisine, art and music) but who lack 'economic capital' (Bourdieu 1984: 12–16, 114–15, 147ff). These 'disadvantaged' members of the world of privilege engage, he says, in a revaluation of the capital that they are able to access as a way of contesting their diminished social status (Bourdieu 1984: 282, 317). Seen through this prism, we might understand the adopted Irishness of some Americans as an attempt to establish social superiority by way of an identity that is not as ethically vulnerable to charges of historic imperialism as unhyphenated whiteness, a kind of side-stepping of 'white liberal guilt' that is achieved through the claim, 'it wasn't me who profited from racist social structures; I'm a marginalized Other too'.

6. The possible exception to this claim about Jordan's portrayals of Ireland and the Irish is his 1988 film *High Spirits*. This collaboration with Hollywood is definitely a commodification, a 'Hollywoodisation' of Irishness, that Jordan claims he intended as an exploration of cultural connections and disconnections between the Irish and members of their diaspora in the United States (Pramaggiore 2008: 49). The control of this film was taken out of his hands, he claims, and what was eventually screened is quite different from his own version, locked away, according to him, 'in a vault somewhere' (Zucker 2008: 80).

Bibliography

Biss, E. 2009. 'Nobody Knows Your Name', in *Notes from No Man's Land: American Essays*. Saint Paul, MN: Graywolf Press, pp. 171–83.

Bourdieu, P. 1984. *Distinction: A Social Critique of the Judgement of Taste*, trans. Richard Nice. Cambridge, MA: Harvard University Press.

Burr, T. 1993. 'Here Comes Mr. Jordan: The Movies', Entertainment Weekly.com. http://www.ew.com/ew/article/0,,305518,00.html (accessed 21 July 2009).

Cohen-Solal, A. 2007. 'Introduction', in J. Kulka (ed.), *Existentialism Is a Humanism*, trans. A. Waters. New Haven, CT: Yale University Press, pp. 3–15.

De Curtis, A. 1989. Liner Notes for 'The Best of the Velvet Underground', *Verve* 841: 164.

Grossman, D. 1996. *On Killing: The Psychological Cost of Learning to Kill in War and Society*. Newport Beach, CA: Bay Back Books.

Kearney, R. 1988. *Transitions: Narratives in Modern Irish Culture*. Manchester: Manchester University Press.

Negra, D. 2004. 'Irishness, Innocence, and American Identity Politics before and after 11 September', in Ruth Barton and Harvey O'Brien (eds), *Keeping It Real: Irish Film and Television*. London: Wallflower Press, pp. 54–68.

O'Neill, T. 2006. 'Celt Appeal', *The National Geographic Magazine*. March 2006. http://ngm.nationalgeographic.com/2006/03/celtic-realm/oneill-text (accessed 21 August 2009).

Pramaggiore, M. 2008. *Neil Jordan*. Urbana, IL: University of Illinois Press.

Rea, S. 2007. 'Foreword', in C. Zucker (2008) *The Cinema of Neil Jordan: Dark Carnival*. London: Wallflower Press, pp. ix–xi.

Sartre, J.-P. [1943] 2003. *Being and Nothingness*, trans. Hazel E. Barnes. London: Routledge.

———. [1946] 2007. *Existentialism Is a Humanism*. J. Kulka (ed.), trans. C. Macomber. New Haven, CT: Yale University Press.

————. [1961] 2004. 'Preface', in *The Wretched of the Earth*, trans. R. Philcox. New York: Grove Press, pp. xliii–lxii.

Zucker, C. 1999. 'Interview with Stephen Rea', in *In the Company of Actors: Reflections on the Craft of Acting*. London: A & C Black, pp. 108–23.

————. 2008. *The Cinema of Neil Jordan: Dark Carnival*. London: Wallflower Press.

Filmography

Jordan, N. (dir.). [1992] 2005. *The Crying Game*. Lions Gate Films Home Entertainment.

8

CRIMES OF PASSION, FREEDOM AND A CLASH OF SARTREAN MORALITIES IN THE COEN BROTHERS' *NO COUNTRY FOR OLD MEN*

Enda McCaffrey

> The point is ... there is no point.
> (*No Country for Old Men*, Cormac McCarthy 2005)

In this chapter, I want to demonstrate how we can use Sartrean existentialism to understand the choices and freedom faced by the three main characters in the multiple-award-winning film *No Country for Old Men* (2007) by the Coen Brothers. *No Country for Old Men* is a crime thriller adapted for the screen from the Cormac McCarthy 2005 novel of the same name, which in turn is the first line from the W.B. Yeats poem *Sailing to Byzantium*, first published in his 1928 collection *The Tower*. Directed by Ethan and Joel Coen, the film stars Tommy Lee Jones (Sheriff Ed Tom Bell), Javier Bardem (Anton Chigurh) and Josh Brolin (Llewelyn Moss). It tells the story of a drug deal gone wrong and the hunt for the stolen money across the West Texas landscape in the 1980s. Behind the narrative thread, the film explores the themes of chance, free will, fate and predestination – familiar territory for the Coen Brothers in films like *Blood Simple* (1984), *Raising Arizona* (1987) and *Fargo* (1996).

Two questions, in no particular order, come to mind after watching *No Country for Old Men*: Is existentialism still relevant today and can film philosophise? In an era where the depth of philosophical inquiry has been, arguably, subsumed and reshaped by the surface textuality of cultural relativism and postmodernity, it seems apposite to ask what a philosophy such as existentialism can say to us about Western culture, particularly when one of existentialism's key 'points of departure' (the acknowledgement of the contingency of existence) is itself at the heart of the debate on cultural relativism and postmodern bricolage. It comes, therefore, as a pleasant surprise and salutary reminder to rediscover that Sartre's 1946 *Existentialism Is a Humanism* attests not only to the continuing significance of existentialism in our contemporary cultural era but also to the broader relevance, adaptability and pertinence of philosophy per se, and particularly today. Couched in a connecting discourse on subjectivity, intersubjectivity and universality, Sartre writes:

> In choosing myself, I construct universality; I construct it by understanding every other man's project, regardless of the era in which he lives. This absolute freedom of choice does not alter the relativity of each era. The fundamental aim of existentialism is to reveal the link between the absolute character of the free commitment, by which every man realizes himself in realizing a type of humanity – a commitment that is always understandable by anyone in any era – and the relativity of the cultural ensemble that may result from such a choice.
>
> (Sartre [1946] 2007: 43)

In other words, existentialism, as a humanism, fulfils vital links between 'free/ individual being' and 'absolute being', as well as between 'being temporarily localised' and a 'universally intelligible being' (Sartre [1946] 2007: 44). For Sartre, times change but humankind does not.

In response to the second question, I did not have to go beyond the second part of *Existentialism Is a Humanism*, namely 'A Commentary on *The Stranger*', to be reassured of the relevance of philosophy to art (in this specific case literature, although the applications to visual studies and interpretations are, I believe, apt and Sartre's broader cultural links between art and morality in the creation of and invention of the self lend themselves favourably to comparative study between philosophy and art and the arts in general). Sartre's study of Camus's 'novel', on which he relies heavily on the philosophical work *The Myth of Sisyphus*, informs us that philosophy has an interpretative and instructive purpose in relation to fiction and art; *The Myth of Sisyphus* is referred to as a 'translation' and companion to the novel. Furthermore, Annie Cohen-Solal points to the integral link between philosophy and fiction in her description of the 'deft enunciation of philosophy at the very heart of fiction' (Cohen-Solal 2007: 6). Sartre also tells us that this relationship is a unique one in that the absurd (for Camus) and contingency (for Sartre) operates without justification or explanation: 'Camus is not concerned about justifying what is fundamentally unjustifiable' (Sartre [1946] 2007: 79). Sartre's implication is that the 'descriptive' power of the absurd is enough to convey a philosophy of the absurd. Philosophy therefore has a positive role to play in art and film in the tradition of epistemological inquiry, but in the specific context of the absurd/ contingency, this role is decidedly passive and 'descriptive'. One could argue also that it is even post-epistemological in that the absurd and the contingent are by definition unexplainable, in no need of 'proof', more a matter of 'silence' and as Sartre says more 'in the realm of what is not said' (Sartre [1946] 2007: 80). For Sartre, philosophy in the novel and in art instructs the absurd descriptively, using 'substance', 'content', 'presentation', 'image' and 'perception' to convey 'idea' or 'meaning'. This is the template that we can transfer legitimately to the screen where the apparatus of film production is deployed to capture the post-epistemological truth of philosophy, or as Sartre says: 'the outraged acknowledgement of the limitations of human thought' (Sartre [1946] 2007: 81).

The broader relationship between philosophy and film has produced some recent critical works. William C. Pamerleau argues that it is not a question of simply mapping Sartrean existentialism on to film. Films, he claims, have their own concrete realities ('life on their terms') and thus this relationship is one of mutual engagement in which, for example, films have a key role in testing, amending, extrapolating and strengthening the authenticity of a philosophical idea (Pamerleau 2009: 3). In their co-authored Introduction, Richard Allen and Murray Smith explore, by contrast, the concrete links between Continental philosophy and Anglo-American film theory, with particular and relevant emphasis on the purpose of philosophy to critique epistemology, acknowledging, as Sartre does, that 'post-epistemological philosophy endlessly reflects on its (in) ability to make knowledge claims, paralleling the focus in much modernist art on the limitations and paradoxes of representation' (Allen and Smith 2009: 10). Turning to the Coen Brothers' film *No Country for Old Men* (2007), the aptly titled *The Philosophy of the Coen Brothers*, edited by Mark Conrad (2009), brings together a series of philosophical responses to many of the Coen Brothers' films, including two chapters devoted to the above film. Richard Gilmore links Westerns and Greek tragedies, seeing in the film's characters 'forces' of power, fate, hubris and an over-arching struggle between Dionysian passion and Apollonian reason. Gilmore also underlines the philosophical credentials of the Coens' films. Writing about their films as fictional 'stories' (and echoing Solal's and Sartre's reflections about philosophy and fiction), he says:

> It is certainly true that they are stories, but it is also true that they are in their own ways true stories, that reveal true things about the way the world is and about our ways of being in the world. It is precisely in this way that their movies function like philosophy.
>
> (Gilmore 2009: 76)

Douglas McFarland in his chapter views the Coens' films as examples of moral philosophy at play, where the principal characters are caught between opposing sets of moral values (self-interest and personal versus rational, transcendent and ethical). Both authors would appear to distance themselves from outright existentialist readings of *No Country for Old Men*, although both concur that allusions to existentialist thinking form part of the wider debate of the film's philosophical import. In a passage, for example, that bears comparison with Sartre's analysis of the 'morality of action and commitment', Gilmore states:

> This fatalism ... is definitely based on the idea that you are what you do and that what you have done cannot be undone, what decisions you have made cannot be unmade, and finally what you do, what you have decided, will have its natural consequences in the world, and there is no avoiding or evading those consequences.
>
> (Gilmore 2009: 70)

And in an oblique reference to existential heroes, McFarland claims: 'But unlike other so-called existential heroes, who attempt to create meaning in a meaningless world, Llewelyn Moss remains entangled in ethical categories and will ultimately be judged according to these categories' (McFarland 2009: 167).

In spite of these characterisations in contradistinction to existential values, McFarland frames his debate on moral philosophy in such a way as to invite the reader to draw conclusions that advance further existential investigation. In particular, the choices and dilemmas that Sheriff Ed Tom Bell and Llewelyn Moss face are shaped in order to highlight key Sartrean paradigms: existence precedes essence, secular morality and morality of action and commitment, the self and the Other. Without stating so overtly, McFarland sketches characters who are on the cusp of existentialist crisis or self-invention. My approach, therefore, in this chapter extends McFarland's interpretation of the film's 'moral philosophy' by exploring three characters; one (Anton Chirgurh) who, as we will see, appears to have all the hallmarks of an existential hero but who in fact betrays his radical freedom; another (Sheriff Bell) who, in action and language, maps the crisis of existential choice and freedom, occupying a space in between, inhabiting the interstitial moment of the 'hold still' where world and choice are suspended 'unageing' in a Yeatsian poetic pause. And Llewelyn Moss who embodies existentialist values in their raw, valueless and tragic reality.

Anton Chigurh:
Crime of Passion or Hegelian Terrorist Freedom?

For Sartre, a crime of passion is one committed out of love for political engagement, freedom of self and freedom for others. The opposite of this, that is a crime committed in self-interest, for profit or out of hatred, is a denial of freedom and a form of terrorism. By setting up what is a false distinction between crime of passion and gratuitous murder at the outset of this film, the Coen Brothers invite us to reflect on the significance of passion and freedom as philosophical tools to understand one of the film's key existential directions – engagement for the sake of a cause. In *Dirty Hands*, re-titled aptly in an English translation as *Crime passionnel* (1948), Sartre uses Hugo's murderous act as a way of highlighting crimes of passion as that which is motivated by the greater cause of political engagement. In *No Country for Old Men*, the misuse of the term 'crime of passion' is a cheap reference used by an inmate to justify the murder of a girlfriend in the hope of escaping death row, as well as an allusion used by Sheriff Bell to refer to crimes of yesteryear deemed to be more solvable than the gratuitous and untraceable type of murder we see committed in the film. The Sartrean intertext, however, invites us to explore in more depth the Coen Brothers' juxtaposition of crime of passion with gratuitous murder, particularly in the motivations of characters whose 'gratuitous' actions appear paradoxically to invoke some underlying 'passion'.

Specifically, we can use Sartre's existential play on the word 'passion' to differentiate between Sheriff Bell and Chigurh, and particularly to evaluate to what extent these characters manifest existentialist characteristics. Sheriff Bell is 'passionate' about solving crime; he puts everything into it, but without *success*. By the end of the film, he is full of regrets and missed opportunities which signal a critical failing in his life. Chigurh is not only more inscrutable a character but his behaviour gives rise to a critical problematic: his 'passion' and *raison d'être* is to perpetrate murder! Chigurh is a throwback to the Sartrean fictional character Paul Hilbert in the short story 'Erostratus' from *The Wall* (Sartre [1939] 1975]. Hilbert is a loner and a control freak. He has a revolver which he 'uses' to threaten prostitutes to comply with his sadistic games. He stalks bourgeois concert and theatre goers, and imagines shooting them in the back. At the outset, his revolver is an object, including a sensual object he enjoys carrying in his pocket; it is the source of his control and power. Wasting away in his apartment, he decides finally to go out and murder a man in the street, and then open up randomly on a group of bystanders. Cornered eventually in a toilet, with one bullet left in his gun, he resists the temptation to kill himself and instead surrenders himself to the police.

Hilbert is widely interpreted as a maniac whose crime highlights the impossibility and futility of revolt: 'The only solution against humanism is philosophical ... This solution is to found in thought and not in action' (Idt 1972: 39). The links with Chigurh are therefore obvious: two seemingly deranged psychopaths on the loose with weapons, for whom life is a game of chance. They also happen to share a rejection of society's values. In spite of these comparisons, my reading of Paul Hilbert's actions sets in train a fundamental opposition between Hilbert and Chigurh. At the crux of this difference, and what makes Paul Hilbert a failed existentialist and Chigurh a 'Hegelian terrorist' (Sartre [1945] 2009: 18) is the nature of their respective 'passions'. Hilbert's crime is situated within the context of what Sartre calls '*L'Humain*', not just the 'positive' Humanism implied by the term, but also the positive rejection of Humanism as an impediment to his life. For Sartre, Hilbert's life has been taken away from him by a Humanist consensus which has tried to rob him of his freedom and impose pre-existing values. Hilbert's resentment at this is unformulated at the outset (a thought still in need of processing, Sartre claims) but it exists nevertheless as an internal, organic movement inside him, located in a disdain that has clear physical manifestations (choking, fainting, fear of touching – all of which Sartre implies are part of a premonition to a possible existentialist awakening).

To be clear, Hilbert's violent murder of people on the streets of Paris is of course misdirected and ultimately goes against the grain of existentialist freedom. But Hilbert's resistance to Humanism reveals a more complex picture of intentions and motivations, and opens the door to existentialist predispositions. In contrast to Sheriff Bell, for example, whose life peters out without success, Hilbert is clear that he wants to 'achieve something serious' with his life: 'Don't think I didn't have more serious reasons for hating them' (Sartre [1939] 1975: 42). In order to resist being a part of the history of a Humanism he despises, Hilbert turns to crime 'entirely conceived and organised by myself' (Sartre [1939] 1975: 50). His crime would appear to have all the hallmarks of a 'crime passionnel' – unlike that of the foolhardy inmate in the film and anathema to the sentimental musings of Sheriff Bell – in the way that its passion resides partially in the legitimate rejection of Humanism. For Sartre, the existentialist pre-requisite to Hilbert's crime is that it is founded in an internal, organic struggle of existence over essence, a physical struggle that Sartre says involves blood and sweat. In this sense, Sartre's emphasis on the physical nature of Hilbert's motivation is crucial. Sartre literally fleshes out the anatomy of a pre-existentialist humanism (the possibility of a human and violent response to Humanism) through Hilbert's pre-murderous, corporeal motivations. At the critical point in the text, Hilbert decides not to go through with murder as a matter of conscious reflection, but in the same breath he admits that he had taken the decision to proceed with his crime 'as if my decision had stopped'. Thought abandons Hilbert at this critical juncture but the physical disgust directed towards his target continues to motivate and generate his existential crisis.

As an act registered inside human tissue, owing its legitimacy to a life-blood whose humanity is both part of and transcends the Humanism he despises, Hilbert's crime 'succeeds' in as much as it symbolises a potential subversion of Humanism from within. In the final days before Hilbert's futile crime, he spends his last money on take-outs, indulging in the pleasures of life right up to the point when, penniless, he begins to decompose physically and mentally; his meticulous planning for murder (including his empty attempts at self-fattening as an expression of courage) threaten temporarily to be undone by weakness and second thoughts. But his body holds strong and he commits himself unwillingly to his task:

> Then I knew I was going to start screaming. *I didn't want to*: I shot him three times in the belly. He fell with an idiotic look on his face, dropped to his knees and his head rolled on his left shoulder. 'Bastard', I said, 'rotten bastard'.
>
> (Sartre [1939] 1975: 53 [my italics])

Ultimately, the thoughtless disengagement in Hilbert's crime disqualifies it as a crime of passion and him as a hero of existentialism. That said, there is a predisposition in Hilbert to the rank of existentialist that can be located in a pre-meditative physicality that thrives on its own internal rationale and existential sustainability. Hilbert is an unwitting existentialist who lets his resentment override its usefulness and valid purpose in freedom. Even so, in forgoing the easy option of suicide at the end and thus assuming the responsibility of living, Hilbert offers the possibility of existential life for himself and for others.

It is tempting to read Chigurh as an existentialist hero and there are fruitful lines of investigation that lend themselves to this hypothesis. On the DVD cover and the poster for the film, Chigurh is the central figure of three, flanked on both sides by Sheriff Bell and Llewelyn Moss. This centrality is not just an indication of his striking visual appearance but it is also a sign of his importance at the heart of the film's narrative identity and philosophical significance. In the early stages of the film's narrative structure, Chigurh simply appears out of the blue, seemingly unattached by any chronological linearity, popping up in grumpy mood at a gas station then pursuing a cop car and pointlessly killing its occupant. In the second of these episodes, the phrase 'hold still' (uttered as he kills his victim) is repeated in the successive scene by Llewelyn Moss (as he takes aim forlornly at a pronghorn). The Coens would appear to link apparently disconnected scenes as in a poetic pause which serves on the one hand to underline the facticity of life in the Wild West, but also to nudge viewers in the direction of their cinematic *modus operandi*; spatial images generate meaning and ideas and here the prophetic 'hold still' places the spotlight on the very meaning of contingency in this Texan wasteland.

At first glance, Chigurh would appear to embody the doctrine of existentialism in action and in philosophy. In the now celebrated scene with the gas attendant where the latter is asked to choose life or death on the toss of a coin, Chigurh evokes the twin existentialist paradigms of essence/existence and choice. His anger at the attendant's pleasant 'meddling' is channelled into a Sartrean critique of the secular morality of civil society based on the *a priori* existence of 'goodness'. Believing himself to be only passing the time of day as an expression of genial courtesy, the value of the gas attendant's life (his essential humanity) is brought into question; he is accused by Chigurh of 'putting it up all his life', indeed Chigurh's greater wrath is reserved for the attendant's confession that he 'married into the business' – an example of Hilbertian disgust at a life of cosy inheritance and secular morality that Sartre demeans in *Existentialism Is a Humanism*. The process of how roles are inherited, socialised and institutionalised, and then legitimised (in this case via marriage) is anathema to the killer Chigurh, whose own existence has to be reinvented after each murder. Each one is tantamount to the erasure of a previous human essence, a skill he becomes so accomplished in that he is hyper-hygienic in leaving no traces. This scene also echoes a later exchange between Carson Wells (Woody Harrelson), a bounty hunter hired to 'take out' Chigurh, and Chigurh himself when the latter interrogates Carson at gun point: 'Let me ask you something. If the rule you followed brought you to this, of what use was that rule?' In a veiled Sartrean allusion to the metaphorical waste of a life predetermined by values and rules that 'tell you what you ought to do', Chigurh juxtaposes his own vacant 'values' of disdain and worthlessness before shooting Carson in cold blood.

The absence of an authentic value system in Chigurh is further intimated in the riposte 'You don't have to do this', first used by Carson Wells in his exchange with Chigurh and repeated in the scene between Carla and Chigurh at the end of the film. Both scenes highlight Chigurh's ethical wasteland. In both exchanges, Chigurh does not respond to the moral reproaches inferred by the riposte; to do so would be a tacit acknowledgement of the secular morality he opposes. As Richard Gilmore says: 'In both instances, he subjugates his desires to the flip of a coin, to chance. That is his principle. It is the principle that keeps him from a certain kind of vulnerability' (Gilmore 2009: 65). The toss of the coin therefore becomes Chigurh's new 'ethical' benchmark. It erases the consideration of the *a priori* and the *a posteriori*, and defines his alternative 'existence' as one created on the randomness of choice. In requesting Carson and Carla to choose life or death on the toss of a coin, Chigurh is not just deferring choice to the realms of gratuity but he is also handing responsibility over to 'fate' in an act of bad faith that prevents him from taking responsibility for his own ethical choices. Douglas McFarland would appear to concur with this evaluation:

> In an instant he has created a world with its own arbitrary and simple rules ... Categories of justice and assumptions of responsibility cease to have meaning ... Chigurh has shattered complacency ... and catapulted the proprietor into a realm of contingent circumstances, random eruptions of violence, the dehumanised face of chance, the grim necessity of luck, and the quirkiness and perversity of Life.
>
> (McFarland 2009: 171)

Notwithstanding the perverse rationality that leads Chigurh to kill as a matter of twisted principle, he remains faithful to these twisted 'principles' right up to the penultimate scene when, a casualty himself in a higher clash of contingencies,[1] he finds himself escaping a car crash only to be befriended by two suburban teenagers on bikes. In a scene reminiscent of Moss's earlier offer of money in exchange for clothes to cover his bloodied body which allows him to cross the border to Mexico (an act of desperation, self-preservation and mutual exploitation), Chigurh forgoes any opportunity to feel morally obliged to return the favour to the boys by insisting on paying for the garments they wilfully hand over to him. Payment also buys the boys' secrecy and their promise not to reveal his existence. For Chigurh, nothing is a given in life; every situation/person/item has a price and in his world all exchange is calibrated in terms of unreciprocated supply and demand.

However, and crucially, Chigurh is not a hero of existentialism. He is in fact an anti-hero. He is a survivor at any cost. In contrast to Sartre's Paul Hilbert, the unwitting existentialist who misapplies his legitimate disgust, Chigurh is bereft of any existential teleology and takes pleasure in murder for its own sake. He kills not for a cause or a passion but for the sake of it – and for money. At a superficial level, there are comparisons between the two regarding the gratuitous nature of their killings. Hilbert's behaviour hints at this gratuity in his murder of only six people, a number only predetermined by the number of chambers in his revolver. This gratuitousness, however, is both contained (by the object of the revolver itself) and by the fact that the victims will not only be limited in number but in the totality of shots fired (including the final one reserved but unused for himself) they represent the premeditated 'success' of his action. In other words, the indiscriminate act of murder is discriminated as a *fait accompli*. As such, Hilbert's crime is a misguided act, existentially, but a controlled action that also symbolises his refusal of Humanism. Chigurh's crime on the other hand is indiscriminate slaughter, an arbitrary consequence of his rejection of Humanism (not sourced in this rejection as Hilbert's is in the subversive potential of '*L'Humain*'), and indeed a product of Humanism's more debasing characteristics: greed and money. Freedom, Sartre reminds us, does not reside inside oneself. It is not an essence or a property. One becomes free through a 'passion' to be free. Chigurh fails outright in this respect and Hilbert abuses his freedom:

> He [Man] doesn't exist first, and then be free later. He is free by the fact that he exists … But man, who is thus condemned to freedom, still has to free himself, because he doesn't immediately recognize himself as free, or, because he misunderstands the meaning of his freedom.
>
> (Sartre [1945] 2009: 17)

I would contend, therefore, that Hilbert's crime falls short as a 'crime passionnel' even though it is inspired in the first instance by a thirst for freedom which then goes awry. Chigurh's crime, on the other hand, is a 'crime impassionnel' because it is a means to an end and thus 'counter-freedom'. Like Mathieu, the protagonist of Sartre's *Iron in the Soul* (*La Mort dans l'âme*), Chigurh 'is the incarnation of this complete uncommittedness that Hegel calls "terrorist freedom"' (Sartre [1945] 2009: 18).[2] Chigurh is not free because he has not been able to commit himself to anything other than profit. Sartre describes this type of false freedom as 'the freedom of indifference, freedom in the abstract, freedom for nothing. Mathieu's not free, he's nothing, because he's always on the outside' (Sartre [1945] 2009: 18).

Sheriff Bell's Cowardice

In the opening voice-over Sheriff Bell recalls an apparently insignificant anecdote about a young man who killed his girlfriend in a fit of uncontrollable rage. In the ensuing court case, the plaintiff explains his murder as a 'crime of passion'. The sheriff claims not to know what a crime of passion is – for him murder is just 'plain murder', and more generally symptomatic of how society has changed. The distinction between a crime of passion and plain murder, as we have seen in the case of Chigurh, sets up one of the film's principal existential binaries between authentic engagement and terrorist freedom. However, for Sheriff Bell, the (mis)understanding between a crime of passion and plain murder takes us in a different direction from the distinction highlighted for

Chigurh. The crime of passion, to which the sheriff appears to give short shrift as a lame excuse for murder, situates crime/murder in a context where sentiment might have played a contributory role (passion is here synonymous with emotion, not existentialism). By contrast, plain murder, or as the sheriff refers to it 'the crime we see today', poses a different problem in that it can be random, indiscriminate and clues to the guilty party are often impossible to come by. Ironically, this opposition highlights a central psychological schism, not as we might expect in the mind of the youth (who subsequently confessed there was no passion to his crime and was then summarily executed) but in Sheriff Bell himself.

For him, the crime of passion alludes to a bygone time, a Yeatsian time of 'aged men as paltry things ... tattered coats upon a stick', an era of previous generations of sheriffs in whom Bell placed great pride and solidarity. It was a time when there was an expectation that any sheriff worth his salt had a very good chance of solving a crime because in those days criminals were either psychologically flawed, driven mad by 'passion' and thus susceptible to leaving traces behind, or they were simply not smart enough to get away with crime. The law, in effect, was the supreme arbiter; faith in it was unquestioned because the law guaranteed solutions, results and the punishment of wrongdoing. For the sheriff, this age of certainty has now been replaced by an age of uncertainty; murder happens now in ways that make it impossible to solve. Unlike Chigurh's failed crime of passion as an expression of self-interest and the renunciation of radical freedom, Sheriff Bell views the crime of passion as an ethical/legal benchmark, a means of rationalising his understanding of moral and legal codes, endorsing their legitimacy and making judgements on right and wrong. Locked in his history of Humanism, the sheriff regrets the passing of an era where the crime of passion was literally a crime motivated by selfish passion and thus morally and legally unambiguous. Importantly, though, the paradox of the sheriff's current dilemma is that his inability to solve plain murder makes him question who he is and what he has been doing all his life. Gilmore points to a possible way forward:

> One has the sense ... that things are out of alignment, that balance and harmony are gone from the land and the people. It is Yeats' vision, and certainly Nietzsche's as well, that it is the artist/philosopher who is most needed to help restore balance. It may not in the end be the doer as much as the thinker who is needed to help us see our losses and where we might find the gains to make us whole.
>
> (Gilmore 2009: 74)

If philosophy invites us to rationalise and give meaning to the world we live in, then this assumption is undermined from the first few lines of the film. Sheriff Bell, proud of his stance in refusing to carry a gun (again a throwback to yesteryear), admits failure in being unable to understand the modern world of crime. In spite of his adaptability to modern methods in crime scene investigatory techniques, his much vaunted 'linear' thinking, unmatched knowledge of the West Texas terrain and uncanny ability to 'read signs', he continues to admit his impotence in being unable to understand the gratuity of modern murder and make sense of his own human values in a seemingly meaningless world. His scoping of the aftermath of the drug massacre is unparalleled in its professionalism and analysis, but this 'knowledge' is subsequently found wanting, as he comes to be defined as always being one step behind the murderer/the object of his knowledge. This 'lack' takes place in an age of technology where tracking crime is impossible but where the perfect, traceless, unprovable crime is possible (which Chigurh demonstrates at every turn). The sheriff's life and career have been founded on the pursuit and successful solving of crime. However, his hubris and arrogance as a lawman who travels gunless and insists on imposing his own outdated methods of sleuthdom on the Wild West come unstuck as his human fallibility clashes with the gratuitously unclassifiable. This clash of the human and the arbitrary is framed as a process of deferral (what Sartre calls the 'discrepancy between the perceptions of facts and their meaning') (Sartre [1946] 2007: 93).

It is a notion cleverly conveyed by the Coen Brothers in a series of scenes where on one particular occasion the sheriff arrives at Moss's trailer only to find Chigurh has beaten him to it; the replicated image of the sheriff drinking a bottle of milk in the reflection of the TV screen neatly mirrors Chigurh's exact same actions just moments earlier. Implicitly, the sheriff may be on his trail but the prospect of sheriff and Chigurh 'meeting' or 'coinciding' is remote, a prospect nonetheless that the Coens flirt with stylistically, notably when the sheriff (against all conventional police wisdom) returns alone to the scene of Moss's murder, unaware that Chigurh is lurking in the hotel room's ventilation shaft. Although his intuition tells him that Chigurh is present, the sheriff chooses crucially not to act on his intuition which makes his refusal to confront Chigurh all the more problematic and cowardly. Bemoaning himself as eternally 'mismatched' and fatefully at odds with the world and the incomprehensible 'gyre' of modern crime, the sheriff misses a critical opportunity to break with his past, 'take out' Chigurh at his own game and triumph over chance. It is the closest the sheriff gets to turning the tables on Chigurh by predicting his next move and thus solve the riddle of gratuitous 'plain murder'; metaphorically, it is also the closest the pursuit of knowledge gets to its goal, the closest the thing gets to itself phenomenologically, the closest reason comes to circumnavigating the chaos of randomness, and the nearest viewers get to a defining moment when contingency (exemplified in Chigurh) is successfully mapped. Most importantly, I would contend that it is also the closest the sheriff comes to a Sartrean existentialist 'point of departure' where 'the absolute truth of consciousness' confronts itself in a 'moment of self-awareness' revealing man's freedom from the material world' (Sartre [1946] 2007: 40–41).

This is a confrontation that does not happen for Sheriff Bell. Missed opportunity or deliberate act of Sartrean cowardice, he returns to the rule of secular morality, expressing incredulity at the dismal tide of crime ('hard to believe' he rues) and eventually sinking deeper into a defeatist quietism of dreams and dashed hopes, excoriating God for not having come to his rescue. Knowledge of self and of the world has failed the sheriff, leaving him exposed to the vagaries and dangers of chance. His demise, however, is compounded by a double failure to reinvent himself; his indulgent introspection at the film's *dénouement* (questioning why knowledge has not produced meaning and answers to life's problems, and his sense of bewilderment at his abandonment by God) has thwarted all possibility of a projection of self and embrace of the anguish of his abandonment in a new existentialist subjectivity. Gilmore also confirms this sense of failure at the end of the film. However, whereas my reading highlights the sheriff's cowardice in refusing to adapt to the 'gyre' of modern crime, Gilmore glorifies this failure as the endorsement of a new wisdom: 'Bell knows that he is no match for Anton Chigurh. What he has done, however, is bear witness to certain events. This too has an important role to play for the sake of humanity' (Gilmore 2009: 77).

This emphasis on bearing witness reflects Gilmore's more optimistic reading of the film as a chronicle of the times and its privileged heritage as a journey in a poet's assimilation by the continuum of eternity (not forgetting the elevated status of the sheriff himself as a poet/philosopher of his age). In this sense, Gilmore's conclusion forms part of a rich seam of intertextual, literary and artistic connections, but I would also argue there is a danger in taking Sheriff Bell's admission of failure too far; after all, this is a sheriff who, in spinning a yarn about cows, bullets and ricochets, managed to prise crucial information from Moss's wife Carla about her husband's whereabouts, only for this information to be leaked and lead to Moss's subsequent murder, and all this in spite of the sheriff's assurances that Moss would remain safe. If there is something we can be sure of about the sheriff it is that, despite his years of experience, he knows nothing and can guarantee even less. So Gilmore's equivalence between failure and wisdom overshadows a more fundamental flaw in Sheriff Bell's (mis)understanding of the world. His personal failure represents a deeper, systemic failure of reason and knowledge to understand the gratuitous nature of modern crime (symbolised most graphically by Chigurh's cattle stun gun). While Gilmore's reading reflects in part the sentiment of Yeats's *Sailing to Byzantium* in which knowledge is limited by man's mortal condition and can only be rectified in a process of poetic self-immolation 'in the artifice of eternity', it still does not detract from the key point that in the failure of human knowledge to decode the absurdity of life, Sheriff Bell had the choice to acknowledge this failure or become one of its victims. He chose the latter.

Llewelyn Moss and a Clash of Sartrean Moralities

If West Texas is no country for old men, the prospects are not much better for the younger generation, condemned as we see to 'goin' to hell' even from the age of fourteen. If senescence is no guarantee of wisdom and knowledge, what hope is there for youth? Of course, Yeats's solution to this age/knowledge conundrum was to take flight to the Eastern city of Byzantium and find meaning in the ivory tower of Art. There is no such escape for the denizens (young and old) of desert existence in West Texas, 'vases communicants' of Voltairean acausality and unknowableness. This is their lot, choosing to engage positively in a different morality. A case in point is Llewelyn Moss. McFarland does not classify Moss as an existential hero because he 'remains tangled in ethical categories and will ultimately be judged according to these categories' (McFarland 2009: 167). In fact, he proceeds to characterise Moss as 'unable to avoid the entanglements of a situation that has a "dialectic" in its relation to the idea of moral conduct' (McFarland 2009: 167).

It is accurate, on one level, to say that Moss is caught between a need to authenticate himself and a normative set of moral values. There is also sufficient evidence to argue that the emotional pull of his wife, her mother and his own feelings of guilt (all of which, lest we forget, conspire in his eventual murder) situate Moss in a Sartrean 'secular morality' which Sartre describes as the antithesis of existential heroism because it indulges one in a quietism of predeterminism. However, the critique that Moss's 'moral values' are not based on reason but on religious faith (as McFarland suggests) does not advance McFarland's position any further given, as I have argued, that an Enlightenment faith in reason is not the answer to understanding gratuitous murder anymore than religious faith is, and indeed a blind faith in reason and knowledge, including his innate intuition, has exposed the limitations of Sheriff Bell and his vacuous attempts to rid West Texas of gratuitous murder.

I would propose, therefore, an alternative reading of Moss's ambivalence, which takes account of these ethical categories but which frames him from the outset as a tragic existential hero (that is as a character who renounces secular morality, projects himself as a new self beyond this morality but whose demise comes tragically at the hands of terrorist freedom). Unlike Sheriff Bell whose struggle to understand the world of modern crime is an act of cowardice, Moss lives and experiences his alienation in his actions, choices and decisions. We are first introduced to him as a nomad in the desert, an eponymous drifter who lives off the land and his own self-acquired skill in shooting pronghorn; his Vietnam blues and trailer lifestyle, coupled with his new-found 'profession' as welder, bear witness to a washed-up life on the fringe. Moss and his actions embody acausality; an 'unsuccessful' rifle shot leads illogically and ironically to blood tracks in the dirt and the promise of a wounded pronghorn, only for the blood to reveal the presence of a limping doberman, which in turn leads Moss to a drug bust and the fated loot. Ironically, it is his return to the scene of the drug bust the next day (a move mirrored later in the film in the sheriff's fated return to the scene of a crime – both further demonstrations of the triumph of inconsequentiality over sense and reason) that proves significant in the film's acausal trajectory, in Moss's 'ethical' profile and in his existentialist self-projection. McFarland, as noted, explains Moss's return to help the lone survivor as a moral choice, motivated by (religious) compassion and an obligation to pre-established values. He suggests that Moss is unable to suspend these ethical concerns and create his own set of moral values; this amounts to his failure to link authenticity with moral obligation. For McFarland, this obligation contradicts the 'audience's perception of Llewelyn Moss as the existential loner' (McFarland 2009: 169).

Moss's retreat to determinism and what Sartre terms 'inherited' feelings and values that 'have a priori existence' flies in the face of an existential reading of Moss's actions. However, I would contend that 'obligation' is too strong a word to define Moss's reactions in this specific and crucial scene. Furthermore, to categorise his compassion as an expression of 'faith in the redemptive power of Christ's sacrifice' (McFarland 2009: 169) is stretching not only Moss's theological imagination but also that of the audience. The wider implication of McFarland's analysis is that the 'existential loner' must by definition be bereft of ethical compassion. Sartre claims that 'no general code of ethics can tell you what you ought to do; there are no signs in this world' (Sartre [1946] 2007: 33). Equally, Moss, in my view, is the last type of person, given his background and lifestyle, to sign up to a 'general code of ethics'. The critical difference here is that Moss's ethics are not determined by a pre-existing general code. On the contrary, they are co-existent with his self-authentification. Moss's compassion is existentialist firstly in its acknowledgement of the existence of others as a condition of selfhood, and secondly in its responsibility to others as a condition of this existence. Sartre states:

> I cannot discover any truth whatsoever about myself except through the mediation of another. The other is essential to my existence, as well as to the knowledge I have of myself. Under these conditions, my intimate discovery of myself is at the time a revelation of the other as a freedom that confronts my own and that I cannot think or will without doing so for or against me. We are thus immediately thrust into a world that we may call 'intersubjectivity'. It is in this world that man decides what he is and what others are.
>
> (Sartre [1946] 2007: 41–42)

To put this existentialist humanism in context, the real significance of Moss's return to the scene of the drug bust lies in the previous trailer scene when he wakes up in the middle of the night and decides to fill a can with water, collect his stash of money, tell his wife to leave, and depart never to see her again. The final verbal exchange between them is pivotal:

Carla: Llewelyn?
Moss: Yeah?

Carla: What are you doing, baby?

Moss: I'm going out.

Carla: Going where?

Moss: There's something I forgot to do, but I'll be back.

Carla: And what are you going to do?

Moss: I'm fixing to do something dumber than hell, but I'm going anyways. If I don't
   come back, tell mother I love her.

Carla: Your mother's dead, Llewelyn.

Moss: Well then, I'll tell her myself.

We can read this scene in different ways. Moss has lost all take on reality. He does not know what he is saying because his mind is on the money and the dream of a new life. There is also the viewpoint that Moss's decision to return to the scene of the drug bust can legitimately be explained as an expression of laudable empathy within McFarland's 'moral philosophy'. In my view, the above exchange between husband and wife is as much about 'instinct' as it is about moral imperative. Moss has had to rely on instinct as a soldier in Vietnam and as a pronghorn hunter in the Wild West. Indeed, Moss acknowledges that his decision to return to the crime scene is 'dumber than hell', in fact deadly. But he goes back nevertheless. In fact, it is this instinct (as opposed to feeling, obligation or predetermined value) that is the most reliable indication of what Moss is thinking. And in this instance, his instinct is that he is sure to die as a result of this decision, which is effectively what happens. Moss is therefore not in bad faith about his impending death; he accepts it as a condition of his departure and liberty, so much so that he is ready to tell his dead mother that he loves her (i.e. when the dead two meet). Unlike Sheriff Bell who forgoes the opportunity to embrace the 'absolute truth of consciousness confronting itself', Moss's acceptance of his own death, coupled with his SELF-awareness as thing-in-itself (symbolised by his mother's continuing existence in his own consciousness and the knowledge of which is dependent on itself rather than on an outside 'object') is a proleptic preview of his own existential death as an 'essence' and his rebirth as a subjective 'existence'. Conscious of his subjective existence, and out of responsibility to it, Moss returns to help the dying man in the truck. He chooses to go back, not in deference to some code of ethics, but because of an instinctive commitment to mankind ('rely on your instincts', Sartre [1946] 2007: 32) and because of a moment of lucidity in which he sees an opportunity to create his own moral value. Even though the dying man has passed on and Moss's action is deemed temporarily fruitless, it serves more importantly to remind him and viewers of the philosophical urgency of his new-found freedom and broader existentialist 'doctrine'.

When Moss returns to the drug scene, his new life begins. The 'old' Moss is effaced; after his escape from the posse of dogs, he flees to the wilderness, cleansing himself in cooling rapids and self-suturing himself against a backdrop of balmy mountain breezes. His new identity, from hunter to hunted, conjoins with new tropes of 'existence' ('on the run', hitchhiking and keeping one step ahead of his pursuer). From a Sartrean perspective, what we see from this point of the film until Moss's eventual murder is a man who has re-invented himself, whose new 'morality' is not an abstract principle but a Sartrean 'work of art' founded on the assumption of and responsibility for one's actions, and the invention and creativity needed to stay alive. Moss's new value is that of life, living life at its outer edge and with utmost intensity, confronting at every moment his possible death. His murder comes as inglorious and contingent an event as one would have expected; no build-up, no stake-out, no holding out for a great escape. We capture him tragically, within a sequence of fast-moving, disconnected clips, slumped on a bedroom floor, and again, in a similar fragmented sequence, laid out unceremoniously in a morgue. Moss's death, seemingly inconsequential and barely noticed within the wider Chigurh-Bell narrative, points paradoxically to the authenticity of his existence, shaped by intuition and self-formation in the face of the knowledge of his death. Not only, therefore, are his moral 'shortcomings' rendered trivial, but he assumes, as a consequence of his subjective existence, a greater ethical responsibility for all mankind: 'In choosing myself, I choose man' (Sartre [1946] 2007: 25).

Conclusion

The human condition is snared by age, by the limitations on what it can know and ultimately by death. For W.B. Yeats, this undesirable state could only be eliminated by the efforts of the soul and the cleansing fire of art to 'gather him into the artifice of eternity', symbolised by Byzantium's transformation into the timelessness of art. In *No Country for Old Men*, the principal characters face the same constraints imposed by knowledge and death, and a more acute (visual) awareness of the insignificance and nothingness of life in West Texas. But, whether Byzantium or Texas, existentialism is seen to remain relevant because of Sartre's confirmation of the fundamental relationship between the 'absolute character of the free commitment ... and the relativity of the cultural ensemble that may result from such a choice' (Sartre [1946] 2007: 43). The three main characters in this film reflect in different ways the validity of this eternal relationship. Unlike one of his nearest Sartrean counterparts Paul Hilbert, whose crime of passion is principled in its existentialist disgust for the political class of the bourgeoisie but distorted as an expression of freedom and a form of legitimate action, Anton Chigurh's campaign of murder is without principle, gratuitous save a veiled mercantile motivation and terroristic in its abuse of freedom. For Sheriff Bell, crime of passion is a metaphor for a lost past where he could once apply his reason and knowledge to solving crime. Chigurh and his modern methods of murder pose a challenge to the sheriff to adapt his ways but also to reinvent himself by addressing the contingency and wider facticity of his life. His cowardice prevents him. Stumbling upon stolen money is the pretext for Llewelyn Moss's renunciation of normal ethical categories and the assumption of a new existentialist identity founded on authenticity and intuition. While Yeats may invoke the magnificence of Byzantium and its 'monuments of unageing intellect' to inspire transcendence through art, the Coen Brothers have their own customised artifice of the desert (flat, immanent and lifeless) to flesh out an equally transcendent existentialist bio-technology of the self.

Notes

1. The iconic night scene in which Chigurh, in pursuit of Moss, slows down in his car to take aim at a bird (and misses) is another example of Chigurh falling victim to a higher/ other natural contingency. His thirst for control, facilitated narratively and structurally, by the transponder that keeps him artificially on the heels of Moss, is illusory. Once bereft of the transponder, he is powerless and vulnerable, forced to rely on instinct and prosaic methods (telephone, threats, hunches) to hunt his prey.
2. See Sartre's interview with Christian Grisoli where he talks about this concept of Hegelian terrorist freedom (Sartre [1945] 2009). For more specific reading on the concept of Hegelian freedom, see the sub-section 'Spirit' and the chapter 'Absolute Freedom and Terror' in *Phenomenology of Spirit* (Hegel 1979).

Bibliography

Allen, R. and M. Smith (eds). 2003. *Film Theory and Philosophy*. Oxford: Oxford University Press.

Cohen-Solal, A. 2007. 'Introduction', in *Existentialism Is a Humanism* [including A Commentary on The Stranger], J. Kulka (ed.), trans. C. Macomber, notes and preface by A. Elkaïm-Sartre. New Haven, CT: Yale University Press, pp. 3–15.

Conrad, M.T. (ed.). 2009. *The Philosophy of the Coen Brothers*. Lexington, KY: The University Press of Kentucky.

Gaughran, R. 2009. '"What Kind of Man Are You?" The Coen Brothers and Existentialist Role Playing', in M.T. Conrad (ed.), *The Philosophy of the Coen Brothers*. Lexington, KY: The University Press of Kentucky, pp. 227–42.

Gilmore, R. 2009. '*No Country for Old Men*: The Coens' Tragic Western', in M.T. Conrad (ed.), *The Philosophy of the Coen Brothers*. Lexington, KY: The University Press of Kentucky, pp. 55–78.

Hegel, G.W.F. 1979. *Phenomenology of Spirit*, trans. by A.V. Miller. Oxford: Oxford University Press.

Idt, G. 1972. *Le Mur de Jean-Paul Sartre. Techniques et contexte d'une provocation*. Paris: Larousse.

McCarthy, C. 2005. *No Country for Old Men*. New York: A.A. Knopf.

McFarland, D. 2009. '*No Country for Old Men* as Moral Philosophy', in M.T. Conrad (ed.), *The Philosophy of the Coen Brothers*. Lexington, KY: The University Press of Kentucky, pp. 163–78.

Pamerleau, W.C. 2009. *Existentialist Cinema*. London: Palgrave Macmillan.

Sartre, J.-P. [1939] 1975. 'Erostratus', *The Wall*. New York: New Directions Publishing.

———. [1945] 2009. 'Interview at the Café Flore', *The Last Chance. Roads of Freedom IV*, trans. C. Vasey. London: Continuum, pp. 14–21.

———. [1946] 2007. *Existentialism Is a Humanism* (including A Commentary on *The Stranger*), J. Kulka (ed.), trans. C. Macomber, notes and preface by A. Elkaïm-Sartre. New Haven, CT: Yale University Press.

———. [1948] *Les Mains sales* (*Dirty Hands*). Paris: Gallimard.

Yeats, W.B. [1928] 2007. *The Tower*. London: Macmillan.

Filmography

Coen, J. (dir). 1984. *Blood Simple*. River Road Productions.

———. 1987. *Raising Arizona*. Circle Films.

———. 1996. *Fargo*. Working Title Films.

Coen, E. and J. Coen (dirs.). 2007. *No Country for Old Men*. Scott Rudin Productions.

9

'AN ACT OF CONFIDENCE IN THE FREEDOM OF MEN': JEAN-PAUL SARTRE AND OUSMANE SEMBENE

Patrick Williams

The work of art, from whichever side you approach it, is an act of confidence in the freedom of men.

(Sartre [1948] 2001a: 47)

'It was the best of texts. It was the worst of texts.' – as Dickens might have said: *Existentialism Is a Humanism* was simultaneously seen by some as the best of Sartre, because it was popular, and by others as the worst – because it was popular. The enormous popular success of this brief lecture transcript made philosophy seem accessible, even fashionable. One instance of that popularity was that, as Simone de Beauvoir complained, she and Sartre could no longer go to the Café Flore for a drink without being mobbed by admirers. At the same time, particularly for academic commentators in the years following its publication, one of the main problems with *Existentialism Is a Humanism* was precisely the fact it offered a popular – in their view over-popularised – version of philosophical analysis.[1] As a result, numerous studies of Sartre mention it only in passing if they mention it at all. Manser, for example, in *Sartre: A Philosophic Study* (1967), refers to it as 'the unfortunate lecture', and has nothing more to say about it. Such dismissals are ill-founded, even if Sartre himself subsequently expressed reservations about certain aspects of his lecture. Despite the existence of these problems and contradictions, and, even more so, despite the currently unfashionable status of existentialism which represents the flip side of its earlier popularity, *Existentialism Is a Humanism* offers a surprisingly rich resource with contemporary relevance. This chapter will draw on *Existentialism Is a Humanism* and another important work published just two years later *What Is Literature?*, as the basis for an analysis of *Moolaadé* (2004), the challenging final film by the great Senegalese director Ousmane Sembene, who died in 2007.[2]

Set in a geographically unspecified African village, (actually Djerisso in Burkina Faso, a rare move outside Sembene's native Senegal), *Moolaadé* tells the story of one woman's act of defiance which turns into a more general movement of resistance to traditional patriarchy and its often brutal practices of gendered power. Collé (Fatoumata Coulibaly), the central character, takes in four young girls who have run away from the traditional ceremony of female genital mutilation (two others commit suicide rather than submit to the practice). Although, like every other woman in the community, Collé has herself undergone the horrors of excision and infibulation (commonly misleadingly referred to as 'female circumcision'), she had previously refused to let it be done to her daughter, Amasatou (Salimata Traore), with the result that Amasatou is regarded as 'unclean'. Invoking the power of Moolaadé, or religiously-sanctioned asylum, Collé cordons off her house to protect the four girls, and embarks on a struggle where her opponents include all the men of the village, especially its council of elders (her husband, somewhat reluctantly, among them), the Salindana, the powerful group of women whose 'profession' consists of performing the genital mutilations, as well as numbers of the village women who fear the effects of Collé's transgression. While Collé resists ongoing emotional pressure, personal threats, religious imprecations, and, in the end, a brutal public whipping, the male elders try to prevent the further spread of unacceptable, potentially subversive, ideas among the women by confiscating their transistor radios, which connect them to the outside world. Collé's brave individual stand eventually leads to a collective resistance on the part of the women of the village, as well as to the decision by the son of the chief, recently returned from Europe, to defy his father, and his community's traditions, in marrying his fiancé, the 'unclean' Amasatou, and inaugurating a new era of freer male–female relations, less circumscribed and less 'circumcised'.

Moolaadé was the second part of a projected trilogy by Sembene, the first instalment being *Faat Kine* (2000), another study of a strong female character, while the final, unfinished, *Brotherhood of Rats* would have focused on urban issues and state corruption. Critics have made much of the trilogy as portraying 'the heroism of everyday life', but this was an idea which had been important to Sembene since at least the 1970s, as he said of himself in an interview from 1976: 'being concerned somewhat with history and the heroism of everyday life …' (Downing 1987: 41), and arguably something which his films from *Borom Sarret* (1963) onwards portray. While Sartre himself does not use precisely this expression, it is a concept he would fully support, and at this point it is appropriate to outline some of the relevant positions in *Existentialism Is a Humanism* and *What Is Literature?* before moving on to the analysis of the film.

It would be tempting to call *Existentialism Is a Humanism* a transitional work, if Sartre's whole intellectual career were not one of change and movement, reflection and reworking. Like many of his other works, it represents an attempt to grapple with the complex, and changing, political and intellectual environment of his time – and, as he commented on various occasions, Sartre was someone who aimed to 'write for his time'. Given how simply he sets out what the twin terms of existentialism and humanism mean to him, it is remarkable that critics – even if they did not faint like the audience members mentioned above – understood so poorly. Although there are earlier Christian versions of existentialism, typified by Kierkegaard, Sartre's is firmly atheistic, and in a world without God, human beings can only be what they make of themselves:

> Man is not only which he conceives himself to be, but that which he wills himself to be, and since he conceives of himself only after he exists, just as he wills himself to be after being thrown into existence, man is nothing other than what he makes of himself. This is the first principle of existentialism.
>
> (Sartre [1946a] 2007: 22)

As Sartre says again and again, human beings are to be understood not simply in terms of intellectual or philosophical models of human nature or human existence, but also, and more importantly, in terms of the actions they carry out, and which collectively constitute their being. Also, the fact that existentialism is a philosophy based in action stands as a rebuttal of the frequent accusation that it recommends passivity or quietism. Human action is, for Sartre, inescapably future-oriented: it is a 'project', both in the sense of a deliberate task to be accomplished, and in the literal sense of something thrust or thrown forward (into the future), and the notion of the project comes to help define both existentialism and humanism. In terms of the latter, Sartre says:

> But there is another meaning to the word 'humanism'. It is basically this: man is always outside himself, and it is in projecting and losing himself beyond himself that man is realised; and, on the other hand, it is in pursuing transcendent goals that he is able to exist.
>
> (Sartre [1946a] 2007: 52)

while the former is construed as follows:

> Man is nothing other than his project. He exists only to the extent that he realises himself, therefore he is nothing more than the sum of his actions, nothing more than his life. In view of this, we can clearly understand why our doctrine horrifies many people.
>
> (Sartre [1946a] 2007: 37)

If existentialism is centrally preoccupied with the question 'What is existence?', it does not ignore the additional, and more challenging query, 'What is a good existence?' Despite being attacked as immoral, existentialism is in fact grounded in moral and ethical thought, to the extent that one might wish to rename Sartre's lecture *Existentialism Is an Ethics*. Human actions, the construction of the human project, involve making choices, and these choices carry an ethical dimension: 'Man makes himself; he does not come into the world fully made, he makes himself by choosing his own morality, and his circumstances are such that he has no option other than to choose a morality' (Sartre [1946a] 2007: 46).

However, in case existentialism might be seen as a philosophy concerned only with the individual (which is precisely how a number of commentators have regarded it), the supposedly 'individual' morality reveals a generalised ethical stance:

> When we say that man chooses himself, not only do we mean that each of us must choose himself, but also that in choosing himself, he is choosing for all men. In fact, in creating the man each of us wills ourselves to be, there is not a single one of our actions that does not at the same time create an image of man as we think he ought to be. Choosing to be this or that is to affirm at the same time the value of what we choose, because we can never choose evil. We always choose the good, and nothing can be good for any of us unless it is good for all.
>
> (Sartre [1946a] 2007: 24)

The movement from a necessary starting point in individual subjectivity to an inescapable ethically-grounded involvement in the wider collectivity, or humankind as a whole, is key to the (frequently overlooked) political dimension of existentialism. It is also, as we shall see, central to the action in Sembene's film.

If *Existentialism Is a Humanism* is indeed a transitional work, as mentioned above, then one transition it is in part effecting is Sartre's movement – complex, and often tentative at this period – towards Marxism, an affiliation he shares with Sembene, though the latter's engagement with Marxism was both more long-term and more unequivocal. The question of the political involvement of writers and cultural producers is dealt with at length in *What is Literature?* where the concept of committed literature (*la littérature engagée*) forms probably the most important, as well as the most controversial, aspect of the discussion. The effect of the controversial nature of committed literature can, however, lead even the best critics to misunderstand Sartre. In his book *Sembene: Imagining Alternatives in Film and Fiction* (2000) David Murphy is eager to remove Sembene from the contaminating effect of commitment:

> Sembene himself has argued that this notion of 'engagement' (or commitment) as applied to the artist is something of a misnomer. In his view, life itself is a form of commitment: 'each time I walk out into the street, I'm aware that people are committed. The daily struggle to improve our society is commitment. Why do we only speak of the artist in terms of his/her commitment?'. This argument serves a double purpose: firstly, it attempts to do away with the category of the 'committed writer' by describing 'engagement' as a universal condition; secondly, and consequently, he seeks to distance himself from the negative image of the 'committed writer' who writes worthy, committed but fundamentally dull works.
>
> (Murphy 2000: 7–8)

Clearly, Murphy is unhappy with what he sees as the implications of commitment, though arguably he, and, it would appear, Sembene, are misunderstanding the Sartrean concept. For Sartre, commitment is certainly not something separate from everyday life, quite the contrary, but the position – and therefore the responsibility – of the writer or filmmaker is fundamentally different from ordinary members of society. We are indeed all 'situated', as Sartre terms it, and all potentially committed, though most people remain oblivious of the fact. It is therefore the task of the writer to demonstrate his/her commitment by making people aware of the truth of their situation (as economically exploited, ideologically misled, politically oppressed, or whatever), and thus 'doing away with the category of the committed writer' would be a serious error. This form of politicised consciousness-raising activity which Sartre indicates, particularly carried out through the medium of film, has been one of the guiding principles of Sembene's long career, and as a result it is hard to see in what way he does not represent the epitome of the committed writer/filmmaker. Also, the idea that committed writers produce 'worthy ... but ... dull works' (which Sembene does not in fact appear to mention) has no basis in Sartre who, on the contrary, argues that commitment is likely to result in the production of works of higher quality, not least because of their combination of critical insight and generosity of spirit.

In addition, Sembene typically refers to himself as a 'militant', saying also that he wants to create a 'militant cinema' (Busch and Annas 2008: 202). It is hard to imagine how a militant (and a Marxist) would not consider themselves to be committed, and indeed, in Sartre's terms, that avoidance of commitment would be possible only at the cost of extreme 'bad faith' (*'mauvaise foi'*), in other words, self-deception, and self-alienation. Of the (militant) interweaving of the individual and the collective he has this to say: 'We must militate, in our writings, in favour of the freedom of the person and the socialist revolution. It has often been claimed that they are not reconcilable. It is our job to show tirelessly that they imply each other' (Sartre [1948] 2001a: 213). For his part, Sembene says: 'My concern is to make the problems faced by my people public. I view cinema as a political weapon. I own to the Marxism-Leninism ideology. But I'm against a "cinéma de pancartes" (cinema of placards)' (Busch and Annas 2008: 22).

The meeting over Marxism is just one of the ways in which the unlikely convergence of these two differently iconic figures occurs. On the one hand there is Sartre: philosopher, product of the most elite forms of French education, the École Nationale Supérieure and the *agrégation* examination, showered with honours for his writing (including the Nobel Prize for Literature, which he turned down); on the other, Sembene, largely self-educated, former dock-worker and trades union organiser, struggling to achieve recognition for African cultural production, particularly in the form of filmmaking (to the extent that he is commonly referred to as 'the father of African cinema'). On the face of it, they could hardly be more different, the militant representative of formerly colonised Africa, and the most famous mid-twentieth-century intellectual from the country that colonised him. In fact, on a range of the issues which are most important to them, from the need for cultural producers (above all, writers and filmmakers) to be socially responsible, to the urgency of a politics of anti-colonialism and anti-imperialism (in its form of capitalist globalisation), they have a great deal in common. Like Marxism, anti-colonialism was a position to which Sartre came gradually, but even at the time of *Existentialism Is a Humanism*, a first step in the shape of a universalising anti-racist humanism was in evidence:

> Consequently, every project, however individual, has a universal value. Every project – even one belonging to a Chinese, an Indian, or an African – can be understood by a European … There is universality in every project, in as much as any man is capable of understanding any human project … In this sense, we can claim that human universality exists, but it is not a given; it is in perpetual construction. In choosing myself, I construct universality; I construct it by understanding every other man's project, regardless of the era in which he lives.
>
> (Sartre [1946a] 2007: 42–43)

It is time to turn in more detail to this very 'African … project', *Moolaadé*. Interestingly, Sembene claimed that it was his 'most African film', though precisely why that would be the case, given that all his films are representations of Africa, is not immediately clear (and Sembene's answers in interviews do not always help, either). One possibility would be that although his films have concentrated on subjects which were, in their different ways, 'difficult' – the hidden history of French colonial atrocities, post-colonial corruption in 'independent' Africa, the negative effects of supposedly benign Western aid – *Moolaadé*, in its focus on female genital mutilation, is the one which could be seen as most intimately African in its difficulty: a practice which is both widespread (carried out in 75–80 per cent of African countries) and usually too sensitive to be discussed openly. As Sembene said in a 2004 interview:

> I should confess that I did not have the courage to put all my findings in my film. Because then it would become propaganda. I have been investigating this issue with these women for a long time. It's very difficult in Africa for women to talk to you about their intimate lives, their private lives. But once you manage to have their confidence …
>
> (Sembene 2004)

Like several of his other films, *Moolaadé* was the result of Sembene's own growing awareness of a particular issue, though in his case, the awareness of female genital mutilation as a significant problem apparently does not date back very many years: 'Myself, until eight years ago, I used to find excision to be the normal practice' (Sembene 2004). On the one hand, this is a salutary reminder of just how difficult it can be to create recognition of certain social problems, even in those who are generally alert to such problems. On the other hand, this recent *prise de conscience* can seem strange, given that Sembene mentions female genital mutilation in his 1957 novel *O Pays, mon beau peuple!* One difference may be the fact that in the intervening years African women have been speaking out more openly about a practice they find intolerable, and that emergence of indigenous agency is important. One of the repeated (if arguably misplaced) criticisms of Alice Walker and Pratibha Parmar's film *Warrior Marks* (1993) was that two Western women were importing and imposing their sense of the limits of ethically and medically acceptable behaviour on African people and societies, in a manner reminiscent of the days of empire.

The ability of African women, or even young girls, to ask for an end to oppressive traditions is present from the start in *Moolaadé*. After the opening sequence showing quiet daily (un-heroic?) activity in the village, the calm is shattered by four girls who burst into the compound of Collé, the central character, and ask for her protection. They are among six who have run away from the 'purification' ceremony because they do not want to be excised. This unprecedented refusal on the part of the girls is matched by the equally unprecedented decision of Collé not to return them to the Salindana, the quasi-priestly female society which carries out the genital mutilations, but instead to invoke the Moolaadé of the title, a form of sanctuary which is grounded in tradition and supported by spirit forces too powerful even for the chief and male elders to challenge. The choice of Collé for shelter is not an arbitrary one on the part of the girls, however, since seven years previously she had refused to have her daughter Amasatou undergo genital mutilation. This important group of choices – individual, but interlinked, and increasingly collective – epitomises what, from an existentialist perspective, Sartre sees as the nature of human life. Choice is unavoidable – as Sartre says, even refusing to choose is a form of choice – but inevitability does not make choosing any easier. These initial choices not only involve going against generations of tradition supported by the fearsome combined power of patriarchy and religion, they also involve assuming a level of autonomy not typically allowed to women – the ability to choose in the first place, to speak out, to defy.

Collé's original decision appeared to have remained at the level of the individual: it did not disrupt her family life, still less the life of the village (so much so, that some of the male elders were unaware that she had made it). Remarkably, it did not seem to have harmed Amasatou's chances of marriage (again, presumably because of male ignorance of the [non-]event) – remarkably, because the status of '*bilakoro*' (non-excised) would normally mean that a woman would never find a husband in that society. Her decision to protect the girls, however, has an ineluctable collective dimension, and as a result, family life, community life, gender relations, hierarchies of power and control are all changed or threatened with disruption in various ways. The collective implications of choice are clear to Sartre: 'When we say that man chooses himself, not only do we mean that each of us must choose himself, but also that in choosing himself, he is choosing for all men' (Sartre [1946a] 2007: 24).

Choices must also be made as far as possible in the light of their effects and consequences, in part because the 'choosing for all men' involves a responsibility towards them. The question of whether her choices are the right ones, not just for herself but even more for those whom they will affect, is a difficult area for Collé throughout the film. As mentioned, it seemed as if Amasatou's avoidance of genital mutilation had not stood in the way of her getting married, but when the chief learns of her condition, he breaks off her engagement to his son and heir Ibrahima (Théophile Sowié), who has just returned from France. Amasatou's anger at her mother following this is, however, far exceeded by that of almost the whole village at Collé's choice to prioritise the rights of young female bodies over the maintenance of community ritual. Although it seems as if Collé might have to face this combined anger on her own, her choice is vindicated by the help she receives from Hadjatou, her husband's first wife. Even though Collé's decision could be seen as undermining Hadjatou's authority as elder wife within the household because she was not consulted about offering asylum, she chooses to stand by Collé, becoming her strongest supporter, and, by the end of the film, the loudest voice calling for the complete eradication of genital mutilation.

From an existentialist point of view, there is nothing – whether God, an absolute moral code, or anything else – which can act as ultimate guarantee for the choices we are compelled to make. One result of that is the condition of 'abandonment', where 'man is condemned to be free' and 'responsible for everything he does' (Sartre [1946a] 2007: 29). Another is the possibility of assessing choices and actions on the basis of their being made either in good or bad faith. Bad faith is analysed at length in Sartre's earlier work, *Being and Nothingness* ([1943] 1989). In the context of *Existentialism Is a Humanism*, it consists of various forms of insincerity, characterised by a refusal to reflect on behaviour or analyse aspects of existence, persisting in unexamined attitudes and the perpetuating of practices which constrain rather than liberate. This kind of perpetuating of practices results in what Sartre in the later work *Critique of Dialectical Reason* ([1960] 1976) called the 'practico-inert', where the productive aspect of human activity as praxis has progressively solidified into something more lifeless.

The clearest, but by no means the only, example of deadening repetition in *Moolaadé* is the ritual of genital mutilation. Unexamined, unquestioned either by its practitioners or those it is practised upon, its survival is premised upon a collective act of bad faith, which is fundamentally challenged by Collé in the film, and by women like her in the real world.[3] The bad faith of his opponents in this area is made clear by Sembene:

> Of course, I faced a lot of pressure not to make this film, but I refused to kneel before that pressure. This is a very sensitive issue. Many in Africa say it is our culture. But what they're saying is a way of escaping from reality. They are hiding behind the

tradition. They don't think of the reality of what is being done to women. To me it is butchery.

(Sembene 2005)

A thoughtful engagement with questions of tradition and ritual has been a trademark of Sembene's creative output: polygamy, for example, is tackled in two of his best works, the novel *God's Bits of Wood* ([1960] 1970), and the film *Xala* (1975). Part of his approach is the necessary defence of African practices in the face of continuing Western denigration, both in terms of the intrinsic value of the practices, and also of their utility as constituents of communal identity or as the focus for anti-colonial resistance. At the same time, his historically- and culturally-aware understanding of how tradition and ritual operate in society is anything but an unreflective, bad-faith justification of past practices. As he said in the 1975 lecture *Man is Culture*: 'If the demand for the ancient culture was a just cause, the servile imitation of it checks progress. The obligation to do today as the ancestors did is a sign of intellectual deficiency. What is worse, it reflects a lack of control over daily life' (Sembene 1979: 9). In *Moolaadé*, the male elders attempt to justify female genital mutilation by saying that it 'goes way back', and that it is required by Islam. On the second point, they are factually refuted by Collé, who has heard on the radio the Grand Imam declaring that it has nothing to do with Islam. Regarding the first point, Sembene is more concerned about whether it and other practices have any contemporary validity:

> Whatever the origin – which we now know, but that is not the question – female circumcision [*sic*] is something outdated in Africa. The primary motives are not the same any more. We do know that it is an attack on women's and men's rights. I am against it ... because it is absolutely useless.
>
> (Interview on *Moolaadé* DVD)

The question of contemporary relevance might (with some justification) look like another take on one of the most fought-over binaries in relation to discussions of African culture: tradition versus modernity, and this, too, surfaces in the film in the context of the choices made and actions taken. The fact that the (extremely modest) access of the women of the village to modernity, in the shape of battery-powered radios, is vetoed by the bad-faith decision of the elders shocks newly-returned Ibrahima, who is in the middle of setting up his television – which he is told he will not be allowed to use. The elders' attempt to deny the existence of the modern world is unacceptable, and it is significant that in the final, slightly farcical, confrontation with his father, Ibrahima's confirmation of his (good-faith) choice to side with the rebellious women is his parting shot: 'From now on, I'll have the television on!', while the film's final visual sequence moves from the smoke rising from the women's radios, confiscated and set on fire by the men, via the towers of the ancient village mosque, to a television aerial.

Ibrahima's decision is one example, though not the most ideologically significant, of Sartre's point that although bad faith may be a chosen position, it is not something the individual is thereby permanently condemned to. More interesting is the easy-going Ciré (Rasmane Quedraogo), Collé's husband, who is reluctantly pressured by his elder brother Amath (Ousmane Konaté) into acting like a (traditional) man, and making use of 'the unlimited powers of the husband' to bring Collé into line. This behaviour in bad faith reaches its climax in the appalling public whipping of Collé in an attempt to force her to utter the words which would end the Moolaadé and thus allow the girls to be taken away for 'purification'. Ciré fails, and in a sense is publicly humiliated, thanks to a combination of Collé's strength of character, the vocal support she receives from the women, and the intervention of the itinerant merchant Mercenaire (Dominique Zeïda). Rather than this resulting in a desire for revenge on his wife, however, he subsequently takes her side, smiling and nodding during her courageous confrontation with the council of elders, and standing up to his domineering older brother, threatening to 'deal with him' if he touches Collé. When Amath tells him that he is betraying the men folk, Ciré's reply is 'It takes more than a pair of balls to make a man!'.

Mercenaire's intervention to stop the whipping of Collé, and which will have fatal consequences for him, is important because of his position as outsider and Other to the collective identity of the community. Sartre says: 'I cannot discover any truth whatsoever about myself except through the mediation of another. The other is essential to my existence, as well as to the knowledge I have of myself' (Sartre [1946a] 2007: 41). In different ways, Mercenaire acts as the Other who delivers truth and self-understanding, though to the extent that the community is operating from a position of bad faith, they are unwilling to acknowledge that. Part of his otherness resides in the connotations of his nickname: his apparently greedy, 'mercenary' and profit-driven business practices belong to a world Ibrahima is familiar with – as Mercenaire reminds him – but which is entirely foreign to the village. In addition, mercenaries are 'bad' soldiers, as Amasatou points out; and Mercenaire admits to Ibrahima that he was dishonourably discharged from the army. Another aspect of his otherness is his modernity: material, in his merchandise; more subversively in his attitudes – the child marriages common in the village are no better than paedophilia; husbands do not have the right to whip their wives.

The irony is that Mercenaire is not the bad person his nickname implies. Although he was thrown out of the army, it was for revealing the corruption of his superior officers in the UN peace-keeping missions; although his morals are not those of the village (he is seen as an inveterate womaniser), in ending the whipping of Collé he makes one of the most moral decisions in the film, one which, as mentioned, costs him his life. Mercenaire thus embodies one of the problems of identity for existentialists: the extent to which we may come to inhabit an identity which is given to us by others, rather than authentically constructed by ourselves through our choices and actions. That this is more than just a problem for the individual is demonstrated in different ways by Sartre and Fanon in relation to the twentieth-century's two largest groups of victims: Jews and colonised people. Sartre examines the former in his other 1946 work *Anti-Semite and Jew*, where he says of the question of imposed identity: 'The Jew is one whom other men consider a Jew: that is the simple truth from which we must start' (Sartre [1946b] 1995: 69). In the context of anti-colonial struggle in Africa, Fanon in *The Wretched of the Earth* looks at the way in which colonialism creates the category of 'native' for the people it oppresses: 'In fact, the settler is right when he speaks of knowing "them" well. For it is the settler who has brought the native into existence and who perpetuates his existence' (Fanon [1961] 2001: 28).

The struggle of the colonised people against false, imposed identities and what they justify in terms of control and subjugation is part of the fight for freedom in all its forms. This finds its contemporary counterpart in many post-colonial countries, where the process of national independence has not produced the necessary social liberation, and different freedoms remain to be fought for, as the story of Collé so graphically demonstrates. From an existentialist perspective, the apparently individual drive towards freedom turns out, once again, to in fact be a process with a collective goal: 'We will freedom for freedom's sake through our individual circumstances. And in thus willing freedom we discover that it depends entirely on the freedom of others, and that the freedom of others depends on our own' (Sartre [1946a] 2007: 48). While Collé's fight for her own freedom is the catalyst for the assertion of other freedoms, especially those of the women of Djerisso, it is unlikely that it could have been successfully accomplished without the simultaneous, dialectical, emergence of those other freedoms to support and maintain what she was fighting for.

The liberation of the women may be the main focus of the film, but the liberation of (some) men, such as Ibrahima and Ciré, nevertheless occurs alongside it. This is important, since in Sembene's opinion it is African men who are currently much more in need of liberation. While that may be true at the level of their thinking (as we have seen, it is the men who are particularly prone to attitudes grounded in bad faith), it nevertheless remains the case that women like Collé urgently require the freedoms which are withheld. As Sembene says:

> It is a struggle for the liberation of African men and women that we are going to conduct head-on. Because it [female genital mutilation] is useless ... But the film is about freedom. The freedom of individuals, their freedom of choice.
>
> (Interview on *Moolaadé* DVD)

Although Collé's choices and her fight for freedom are at the centre of the film, it is significant that the final word belongs to Amasatou as she looks challengingly at her fiancé Ibrahima and says: 'I am, and will remain, a *bilakoro*'.

Another generation, another choice, another statement of female freedom, a condition that men must come to terms with.

Freedom is a term which brings together Sartre's and Sembene's understanding of the role of the artist, as well as existentialist concepts of human existence. For existentialists, freedom is not just something to be willed, as in the earlier quotation, but above all something which has to be enacted: 'the ultimate significance of the actions of men of good faith is the quest of freedom in itself' (Sartre [1946a] 2007: 48); and one particularly important form of the enactment of freedom is cultural production. In *What is Literature?* the work (book, film, or whatever) figures the complexly reciprocal and dialectical freedoms of the writer and reader, or cultural producer and audience. The work itself stands as an expression of the freedom of the writer; at the same time, it is addressed to the freedom of the reader in the particular form of an appeal. The work describes a world which is unsatisfactory (Sartre takes that unsatisfactoriness as axiomatic), and calls – however subtly – for (freely chosen) action to change it, in the name of the freedom of all. The appeal does not only work in one direction, however: 'Here there appears the other dialectical paradox of reading; the more we experience our freedom, the more we recognise that of the other; the more he demands of us, the more we demand of him' (Sartre [1948] 2001a: 38). The demands of the audience are something which Sembene welcomes. In a manner which recalls, but goes far beyond, Brecht's strategies for interacting with the audiences of his plays, Sembene for many years toured his films around Senegal and beyond, screening them for free, and initiating debates with the audience afterwards, inviting comments, criticism and suggestions on how to improve both visual representation and political analysis.

The first step on the road to freedom is the perception of the truth of one's situation, and so both Sembene and Sartre attach great importance to culture's ability to reveal that truth, Sembene's favourite image of his cinema being that of 'an evening class' where his people could learn more about history, culture and politics. On the one hand, *Moolaadé* shows this process of individuals and groups coming to consciousness, and thence to different degrees of freedom. On the other, as well as simply showing this, it also enacts the process in the real world: unusually for one of Sembene's films, it was dubbed in a variety of African languages, in order to be used as a means to fight female genital mutilation across the continent, with empowerment and agency as the best justification for cultural production:

> But if perception itself is action, if, for us, to show the world is to disclose it in the perspectives of a possible change, then, in this age of fatalism, we must reveal to the reader his power, in each concrete case, of doing and undoing, in short, of acting.
>
> (Sartre [1948] 2001a: 224)

For his part, Sembene has this to say:

I have to talk to my people all my life. I listen to them. I show them their situation and force them to take responsibility for their own future, and that of their children and grandchildren. That is the role of the artist. It is an eternal duality.

(Interview on *Moolaadé* DVD)

Apart from the idea of life as a continuous dialogue with the people, this might almost have been written for him by Sartre.

In his Preface to Sartre's 1964 collection of essays translated as *Colonialism and Neocolonialism*, Robert Young says:

The writings collected in this volume illustrate Sartre's developing response to colonialism: moving from the ethical to the political, from a preoccupation with individual freedom to intellectual and political commitment, and the moral demand for an assumption of responsibility for each individual's role in history.

(in Sartre [1964] 2001b: viii)

On the basis of what we have seen in the course of this chapter, it is possible to argue that, far from this polarised 'from … to' view of Sartre's intellectual concerns, all of the above – the ethical and the political, individual freedom and political commitment, the assumption of responsibility – are contained in the early works of the often underrated Sartre-the-Existentialist, above all in that best and worst of texts, *Existentialism Is a Humanism*. In addition, in a manner of which Sartre would have wholeheartedly approved, they live on, powerfully embodied in the cinematic oeuvre of Ousmane Sembene, his 'act of confidence in the freedom of men'.

Notes

1. An indication of the level of understanding to which Sartre was addressing himself is the reported fact that the opening reference to existentialism as a humanism provoked fainting among the audience (Greene 1960: 13).
2. For an overview of Sembene's career and analysis of his films, see the chapter on him in Murphy and Williams (2007).
3. Interestingly, Fatoumata Coulibaly, who plays Collé, had already been involved in trying to get the issue of female genital mutilation aired on Malian television, only to find herself censored by her bosses.

Bibliography

Busch, A. and M. Annas. (eds). 2008. *Ousmane Sembene Interviews*. Jackson, MI: University of Mississippi Press.

Downing, J.D.H. (ed.). 1987. *Film and Politics in the Third World*. New York: Autonomedia.

Fanon, F. [1961] 2001. *The Wretched of the Earth*. London: Penguin.

Greene, N. 1960. *Jean-Paul Sartre: the Existentialist Ethic*. Ann Arbor: University of Michigan Press.

Manser, A. 1967. *Sartre: A Philosophic Study*. London: Athlone Press.

Murphy, D. 2000. *Sembene: Imagining Alternatives in Film and Fiction*. London: James Currey.

Murphy, D. and P. Williams. 2007. *Postcolonial African Cinema: Ten Directors*. Manchester: Manchester University Press.

Sartre, J.-P. [1943] 1995. *Being and Nothingness: An Essay on Phenomenological Ontology*, trans. H.E. Barnes. London: Routledge.

———. [1946] 2007. *Existentialism Is a Humanism*, trans. C. Macomber. New Haven, CT: Yale University Press.

———. [1946b] 1995. *Anti-Semite and Jew*, trans. G.J. Becker. New York: Schocken Books.

———. [1948] 2001a. *What is Literature?*, trans. B. Frechtman. Intro. D. Caute. London: Routledge.

———. [1960] 1976. *Critique of Dialectical Reason*. London: Verso.

———. [1964] 2001b. *Colonialism and Neocolonialism*. London: Routledge.

Sembene, O. 1957. *O Pays, mon beau peuple!* Paris: Presses Pocket.

———. [1960] 1970. *God's Bits of Wood*. London: Heinemann.

———. 1979. *Man is Culture*. Bloomington, IN: African Studies Programme.

———. 2004. Interview, *Cinemascope*, online version: www.cinema-scope.com/cs21/int_pride_sembene.htm (accessed 19 January 2011).

———. 2005. Interview, *Socialist Worker*, online version: www.socialistworker.co.uk/art.php?id=6654 (accessed 19 January 2011).

Filmography

Sembene, O. (dir.). 1963. *Borom Sarret*.

———. 1975. *Xala*. Films Domireew.

———. 2004. *Moolaadé*. Ciné-Sud Promotion.

Parmar, P. (dir.). 1993. *Warrior Marks*.

10

CÉDRIC KLAPISCH'S *THE SPANISH APARTMENT* AND *RUSSIAN DOLLS* IN *NAUSEA*'S MIRROR

Jean-Pierre Boulé

The first frame of *The Spanish Apartment* (Cédric Klapisch 2002) aka *Pot Luck* in the United Kingdom sees Xavier, a twenty-five-year-old Frenchman (Romain Duris), word-processing the story which will unfold before us. Xavier goes to Barcelona to study for a Masters in Economics and leaves behind in Paris his girlfriend Martine (Audrey Tautou), having been promised a job at the Ministry of Finance when he returns. Once in Barcelona, he shares an apartment with six other European students. We join him in a series of adventures which will translate into a personal journey that will broaden his horizons. The first frame of *Russian Dolls* (2005), a sequel to *The Spanish Apartment*, situates Xavier writing on his laptop on the TGV.[1] We learn that he is in a mess and then the story reverts to St Petersburg where Xavier, William (Kevin Bishop), Wendy (Kelly Reilly), Martine and Isabelle (Cécile de France) have reunited after five years for William's wedding. The film is shot in Paris, London and St Petersburg.

Most reviews and critical articles on these two films have concentrated on the European cultural experience. The *New York Times* hailed the film as 'an appealing and persuasive picture of European integration' (Scott 2003), and the *Philadelphia Inquirer* talked about 'a love song to the new Europe' (Rea 2003). According to Ty Burr's analysis – the film critic for the *Boston Globe* – the 'young audience [of *The Spanish Apartment*] … saw itself reflected in a movie for the first time: post-Cold War kids for whom national borders were irrelevant'. He observed that 'the film captured the *real* new European Community, and it was giddy with possibilities', adding that *Russian Dolls* had 'a similar sense of wanderlust' (Burr 2006). Ezra and Sánchez (2005) critique in the film the creation of a new transnational identity, noting its failure to engage with a wider socio-historical context.

When reviewing *Russian Dolls*, Burr said that once again Xavier was at a crossroads. The reviewer fell short of comparing Klapisch to François Truffaut, only because of the indulgence with which Xavier is treated and the 'detached comic wisdom' emanating from the film. Truffaut was one of the main protagonists of the French 'New Wave' cinema. *Breathless* (1960), directed by Jean-Luc Godard with a Truffaut script, could be described as an existentialist film in the way its main character pursues freedom, refuses convention and desires to invent his own values.[2] In an interview on *Russian Dolls*, Klapisch points to Truffaut's *The Man Who Loved Women* as the film that inspired him most (Klapisch 2005a). Burr does not openly compare the Klapisch films to existentialist films, but he does ask rhetorically: 'Who's Xavier, anyway, but a twenty-first century variant of Goethe's Wilhelm Meister?' (Burr 2006). Goethe is an interesting comparison given Sartre's use of Goethe as a figurehead in the play *The Devil and the Good Lord*. This play is essentially about a journey of self-realisation (Sartre 1951). Although *Wilhelm Meister's Apprenticeship* was published in 1796, the hero of the novel is commonly understood to undertake a journey of self-discovery. Wilhelm – not unlike Xavier – tries to escape the empty life of a *bourgeois* businessman.

My reading of the Klapisch films will draw parallels with Sartre's *Nausea* and Sartrean existentialism. It will consist of a mirrored mapping of the novel and the two films, reflecting back and forth between them. I set out to go beyond traditional analyses that highlight the appeal of these two films for young European audiences, and to bring out buried existential concerns which find an echo in Xavier's own journey with its resolution (of sorts) by the end of the second film. My approach is an implicit acknowledgement that these two films do not have fixed meanings, that what Barthes called the pleasure of the text can be derived from the interaction between reader/spectator and text/film, that any authoritarian criticism would attempt to fix and limit meaning (Harvey 1978: 111), and that given the plurality of practices that is postmodernity, 'it is hard to see how anyone could now plausibly advance claims for the universal validity of a particular orientation' (Lapsley and Westlake [1998] 2006: xv).

I will focus on a series of Sartrean key concepts in order to open up a dialogue between the novel *Nausea*[3] and the two films before concluding that existentialism is an optimistic philosophy. These key concepts are: freedom, the bourgeoisie, writing, nausea, the roles of the past/present and future, the role of the Other, humanism, commitment and the project. I do not argue that Sartrean existentialism and the Klapisch films are a perfect match. *Nausea* is a philosophical rumination on the contingency of existence (immortalised by a classic encounter between the main character and a chestnut tree, Sartre [1938] 1963: 182–85), whereas the films concentrate on the trials and tribulations of love, notably of a single man looking for the 'woman of his life' (and initially oblivious to forms of socio-political or personal engagement), and arguably has none of the seriousness of Sartre's existential ethical projects.[4] Roquentin and Xavier seem oblivious to the social and political context they live in but the importance of one's social context is something that becomes paramount in Sartrean politics, coined by Sartre's expression 'To live for our time'.

There is nevertheless a social context to Klapisch's cinema.[5] When asked in an interview about *The Spanish Apartment* and the social relevance of his film, Klapisch replied that we are totally implicated in our time, and that social contexts informed his film (Klapisch 2000a).[6] Klapisch's stance, therefore, is somewhat ambiguous; on the one hand he does not accept the label of a committed film director[7] but, on the other hand, he regrets in an interview in June 2000 that people are not more committed and insists that commitment is necessary in life (Klapisch 2000b). It seems that Klapisch shuns the label of 'committed' cinema (perhaps he does not want to be 'stuck' with that label and the legacy it entails) whilst making films which are socially engaged.[8] I hope to shed some light on this ambiguity in the course of this chapter.

Freedom

Freedom is arguably the most important concept in Sartrean philosophy. For Sartre, there are two sorts of freedom. Each individual is born with ontological freedom and Sartre states that there is no difference between being born and being free. The second aspect of freedom is 'freedom within a situation', that is to say freedom limited by the confines of a situation, such as the slave who cannot break free from his chains. During the Occupation of France in the Second World War, because the freedom of France was severely limited by the occupying Germans, Sartre argued that each seemingly innocuous gesture was a victory against the German invaders. By contrast for Sartre, being free 'for nothing' is not freedom; freedom is when we commit ourselves through a project. Hence his famous oxymoron: 'Man is condemned to be free' (Sartre [1946] 2007: 29).[9]

Mathieu, at the beginning of *The Age of Reason*, exemplifies what it is not to be free:

> Mathieu incarnates ... what Hegel calls terrorist freedom, which is really a counter-freedom. He is like Orestes at the beginning of *The Flies*, weightless, without strings, detached from the world ... He is not free, because he hasn't been able to commit himself ... Mathieu's is an indifferent freedom, an abstract freedom, freedom for nothing. Mathieu is not free, he is nothing, because he is always on the outside.
> (Sartre [1981] 2009: 18)[10]

At the beginning of *The Spanish Apartment*, Xavier is unable to commit himself to his girlfriend Martine. In *Russian Dolls*, he is afraid of committing himself to Wendy. In Sartrean terms, Xavier is not free because he is not exercising his freedom. However, were he to *decide* that he did not want to commit himself in love, then that would be acting in good faith.

Bourgeoisie

As a social and political class, the bourgeoisie hold a special contempt in Sartre's philosophy. For him, this class oppresses other classes, robbing them of their freedom, and pretending that its values are universal, essentialist values. At the beginning of *The Spanish Apartment*, we realise that Xavier is well connected to the establishment through his father who attended the ENA[11] and his friend Jean-Charles Perrin at the Ministry of Finance (Vladimir Yordanoff). Xavier's destiny, it would seem, is to be a manager, just like Lucien Fleurier in the short story 'Childhood of a Leader' (Sartre 1939). This career choice would put Xavier in the category of the ruling class, and an arch-enemy of Roquentin, who abhors the bourgeoisie as immortalised in the famous scene in the Bouville museum which ends with the phrase, 'Farewell, you Bastards' (Sartre [1938] 1963: 120–38). For Sartre, 'bastards' are people who believe they have rights and 'try to prove their existence is necessary' (Sartre [1946] 2007: 49). The French couple Jean-Michel (Xavier de Guillebon) and Anne-Sophie (Judith Godrèche) whom Xavier meets on arrival in Barcelona represent a certain type of bourgeoisie that Xavier courts at the beginning of the film. And yet Xavier describes Jean-Michel, the neurologist, as: 'He was just like the jerks I always try to avoid'. Xavier nevertheless will accept staying at their flat and after seducing Anne-Sophie ends up sleeping with her. Anne-Sophie is someone who is totally repressed by her class; she is old-fashioned, sacrifices her life for her husband's career, and lacks self-confidence to the point of being afraid of going out alone. She is withdrawn and retiring. Her freedom has been prised away from her by her class values. She is like the living dead, in Sartrean terms, and her patriarchal husband treats her like a prized possession: 'Get out of that shell, sweetie!' is his patronising way of liberating her. Even as Xavier tries to make her experience the 'real' Barcelona, she finds it dirty and reminiscent of the Third World; he retorts that all she has ever known is gentrified Paris. Xavier's initial affinity with the bourgeoisie gives way to a growing social awareness of its oppressive nature. He can only explore this 'class' further if he continues to engage with it and subvert it from within.[12]

Writing

Sartre devoted half his autobiography, *The Words* (1964), to 'writing'. The dual aim of this work was to denounce what he saw as the myth of the nineteenth-century writer that he had grown up with, encapsulated in the motto 'art for art's sake' (in other words, the creation of a work of art as a sense of plenitude, outside of any socio-political reality), and also to reaffirm the importance of committed writing. In *Nausea*, Roquentin questions what he writes and by the end of the novel speculates on the idea of writing a book which would talk about existence. The strongest common denominator between Xavier and

Roquentin is in fact the act of writing. Roquentin keeps a diary 'in order to understand' what is happening to him and to the world around him (Sartre [1938] 1963: 9), whilst Xavier declares in *Russian Dolls* that writing is synonymous with helping him sort out the mess of his life. The voice-over narration of Xavier resembles the style of a diary. As both *The Spanish Apartment* and *Russian Dolls* unfold, Xavier is seen actually writing these two respective stories. We find out in *Russian Dolls* that, although five years have elapsed, he has not found an editor for *The Spanish Apartment*. To remind himself of his aspirations to be a writer, Xavier puts up in his Spanish apartment a photograph of himself aged around five. Occasionally, the little boy comes out of the photograph to say: 'When I grow up, I want to write books'. This picture is a proleptic vision of his authentic self. It sits in his bedroom to remind him of his original project.

Besides *his* diary, Roquentin is also writing a thesis on a historical character who lived in the eighteenth century (Marquis de Rollebon). When we encounter Xavier again in *Russian Dolls*, the equivalent of Rollebon for Xavier is being a scriptwriter for a soap opera ('Now I write; my job is telling stories'). We see him playing out various scenes in his head, casting friends and acquaintances in the various roles as he tries out his storyline. This gives a dreamlike quality to these passages. Due to the vagaries of globalisation, the rights to the soap opera have been bought by the BBC and the script has to be written in English. Xavier tells the producers that he can write in English and soon he pairs up with Wendy to co-write the script, travelling frequently to London. He also undertakes another job ghost-writing the memoirs of a supermodel, Celia Shelburn (Lucy Gordon). She speaks her memoirs and he writes them down; she tells him he has become her *mirror*, they end up in bed together and he seems smitten by her. Xavier invents love stories whilst Roquentin tries to unravel Rollebon's love life (Sartre [1938] 1963: 24). The mirroring effect continues.

In both novel and film, there is a subtle acknowledgement that these ersatz of writing are inauthentic. Roquentin writes in his diary: 'M. de Rollebon now represents the only justification for my existence' (Sartre [1938] 1963: 105); 'Love, Passion in Venice', the soap opera Xavier is writing for television, fulfils the same function in that Xavier is under the illusion that he is a writer fulfilling his childhood dream. At one stage, Roquentin comes to a realisation about his research on Rollebon: ' I needed him in order not to feel my being', further elucidating that he no longer noticed that he existed, that he no longer existed for himself but for Rollebon (Sartre [1938] 1963: 142–43). Likewise, Xavier is masking his own freedom and spending his time being a script-writer and a ghost-writer, rather than using his talents as a *writer for himself*. From a Sartrean perspective, in order to be authentic and act in good conscience, writing needs to be part of a project, and to reflect commitment on the part of the writer.

Nausea

Nausea is a typical Sartrean physical manifestation experienced when one realises that life is not necessary. Nausea is experienced by Roquentin when he realises the contingency of existence, the fact that we are on earth for nothing and that we are superfluous: 'So this is the Nausea: this blinding revelation? ... I exist – the world exists – and I know that the world exists' (Sartre [1938] 1963: 176). The main character in *Nausea* leads a very solitary life, and even though he does interact with people, he has no real contact with them. What happens to Roquentin is mirrored by what happens to Xavier. At one stage in *The Spanish Apartment*, when Martine breaks up with Xavier,[13] he starts having insomnia, followed by bad dreams and even hallucinations, which Roquentin will also experience. Xavier has visions of Erasmus, the Dutch Renaissance humanist who lived in the fifteenth and sixteenth centuries, in the streets of Barcelona.[14]

Roquentin is also plagued by bad dreams. He complains that he remembers his dreams much too often (Sartre [1938] 1963: 89), including one where he was in the court of the Tsars (Sartre [1938] 1963: 142).[15] He hallucinates too when he thinks there is a monster under water (Sartre [1938] 1963: 116), or that a seat 'exists' and is a donkey's belly (Sartre [1938] 1963: 179–80) before telling us that these manifestations are connected to the fact that he is afraid of existence (Sartre [1938] 1963: 227). Xavier's physical symptoms could be provoked by his own experience that man is alone in the world, fully responsible for creating his own values, and aware that when he chooses for himself, he chooses for the whole of humanity. According to Sartre, this realisation makes people feel dread (Sartre [1946] 2007: 25).

Klapisch shoots a visually dazzling film full of special effects; at times the action is speeded up to fast-forward motion, at other times, it is slow motion. These scenes resemble passages in *Nausea* when Roquentin is gripped by nausea. Animated maps and superimposed images are also used. Whilst some critics have found these special effects irritating, it all adds to the feeling of nausea and points to an existential crisis. In *Russian Dolls*, the clever collages of interrelated images and layered, multiple screens, as well as slow motion reinforces a similar feeling of nausea and gives Xavier's tale a visual support that reflects our postmodern world in its plurality and multiplicity of combinations. According to Marxist film-theory, transgressing cinematic taboos is breaking with existing forms or conventions (Harvey 1978: 82), going back to Brecht and his 'alienation' effect, ' a method of distancing the audience from the spectacle' and of inviting the audience to 'see differently' (Harvey 1978: 74). So, for instance, when Xavier watches Celia catwalk one of St Petersburg's famous streets, the music and slow motion invite us spectators to look critically at the version of 'beauty' in front of our eyes by lending the scene an air of unreality.

At the beginning of *The Spanish Apartment* when Xavier, dressed formally, visits his father's friend to talk about a future career, the fast-forward motion of the people at the Finance Ministry gives the impression of automatons and vacant corridors. The existential questions that Roquentin highlights at the beginning of *Nausea* when he is in Indo-China and he is asked to go to Bengal on an archaeological expedition seem to be implicit in Xavier's mind during the aforementioned scene: 'What was I doing there? Why was I talking to those people? Why was I dressed so oddly? My passion was dead ... I felt empty' (Sartre [1938] 1963: 15).

Xavier's 'nausea' is a symptom, not a cause, of Xavier's alienation and it leads to one of the key stages in his existentialist self-revelation, an existential crisis. As Xavier is listening to but not comprehending his first economics lecture at university (because the lecturer insists on delivering it in Catalan rather than in Castillian), he thinks: 'What was I doing there?'. This could be interpreted as a metaphor for existence since we are on earth *for nothing* argues Sartre. Life is contingent. We have to invent our own path, and we are 'solely responsible' for what we are (Sartre [1946] 2007: 23). At the end of *The Spanish Apartment*, as he is walking through Montmartre, Xavier reflects on his new career at the Ministry of Finance: 'What was I doing there? I didn't know. In general, I have never known why I was where I was'. To make the job more attractive, it is pointed out to him that he will be a young retiree since people working in government retire at fifty-five. His whole future life flashes before him. This career path means his entire existence is predetermined. As his new female colleague points out the Ministry's motto: 'Everything in place. A place for everything', he starts to feel the full horror of predetermined values and of essentialism which squeeze out any sense of freedom. His reaction is to run, and run. Xavier realises that he is free to make his own choices and, as Sartre argues, the consciousness of our absolute freedom is always daunting because we have to invent our own values, and not only for us individually but for the whole of mankind, for when we choose for ourselves, we choose for the whole of humanity. Five years later in *Russian Dolls*, Xavier writes that he is thirty years old and that he has to take stock: 'If I look at my life, it's not impressive. What have I done?'. He looks back at his past and thinks about the various women with whom he has had relationships, concluding that his life is chaotic. He remarks on the paradoxical nature of his life, paid to write love stories when his own life, and his love life, is in turmoil. Xavier's existential crisis, which started with a form of nausea, is the first step towards a form of lucidity.

Past/Present/Future

Sartrean existentialism holds some controversial views about time relations which are consistent with Sartre's wider philosophy. Basically, he claims that we should not be enslaved by our past, and that the future holds the promise of change (Sartre [1943b] 1958: 107–70). *Nausea* begins with an editor's note, and then an 'Undated sheet' before the narration starts with the 'Diary' section. Both Klapisch films have a false start with flash-backs to sequences in Barcelona as the opening credits roll, and Xavier declares in the preamble to *The Spanish Apartment*: 'It begins where it ends'. The first frame of *Russian Dolls* sees Xavier on the TGV, then there is a flash-back to St Petersburg a month previously and shortly after that another long flash-back to the previous year whilst the opening credits roll. Near the beginning of *The Spanish Apartment*, whilst he narrates his arrival in Barcelona, Xavier remarks that 'after you have lived here, walked these streets, you'll know them inside out. You'll know these people ... It'll belong to you because you've lived there. Later, much later, back in Paris, each harrowing ordeal will become an adventure'. Existentialism appropriates the world around us, and uses the present to make sense of the past. Roquentin remarks in *Nausea* that 'for the most common-place event to become an adventure, you must – and this is all that is necessary – start *recounting* it' (Sartre [1938] 1963: 61). The story in both films appears to be told at random, and has a rough-draft aspect, like a diary. There are flash-backs and fast-forwards and Roquentin's comments about his own story could be applied to the two films: 'There are moments when you ... can ... go forward or back ... it has no importance' (Sartre [1938] 1963: 86). Xavier's voice-over conveys at one point that he is not telling us the story in order, since 'order is a real mess'. Roquentin is equally wary of the linearity of story-telling. For him, people talk about true stories when there is no such thing; 'events take place one way and we recount them the opposite way' (Sartre [1938] 1963: 62). He also points out that in relating a story, one may appear to be at the beginning when in fact one has begun at the end (Sartre [1938] 1963: 62). This comment could be mapped out across both Klapisch films. In one of two alternative endings in *Russian Dolls*, when Wendy articulates that she is afraid of what is ahead of them, Xavier tells her not to look ahead. She replies that she cannot help it and that it reminds her of her previous boyfriend (Gary Love); Xavier then tells her not to look back either. He is making a philosophical point here by asking her not to project herself into the future but to live in the present and not to be enslaved by the past. This is one of the main tenets of Sartrean existentialism: one should not be enslaved by one's past and can always change what one has been, hence a coward can decide to become a hero (Sartre [1946] 2007: 39). Sartre stated in an interview that it is the future that decides the meaning of the past (Sartre 1981: 1916). Xavier's take on time, it would seem, is consistent with that of Sartre.

The Other: The Case of Martine/Anny

'Hell is other people' is probably one of the most misquoted Sartrean phrases. It comes from the play *No Exit* (1945b). Within the context of the play, the sentence means that if the Other does not comply with the image of self that is projected, then the Other can make one's life hell. Martine, Xavier's girlfriend in *The Spanish Apartment*, is a character reminiscent of Anny in *Nausea*; Anny used to be the girlfriend of Roquentin.[16] Roquentin paints Anny as an idealist whose main aim in life is to realise what she calls 'perfect moments' (Sartre [1938] 1963: 93). When Martine is upset during a party in *Russian Dolls*, Xavier tells her that she is looking for an ideal guy who doesn't exist: 'Stop dreaming of Mr Perfect!' he exclaims. They seem equally entrapped by some ideal of perfection. Xavier does not understand Martine's feminism (for him, children's books where women are in traditional roles are 'sweet' whereas she finds them sexist) nor does he understand her political commitment. Anny would not be classified as a feminist as the action is set before the 1970s, but she displays some characteristics of future feminists: independent, strong-willed, disinterested in the trappings of a bourgeois marriage, and wanting to pursue her own personal development. Martine, like Anny, is presented as an idealist. She attacks the corroding effects of globalisation and, in the second film, attends an international social forum in Cancún. She is portrayed through Xavier's eyes as blinded by her political idealism.

A meeting between Roquentin and Anny near the end of the novel crystallises things for Roquentin and precipitates his decision to leave Bouville. Roquentin and Anny's paths have not crossed for years when she asks Roquentin to come and see her in a hotel in Bouville. Anny tells Roquentin she has another companion. As their encounter is drawing to a close, Roquentin regrets that he must leave Anny after finding her again, before concluding: 'Anny came back only to take all hope away from me' (Sartre [1938] 1963: 223). To carry on with the process of mirroring, in a key dialogue, Martine helps Xavier to shift his life towards a more authentic existence. Martine telephones Xavier to tell him she has met someone else. On a whim, Xavier goes to Paris to talk to her and it is when he gets back to Barcelona that he starts having the visions and physical manifestations of his melancholy (*Melancholia* was the original title of *Nausea*). At that point, the malaise of both Xavier and Roquentin is encapsulated in Roquentin's statement: 'I am alone ... alone and free. But this freedom is rather like death' (Sartre [1938] 1963: 223).

'I cannot discover any truth whatsoever about myself except through the mediation of another' writes Sartre in *Existentialism Is a Humanism* ([1946] 2007: 41). This statement is illustrated in both Anny and Martine; both are depicted as strong women. Anny upsets Roquentin's complacency when she declares: 'You blow your nose solemnly like a bourgeois, and you cough into your handkerchief as if you were terribly pleased with yourself' (Sartre [1938] 1963: 93). Martine challenges Xavier by accusing him of having compromised his ideals by becoming a soap opera scriptwriter and a ghostwriter. They have an argument where she points out he has done nothing with his life and that his work over the last two years has been 'a lot of crap'. He replies by poking fun at people like her who fight against pollution, exclusion and violence, what she calls 'real things in the real world'. She accuses him of being a parasite, avowing that she is saying all this because she knows he is worth more. Even if he appears hurt at the time, some of what Martine says registers in his subconscious. The two male protagonists are about to make important changes to their lives as a result of their respective encounters with these women who have helped them along the road to self-realisation.

Humanism: The Autodidact/Mr Boubaker

Existentialism Is a Humanism is a paradoxical title. As is made explicit in the text, Sartre is against Humanism as a doctrine which takes humankind as an end and as the supreme value (Sartre [1946] 2007: 51). For Sartre, human beings are not an end in themselves 'because man is constantly in the making' (Sartre [1946] 2007: 52); he is against the cult of Humanism. However, if human beings are put at the heart of an existentialist quest (Sartre will call man 'his own legislator'), then Sartre is happy to state that existentialism is a humanism. One of the characters in *Nausea* who engages most with Roquentin is the Autodidact (Pierre Ogier). Roquentin and the Autodidact meet at the town library, and Roquentin acts as if he thinks the Autodidact is the most uninteresting guy on earth. Soon, it becomes obvious to Roquentin that the Autodidact instructs himself by reading the entire collection of library books *alphabetically*, passing abruptly 'from the study of coleopterae to that of quantum theory' (Sartre [1938] 1963: 49)! The Autodidact is desperate to befriend Roquentin and invites him for lunch in a restaurant where he tries out his 'maxims' on him. His knowledge is so bound up with his programme of learning that, on believing that Roquentin has not heard the ideas expressed in one of his maxims, he utters: 'If it were true, somebody would have thought it already' (158). This is a way for Sartre to poke fun at Humanism.

Mr Boubaker (Zinedine Soualem) is Xavier's neighbour in *Russian Dolls* until Xavier moves in with his friend Isabelle, and there are many parallels between Boubaker and the Autodidact. We are introduced to Boubaker when he wants to borrow a compact disc from Xavier who comments: 'Mr Boubaker is the most uninteresting guy on earth'. Boubaker's knowledge is gleaned not from books but from the radio and he tries to engage Xavier in conversation much like the Autodidact with Roquentin: 'The big bang theory does not work. They said on the radio this morning it may not be true'. Xavier brushes him aside ('Well, no one knows for sure') before fleeing. They both display false knowledge and rely on Roquentin and Xavier to enlighten them and to endorse their specific form of humanism. Roquentin is not prepared to do so, and whilst the debate about humanism is not made explicit in the interaction between Xavier and Boubaker, one senses that he does not approve of Boubaker's values either. Both secondary characters are solitary and illustrate a certain type of humanism (where man is put on a pedestal), which Sartrean philosophy rejects, and which Xavier appears to reject too.

Commitment

After freedom, commitment is another key Sartrean concept. In fact, the two are linked: to commit oneself is to commit one's self freely. The two films form a connected path towards commitment, mirroring Mathieu's own 'road to freedom' in the trilogy of the same name. The key to Xavier's commitment is first to write authentically, which he will only discover at the end of the first film, and second to commit himself in a relationship.

In *The Spanish Apartment*, we encounter Xavier at a crossroads in his life. He makes the decision to go to Barcelona, which will broaden his horizons and make him realise that he is not in love with Martine. Xavier's lived experience in Barcelona will give him the storyline that will become *The Spanish Apartment*. It is only at the end of the film that he will choose his path, and engage his freedom by refusing life as a government employee and deciding instead to write. At the beginning of *Russian Dolls*, he is seen writing, but not as a writer. He makes ends meet by writing soap operas and ghostwriting memoirs; he is an ersatz of a writer and is not being true to himself. Martine points out he has sold himself short by writing this type of 'crap'; she knows he is worth more. He should be doing more with his talent and his freedom to act and not settle for mediocrity.

In *Russian Dolls*, Xavier is also at a crossroads emotionally, since after his relationship with Neus (Irene Mantala) and Kassia (Aissa Maiga), he is now vacillating between Celia and Wendy. Roquentin writes: 'Something is going to happen ... my life is going to begin' (Sartre [1938] 1963: 82). In one of the preambles to *Russian Dolls*, Xavier warns us: 'A monumental event is about to take place in my life. Something really fundamental'. For Roquentin, it is the slow discovery of the contingency of the world (the fact that nothing is necessary and that everything is gratuitous), and for Xavier ... we are left waiting for an answer as the film goes back to the previous year in a long flash-back.

Having taken on the challenge of writing his script for the BBC in English, Xavier goes back and forth to London to work with Wendy on 'Love, Passion in Venice'. They write a love story together and it is a case of art imitating life, life imitating art. Xavier remarks: 'Wendy was always like a sister, like a mirror image'. After her thuggish boyfriend is out of the way, they kiss outside a London park and then go to bed together. But then Xavier meets Celia, and everything changes. When they are in St Petersburg, Wendy declares her love for him, but he betrays her to go and meet with Celia. The latter will in turn drop him as soon as she has a better offer. And he reflects: 'Any guy with a normal constitution would have run after her [Wendy]'. With the reunion of all the Barcelona flatmates for the wedding, Xavier comes to the realisation that he loves Wendy. But when she finally responds to the three messages he has left on her mobile phone, it is to tell him she does not want to see him again, and that she cannot trust him any more.

The long flash-back is over and we are back at the beginning of the film when Xavier uttered the sentence: 'A monumental event is about to take place in my life. Something really fundamental'. Fittingly for two films which describe the main character at a crossroads, it is at the very point when he is about to cross the road with his group of friends that he hails Wendy to come back onto the pavement with him. Presented as a long to medium shot, with the symbolic background of a busy junction in St Petersburg, his body language and facial expressions point to someone looking for the right words to formulate an apology when she slaps him in the face and walks away. What is important is that Xavier has acknowledged his feelings and the implication is that he has decided to commit himself to Wendy. This new 'monumental' change in his life echoes the following sentence from *Existentialism Is a Humanism*: 'Man is responsible for his own passion' (Sartre [1946] 2007: 29). Xavier is taking responsibility and offering a degree of commitment to Wendy whose own view of love is equally non-mythological: 'I just don't see what is beautiful. I fall for the other stuff. I love what's not perfect'.[17]

The Project

The notion of project is paramount in Sartre's philosophy. By means of the project ('my projection of the self', Sartre [1946] 2007: 23), human beings commit their freedom willingly and, according to Sartre, they can only attain existence when they are what they project themselves to be. In other words, 'man is nothing other than his own project' (Sartre [1946] 2007: 37). When Xavier returns to Paris at the end of *The Spanish Apartment*, he is seen running away from the Ministry during his first day on the job. We see a close-up of his feet, and then a medium shot of his face. He has visualised his whole life, as if in a bad film, and it is mapped out in front of him. Defiantly, he proclaims: 'I am going to write'. At the end of *Russian Dolls*, Xavier is seen writing his eponymous memoirs on his laptop on the TGV. As the high speed train arrives in London, he leaves his thoughts suspended in mid-air. What has changed since the beginning of the film? He is no longer writing a love story for a soap opera, or ghostwriting; he is writing about his existence and its struggles (the film script of *Russian Dolls*). Near the end of *Nausea*, Roquentin makes the decision to leave Bouville (based on Le Havre, a port town like Barcelona)[18] in order to go back to Paris, like Xavier in *The Spanish Apartment*. The unity of space in both the novel and the film is striking, including the way both main characters frequent bars as places of lucidity. Roquentin will discover one of the keys to existence in a bar when he asks to hear the jazz record, *Some of These*

Days, and Xavier is told by Juan (Javier Coromina) who runs a local bar that it is in bars that he will learn about Barcelona. Both of them have a penultimate scene in a bar before they leave. Bars are a place where they break their isolation and have contact with the world; bars are spaces of engagement where adventures happen.

Roquentin abandons his historical biography. He realises that an existent can never justify the existence of another existent and that the past does not exist. At the very end of the novel, he flirts with the idea that he could write a book. There is a school of thought that interprets *Nausea* as delivering the message of art for art's sake: the writing of the book he envisages. I would argue that the ending of *Nausea* is much more ambiguous and more grounded in social reality (see Keefe 1976). As the novel unfolds, we see Roquentin's nausea fading only when he hears *Some of These Days*. In his philosophical ruminations, Roquentin understands that the effect the record has on him is linked to existence; even if the record is broken, the melody exists, independently of time. He reflects on the condition of the writer and of the performer of the song, both having cleansed themselves of the 'sin of existing' (Sartre [1938] 1963: 251). It is at this point that the outline of a novel comes to mind. This project points to a philosophical work and, as some have argued, a book such as *Nausea*. The book Roquentin would write would have life as its subject (Sartre [1938] 1963: 252), the same subject-matter of both films. Roquentin's aspiration is to write 'the sort of story, for example, which could never happen, an adventure. It would have to be beautiful and hard as steel and make people ashamed of their existence' (Sartre [1938] 1963: 252). Klapisch's films are adventures and the shame derived from watching these two films would be directed towards those who compromise in life, sell themselves short, and do not try to achieve their potential. Such people would be classified as cowards by Sartre, but cowards only by the actions they have taken (or refused to take), with always the potential to change, for what matters is 'total commitment' (Sartre [1946] 2007: 39). The decision taken by both Xavier and Roquentin to write a book represents an important step in their respective roads to freedom.

'You are free, so choose; in other words, invent'

Are Xavier and Roquentin contented as we leave them, or are they in the throes of despair? Analysing the titles of both films will help us answer this question for Xavier. The French title *L'Auberge espagnole* conveys the idea of a Spanish inn where 'you get what you put in'. Searching in the Larousse dictionary for a further explanation of the term *auberge espagnole*, Xavier comes across the definition used by André Maurois, a twentieth-century French writer: '*Il est de la lecture comme des auberges espagnoles: on n'y trouve que ce qu'on y apporte*'. The translation in the sub-titles does not do justice to the original: 'Like reading, as Maurois said, you get in there and it's pot luck'. One can understand how this translation would work as a perfect marketing opportunity to promote the film in the United Kingdom. However, a more accurate and philosophically appropriate translation would be: '... you get from it what you put into it'. One could hardly find a more existentialist statement. 'Man is nothing other than what he makes of himself' (Sartre [1946] 2007: 22).

The statement by Maurois also applies to reading, and this highlights the role of readers in engaging with texts (or of spectators engaging with films) which is a cornerstone of Sartre's *What is Literature?* (Sartre [1948] 2001). In this literary manifesto, Sartre argues that reading is a pact (in generosity) between writer and reader. He also believes that in exercising freedom (as a writer), a subject unveils the Other's freedom [the reader's] (Sartre [1948] 2001: 41). If we apply this dialectic to the relationship between Xavier and ourselves as spectators, it would go some ways towards explaining why *The Spanish Apartment* was so popular in Europe.

Russian Dolls refers to Russian nesting dolls. Xavier compares women to Russian dolls: 'We spend our life playing this game, dying to know who will be the last one, the teeny-tiny one hidden inside all the others ... You have to open them one by one wondering: "Is she the last?"' (Klapisch 2005a). In philosophical terms, Xavier seems to be looking for some kind of perfect *essence* whereas in Sartrean existentialism 'existence precedes essence' which means that human beings exist first and there is no *a priori* human nature (Sartre [1946] 2007: 22). At closer inspection, Xavier is in fact consonant with existentialist doctrine because he is saying that it is only through experience that one will encounter the 'last' one and realise that this is a myth.

At the beginning of the film, Xavier says: 'Writing is arranging life's stuff'. According to Klapisch: 'As a writer, Xavier is looking for boxes and, at the same time, he is looking for the woman of his life' (Klapisch 2005a). If we bear in mind Klapisch's debt to Truffaut's *The Man Who Loved Women*, he claims in the same interview that he wants to show that 'a couple' is not necessarily synonymous with love, nor is love synonymous with coupledom. His film is a critique of the idea of 'the man or the woman of my life'. In this respect, Klapisch's films are not unlike many of the modernist filmmakers who desired to 'engage in a constant critique of illusionism' (Harvey 1978: 71). Through *experience*, Xavier realises that the love–couple relation is erroneous. Isabelle has already told Xavier that the woman he wants does not exist; princesses only exist in fairy tales but, at that stage, he was not ready to give up and asked rhetorically: 'Why stop dreaming?' Watching the wedding of William to Natasha (Evguenya Obraztsova), Xavier calls it the 'till death do us part masquerade'; for him it is insane but at the same time, he avows being moved. In this example, Klapisch is denouncing a certain ideology (the dominant discourse) but also showing its seductive appeal.

At the end of *Russian Dolls*, Xavier is free because he has disabused himself of the myth of the perfect partner. He realises that Celia, the supermodel he liked to gaze at, is but a dream and not real life. He is also free because he has committed himself to living his passion with Wendy. Had the love story ended with Celia, one could have argued that the film was part of Hollywood tradition where the 'lack … [is] made good by the idealised female who is the object of … desire' (Lapsley and Westlake [1998] 2006: 240) but Celia vanishes and with her Xavier's idealised fantasy whereas Wendy is not an idealised female character. When she declares her love for him, she tells him that she loves what is not perfect in him. 'For existentialists there is no love other than the deeds of love' (Sartre 1948: 37); what counts, therefore, is total commitment.

Russian Dolls shows the difficulties of making a living out of writing, but Klapisch still believes that 'it's important not to totally abandon your dreams' (2005a). In this respect, the film does appear to perpetuate the dominant ideology (the ideology of the ruling power or class) because of its cult of the individual, akin to the hegemonic ideology of liberal democracy, especially in the USA, and central to the American Dream of self-realisation and the history of Hollywood cinema. This is not to say that the two Klapisch films are part of mainstream 'feel-good' cinema. In such feel-good endings to films, there is a strategy of bad faith, since the films tend to entice spectators with the possibility of living authentically while actually constraining them (through narrative and film form) in a position of passive complacency. *Russian Dolls* has two endings. In one of them, Xavier tells Wendy he loves her and they kiss, and in the other ending they kiss without the verbal declaration. These two different scenarios betray a playfulness with the conventions of the romantic film. Before they kiss, Xavier asks: 'Who should say I love you?'. They each in turn think the other one should say it – in the end, neither of them does. This scene allows us spectators to stand back from the action and to deconstruct the myth of the classical love story; Xavier and Wendy's relationship will not play out this myth. In existentialist terms, what is important is that Xavier has resolved to commit his freedom.

Xavier has discovered his freedom, rejected the values of the bourgeoisie, examined his authenticity in writing, experienced nausea, clarified the roles of the past, present and future in existentialist terms, experienced the Other in a positive way, showed that Humanism as an absolute doctrine is to be condemned but that humans are at the heart of our daily experience, and committed himself freely by formulating a project. The subliminal message of both films may be summed up by the existentialist expression: 'You are free, so choose; in other words, invent' (Sartre [1946] 2007: 33). The ending of *The Spanish Apartment* sees Xavier proclaiming that his identity is multiple, European and enriched by all the experiences he has had: 'I am not one but many'. In existentialist terms, he is the sum of his experiences: 'Man is nothing other than what he makes of himself' (Sartre [1946] 2007: 22). Sartre has always maintained, against his detractors, that existentialism is an optimistic philosophy because it advocates that a human being's destiny lies within himself (Sartre [1946] 2007: 40), and that 'man must be invented each day' (Sartre 1948: 226); on the other side of despair, there is hope.

I have argued that both the narrative and the films' form deconstruct meaning and denounce illusion. These two films are not like the majority of films where, according to Marxist-inspired film theorists such as Comolli and Narboni, nothing 'jars against the ideology or the audience's mystification by it. They [films] are very reassuring for audiences for there is no difference between the ideology they meet every day and the ideology on the screen' (Comolli and Narboni 1992: 686). The Klapisch films encourage an existential apprehension on the part of the viewers who are invited to reflect on their own human situation and on authenticity, choice and illusion. Lapsley and Westlake show some of the pitfalls of film theory when they argue that 'certain aspects of the spectatorial experience seem to defeat Theory … its affective component – the emotional experience of watching a film …' (Lapsley and Westlake [1998] 2006: xiv). It is my contention that these two films empower viewers into action, reminding them of their freedom, and a version of optimism lingers on as the final credits roll, the sort that Sartre wanted people to derive from his lecture *Existentialism Is a Humanism*.

Notes

1. TGV: High Speed Train.
2. Like Hitchcock, Klapisch makes appearances in both films. In the former, as a harassed teacher taking students on a school trip; in the latter, as a passenger on the TGV.
3. Published in 1938, *Nausea* by Sartre can be classified as a phenomenological novel. The main character Antoine Roquentin discovers the contingency of existence through the self-reflective act of writing his diary.
4. Sartre told Simone de Beauvoir in conversation that *Nausea* represented the theory of man alone and that he could not escape it (Beauvoir [1981] 1984: 298).
5. I do subscribe to the point of view of Comolli and Narboni that '*every film is political*, inasmuch as it is determined by the ideology which produces it (or within which it is produced which stems from the same thing)' (1992: 684).
6. One has to look at Sartre's trilogy *Roads to Freedom* to find a character who eventually commits himself (Mathieu) as Xavier does at the end of *Russian Dolls*. *Roads to Freedom* consists of three novels: *The Age of Reason* (1945), *The Reprieve* (1945) and *Iron in the Soul* (1948).
7. When asked in May 2008 if he considered that some of his films were politically committed films, Klapisch replied that they simply had a social and political inflection. What he likes to make are entertaining films; generally speaking, apart from Ken Loach, he is not keen on committed films (Klapisch 2008). One could cite Klapisch's films *Little Nothings* and *Good Old Daze* amongst the films he has made which have a social and political edge.
8. Although this chapter concentrates on a comparison between *Nausea* and the two films, it could easily have included a comparison of the films with other novels, short stories and plays written by Sartre, as will be illustrated in the next two sub-headings.
9. Instances of Sartre's work that would provide a useful comparison with the Klapisch films include Orestes in the play *The Flies* (1943a) or Mathieu in the novel *The Age of Reason* (1945a).
10. I have slightly modified the translation.

11. 'École nationale d'administration'. Prestigious business school in Paris where many of France's ministers have trained.
12. The film does convey messages about identity, nationality, and race which all point towards tolerance and heterogeneity, as confirmed by Klapisch in an interview (Klapisch 2000a).
13. She pretends she has met someone but in fact she senses Xavier wants to break up but does not know how.
14. His name is used for the Erasmus scheme which enables higher education students, teachers and institutions in thirty-one European countries to study for part of their degree in another country.
15. Another coincidence is that the Rurik dynasty ruled at the time of Erasmus.
16. There is also an interesting parallel in the sexual relationship between Xavier and Anne-Sophie and Roquentin and the landlady of the *Rendez-vous des Cheminots*.
17. Klapisch said in an interview that his key preoccupation when working on *Russian Dolls* was to give more depth to his story (Klapisch 2005b).
18. At one point, Roquentin mentions having travelled to Barcelona (Sartre [1938] 1963: 40).

Bibliography

Beauvoir, S. de. 1981. *La Cérémonie des adieux*, suivi de 'Entretiens avec Jean-Paul Sartre'. Paris: Gallimard. Ed. used 1984, *Adieux. A Farewell to Sartre*, followed by 'Conversations with Jean-Paul Sartre', trans. P. O'Brian. London: André Deutsch and Weidenfeld and Nicolson.

Burr, T. 2006. 'From France, With Love, Comes "Russian Dolls"'. http://www. boston.com/movies/display?display=movie&id=9011 (accessed 26 January 2011).

Comolli, J.-L. and J. Narboni. 1992. 'Cinema/ Ideology/Criticism', in G. Mast, M. Cohen and L. Braudy (eds), *Film, Theory and Criticism*. Oxford: Oxford University Press, pp. 682–89.

Ezra, E. and A. Sánchez. 2005. '*L'Auberge espagnole* (2002): Transnational Departure or Domestic Crash Landing?', *Studies in European Cinema* 2(2): 137–48.

Harvey, S. 1978. *May '68 and Film Culture*. London: British Film Institute.

Keefe, T. 1976. 'The Ending of Sartre's *La Nausée*', *Forum for Modern Language Studies* 12(3): 217–35.

Klapisch, C. 2000a. *Monsieur Cinéma*, June, interview by J.-L. Brunet. http://www. cedric-klapisch.com/interviews_uk.html (accessed 26 January 2011).

———. 2000b. *Cinélive*, June, interview by Bérénice Balta. http://www.cedric-klapisch. com/interviews_uk.html (accessed 26 January 2011).

———. 2005a. 'Interview with Director Cédric Klapisch', *The Guardian*, 12 June.

———. 2005b. *Studio*, No. 209, interview by P. Fabre. http://www.cedric-klapisch. com/interviews_uk.html (accessed 26 January 2011).

———. 2008. 'Le 7e art en péril? Interview de Cédric Klapisch', interview by R. Péllissier. http://www.evene.fr/cinema/actualite/interview-cedric-klapisch-paris-cannes-visions-sociales-1371.php (accessed 26 January 2011).

Lapsley, R., and M. Westlake. [1998] 2006. *Film Theory: An Introduction*. 2nd ed. Manchester: Manchester University Press.

Mast, G., M. Cohen and L. Braudy (eds). 1992. *Film, Theory and Criticism*. Oxford: Oxford University Press.

Rea, S. 2003. '*L'Auberge espagnole*', *Philadelphia Inquirer*, 30 May.

Sartre, J.-P. [1938] 1963. *La Nausée*. Paris: Gallimard. *Nausea*, trans. R. Baldick, intro. J. Wood. Modern Classics, Penguin Classics.

————. 1939. *Le Mur* (*The Wall*). Paris: Gallimard.

————. 1943a. *Les Mouches* (*The Flies*). Paris: Gallimard.

————. 1943b. *L'Etre et le néant*. Paris: Gallimard (*Being and Nothingness*, 1958, trans H. Barnes. London: Methuen).

————. 1945a. *L'Age de raison* (*The Age of Reason*). Paris: Gallimard.

————. 1945b. *Huis Clos* (*No Exit/In Camera*). Paris: Gallimard.

————. 1946. *L'Existentialisme est un humanisme*. Paris: Nagel. Ed. used 2007, *Existentialism Is a Humanism* [including A Commentary on The Stranger], J. Kulka (ed.), trans. C. Macomber, intro. A. Cohen-Solal, notes and preface by A. Elkaïm-Sartre. New Haven, CT: Yale University Press.

————. 1948. *Qu'est-ce que la littérature?* Paris: Gallimard. Ed. used 2001, *What is Literature?*, trans. B. Frechtman, intro D. Caute. London: Routledge.

————. 1951. *Le Diable et Le bon Dieu* (*The Devil and the Good Lord*). Paris: Gallimard.

————. 1964. *Les Mots* (*The Words*). Paris: Gallimard.

————. 1981. M. Contat and M. Rybalka (eds.). *Oeuvres Romanesques*. Paris: Gallimard.

————. [1981] 2009. *The Last Chance, Roads of Freedom IV*, trans C. Vasey. London: Continuum.

Scott, A.O. 2003. '*L'Auberge espagnole*', *New York Times*, 16 May.

Filmography

Godard, J.-L. (dir.). 1960. *A Bout de Souffle* (*Breathless*). Les Productions Georges de Beauregard.

Klapisch, C. (dir.). 1992. *Riens du tout* (*Little Nothings*). Canal +.

————. (dir.). 1995. *Le Péril jeune* (*Good Old Daze*). Vertigo Productions.

————. (dir.). 2002. *L'Auberge espagnole* (*The Spanish Apartment*, US Title; *Pot Luck*, Canada: English title). Bac Films.

————. (dir.). 2005. *Les Poupées russes* (*Russian Dolls*). Lunar Films.

Truffaut, F. (dir.). 1977. *L'Homme qui aimait les femmes* (*The Man Who Loved Women*). Les Films du Carrosse.

11

BAZ LUHRMANN'S
WILLIAM SHAKESPEARE'S ROMEO + JULIET:
THE NAUSEOUS ART OF ADAPTATION

Alistair Rolls

Until the release of his 2008 epic *Australia*, Baz Luhrmann's corpus consisted primarily of his self-styled 'Red Curtain Trilogy': *Strictly Ballroom* (1992), *William Shakespeare's Romeo + Juliet* (1996) and *Moulin Rouge* (2001).[1] According to a Luhrmann fan site, his talent as a filmmaker lies in his 'determination to reinvent genres and break away from the traditional process of story-telling'.[2] With especial focus on *William Shakespeare's Romeo + Juliet*, we will show how the tragedy of Shakespeare's young lovers is, in fact, simultaneously re-endorsed as a play and redirected and adapted as a film. In Luhrmann's film, as in Shakespeare's play, therefore, the basic plot is the same: two members of two feuding families fall in love with each other, initially in ignorance of the impediment of their respective kinship; their struggle to live their love affair is disputed between the two opposing forces of free will (their choice to love each other, which is promoted by other characters, notably, and perhaps perversely, the priest) and determinism (their fates are apparently pre-ordained by the stars as well as by the hatred of their kinsmen). Ultimately, the tension between the competing pulls of the existential and the essential (itself characterised by the shape-shifting and, in Luhrmann's film especially, gender-bending role of Mercutio) concludes in the most tragic miscommunication.

Within the framework of the struggle between existence and essence that is one of the foci of the present volume, it is interesting to consider the basic principles underpinning the 'Red Curtain Trilogy', as offered by the abovementioned fan site:

> 1) the audience knows how it will end right from the start; 2) the storyline is thin and simple; 3) the world created in the film is one of heightened reality; and 4) there is to be a specific device driving the story [Shakespeare's verse, in this case].

If we suggest that the specific device of point 4 above is provided in life itself by an individual's 'situation', the first three points closely resemble Jean-Paul Sartre's existentialist credo, and particularly the chilling epiphany of *Nausea*, which Philip Thody considers important enough to use to open his basic introduction to Sartre's thought: 'Everything that exists is born for no reason, carries on living through weakness, and dies by accident' (Thody and Read 1998: 3).

The aim here is to show not simply how Shakespeare's plot functions according to the same basic principles as existentialism, nor indeed merely how Luhrmann's film highlights this aspect of the play, but rather how the interconnectedness of *William Shakespeare's Romeo + Juliet* and *Nausea* allows us to revisit Sartre's novel of 1938 in the way that it, too, 'actively promote[s] audience participation'.[3] To this end, this analysis will focus on Luhrmann's use of song, which, in addition to staging a modernisation of Shakespeare's tragedy, operates as a doorway,[4] binding his film to Sartre's novel, and its own staging of a song, even as it marks its autonomy. Like Sartre's theory of nothingness, then, Luhrmann's very specificity, that which distinguishes his work from that of others, also serves to highlight his use of a recognised artistic medium, which embeds him in a world and links him to other texts. Both texts, Luhrmann's film and Sartre's novel, will be reconsidered as filmic and literary entities.

In the way that Luhrmann's film stages the adaptive process, through which it marks its difference from and debt to the play that it is showcasing, it will be seen to exist less like the contemporary novel that Roquentin aims to write in *Nausea*, a work of literature whose meaning coincides with itself and which, as such, can save him from the contingency of the human condition, and more as a free subjectivity. If we are to believe Sartre (the Sartre of 1938, at least), literature's salvatory force lies in the transparent fixity of its meaning: a novel is thus an inanimate object, what Sartre terms a 'being-in-itself'. As such, it coincides perfectly with itself, constituting the full extent of its own meaning. In other words, it is what it is. A conscious being, or 'being-for-itself', on the other hand, is always different from itself to the extent that its ability to project its consciousness onto the world always divorces a part of self – the thinking part or 'cogito' – from the visceral frame, the body by which we are recognised by others as being ourselves. Here, Luhrmann's film will be shown, through a detailed examination of the intertextual dynamics of its musical score, to be 'typical Luhrmann', that is individual and self-referencing, precisely in the way that it differs from itself. Always already grounded in Shakespearean prose (and fated by its literary lineage) it equally always tends beyond itself into otherness, freeing itself from pre-ordained meaning (via interaction with other texts, which it achieves through the active audience participation that Luhrmann so keenly solicits, and which sees it become interwoven in an intertextual web of references). This is how *William Shakespeare's Romeo + Juliet* functions as a being-for-itself; this is how, as a film, it is not what it is (Luhrmann's film) and is what it is not (Shakespeare's play). In this way, the film functions, both in relation to itself and to the world in which it exists, like the very world that Luhrmann wishes to stage: 'at once familiar yet distant and exotic'.[5] And since this existential condition, this way of differing from self, is fundamental to an analysis of Sartre's *Nausea*, this key text must in turn be reread. For, the literary flagship of existentialism also performs its existentialism by both being and not being a novel about existentialism...

* * *

In a recent feature article on the art of adaptation, Salman Rushdie seeks to ascertain what exactly is so wrong with the ever-increasing tide of cinematic, dramatic and novelistic 'translations' of existing artistic works. The problem seems, inescapably, to boil down to a 'question of essences' (Rushdie 2009: 4). Clearly, from our perspective of Sartrean existentialism this recalls a much-used and, arguably, rather hackneyed axiom: existence precedes essence. While we should not wish to accuse Rushdie of wanting to have his cake and eat it – indeed, he manages his cake expertly – his negotiation of existence and essence allows him the necessary elbow room to move from, without abandoning, a healthy off-loading of spleen towards a more nuanced position in regards to the adapted work of art:

> The question raised by the adaptive excesses of [Charlie Kaufman's] *Adaptation* is the question at the heart of the entire subject of adaptation – that is to say, the question of essence. 'Poetry is what gets lost in translation' said Robert Frost, but Joseph Brodsky retorted: 'Poetry is what is gained in translation', and the battle lines could not be more clearly drawn.
>
> (Rushdie 2009: 4)

Rushdie's point is that one can align oneself with both camps, and he insists that he is able to do this because he is 'defining adaptation very broadly, to include translation, migration and metamorphosis, all the means by which one thing becomes another' (Rushdie 2009: 4). It is precisely in this alignment with both camps that we should seek to frame our answer to the question that Annie Cohen-Solal poses (albeit rhetorically) in her introduction to the Yale edition of *Existentialism Is a Humanism*: 'And, as we contemplate such a diverse career, what can these two documents, taken out of context, convey to us today?' (Cohen-Solal 2007: 13).

The two documents to which Cohen-Solal refers are the essays *Existentialism Is a Humanism* and 'A Commentary on *The Stranger*' ('Explication de *L'Etranger*'). That we, as contributors to this volume, believe in the value of translation and adaptation – and thus, implicitly, in the broad definition given by Rushdie – goes without saying; what must be stated explicitly is that Sartre's essays, as all his works, gain immeasurably from being taken out of context. That is to say that the vast work of Jean-Paul Sartre weighs, at times, too heavily on each of its individual parts. Hence Sartre's need to justify his own philosophy in *Existentialism Is a Humanism*; hence, too, the value of translating and adapting Sartre; and hence, finally, the importance of juxtaposing these two particular essays. What we see brought together in this translated volume are the key attitudes of Sartre the writer of existentialist phenomenology and Sartre the reader of fiction. The adaptation implicit in Cohen-Solal's question is a call for us to impose, retroactively, the latter position on the former. Such a translation of positions captures the tension inherent in Rushdie's take on adaptation. By reading Sartre's skill as a critical reader back into his philosophical writings we are doing two things: first, we are investing an already completed, existent, work with the 'essence' of our meaning; second, we are exposing the essence that preceded the existence of the work, its telos. In this way, our adaptation of Sartre's work exposes the way that works of art are both beings-in-themselves (completed, immutable and, apparently, self-founding) and beings-for-themselves (intentional, virtual texts, always-already primed for actualisation as 'meaning' at their interface with the reader).

The context from which we wish to extricate the individual Sartrean work is existentialism itself, and the paradigm inferred from Cohen-Solal's question is that of a deconstructive reading praxis.[6] Or rather, what is apparent to us is that Sartre's ability was to adapt. Indeed, his whole philosophy is about adaptation. As he himself was at pains to state, his is not a digestive philosophy: meaning is not absorbed passively from the world but rather it is constructed by the outpouring of consciousness onto it, in situation. Translated onto the textual realm, this is a poststructuralist reading praxis: literature is not transparently – or essentially – meaningful but infinitely (re)created by the reader. The reader gives the text its facticity; the gap between us and the works we read is the same negating strip that simultaneously ties the being-for-itself to the world and separates her from it. Like Rushdie, we come full circle: adaptation takes Sartre out of his context only to put him back into it. And nowhere, we should suggest, is this adaptive circle more powerfully articulated than in Sartre's most famous work on contingency, his philosophical novel, *Nausea*. Our aim in this chapter will not be to apply a simple mapping (after all, one thing never becomes another *simply*) but to examine the dynamics of Rushdie's triptych of translation, migration and metamorphosis at the interface of Sartre's novel of 1938, *Nausea*, and Baz Luhrmann's film of 1996, *William Shakespeare's Romeo + Juliet*.

Perhaps the most striking thing about *William Shakespeare's Romeo + Juliet* is the way that it embraces and reflexively stages its modernising mission. Indeed, a brief survey of prominent Internet sites reveals 'modernisation' to be something of a watchword for Luhrmann's film. One popular site declares that 'the film is a modernisation of Shakespeare's play, designed to appeal to a younger audience',[7] while user comments on the Internet Movie Database agree that it is modernised.[8] Writing for the same site, Alexander Lum notes further how, despite being 'updated to the hip modern suburb of Verona', it still '[retains] [the play's] original dialogue'.[9] Such comments plunge us into the very myth of modernity itself, which, as David Harvey has noted, 'is that it constitutes a radical break with the past' (Harvey 2003: 1). In the way that it pushes forwards into the markedly modern, as signposted with costume, settings and props, while at the same time extending back to the original play, Luhrmann's film functions as a reading of modernity itself. Its reflexivity is a tribute to this, and as commentators have suggested, the film's deliberately 'hybrid background' means that it is 'easy to lose the story in the style'.[10] In this way, the film adopts elements of Modernism as well, with style serving to alert the reader to the need for active engagement with the story as opposed to aiding and abetting passive absorption of it.

The film's modernity is evident as early as the title itself, *William Shakespeare's Romeo + Juliet*, which exposes the complex nature of adaptation. The film is quite clearly Baz Luhrmann's, but *Romeo and Juliet*, stylised or not via the inclusion of the + symbol, remains strongly attached to William Shakespeare. This paradoxical identity of the adapted work recalls the condition of Sartre's being-for-itself. By highlighting its lineage in this way, the film is what it is not and is not what it is: it is pointedly not Shakespeare's play, but an adaptation of it. Yet on the other hand, there is clearly a way in which it would be facetious to deny that the film is Shakespeare's play. Just as the human being fails to coincide with self, *William Shakespeare's Romeo + Juliet* forever oscillates between the mutually exclusive poles of Shakespeare's play (as virtual template) and Luhrmann's adaptation (as existent production or actualisation). Reflexivity, then, reminds us of the film's status as always already in adaptation and the continuous morphing into otherness of all identity (be it human, filmic or textual).

The juxtaposition of Sartre's stentorian authorial voice and his openness to what Roland Barthes terms the 'writerly text', as offered in *Existentialism Is a Humanism*, is suggestive of the degree of negotiation necessary to broach 'existentialist' literature in a way that is productive of, and not dependent on, meaning. Our purpose here is to show how the modernisation of Baz Luhrmann's *William Shakespeare's Romeo + Juliet* parallels Sartre's development of the philosophical novel in *Nausea*. Both are auto-antonymic, offering strikingly non-synthetic juxtapositions of mutually exclusive terms, and both have recourse to the mechanics of Freudian fetishism, which inasmuch as it both symbolises and screens a significant absence, or other, serves as a point of articulation between key poetic tropes of (a recognisably French take on) modernisation and the world-view of Sartrean existentialism.

The most prevalent and subversive trope displayed by Luhrmann's film and Sartre's novel is inversion. As mentioned above, the most famous existentialist precept is that of existence preceding essence. And this is a dilemma that underpins Shakespeare's tragedy itself. It is clearly encapsulated in that most famous of lovers' complaints 'O Romeo, Romeo! wherefore art thou Romeo?' (Shakespeare [1594] 1991: 772 – II. 2. 33). On the one hand, Juliet (Claire Danes) is asking why the man who has just come into her world should have to bear a name that makes her marriage to him impossible. On the other hand, she is also exposing the underlying tension of the play, according to which Romeo (Leonardo DiCaprio) and Juliet are at once the issue of 'the fatal loins of [these] two foes' and 'a pair of star-cross'd lovers' (764 – prologue, lines 5–6). They are, apparently, doubly fated, by a genetic predisposition and a destiny dictated celestially. While Sartre simply dismisses extra-terrestrial forces, he takes more time to argue against the capacity of hereditary factors to impinge on human freedom. Predispositions are not, after all, what we are; their coincidence with, and impact upon, us is negated by that same nothingness that links us to the world in which we act, and we surge forwards forever away from them although never quite leaving them behind. Whether their fate is sealed by loins or stars, the language that speaks their love is couched in essence: why is Romeo Romeo? And why must she be Juliet? If the two lovers could continue to exist free from their names, as existents in Sartre's universe, their love could, Juliet hopes, survive. And yet, such essential Love *is* in an unqualified, non-situated sense and is unable to *exist* precisely because existence and essence stand opposed. In Sartrean discourse, existence only cedes its place to essence in the final act of death itself, at which point an individual finally coincides with the sum total of her past actions. In these terms, therefore, it is logically impossible for Romeo and Juliet to exist in a contingent universe: in short, their very conjuring on the stage signs their death warrant. As David Horowitz notes: 'Death of lovers, which is a fundamental figure in the romantic world image, signs the fact that love is absolute in a world of relatives: lovers must die in order to be born to each other' (Horowitz 1965: 4).

It is, of course, possible to discuss Luhrmann's adaptation in terms of a linear progression from one state towards another. It is equally possible to talk of a systematic and vertiginous troubling of terms, a blurring of existence and essence. Both readings can equally be mapped fairly simply onto *Nausea*, with Juliet's famous line becoming a heart-rending and fundamentally nauseating realisation of the raw contingency of existence. But the arts of adaptation and modernisation rely on a lovers' discourse, a language of mirrors whose inverted images are always already present to parallel existential reality.

In *William Shakespeare's Romeo + Juliet* the famous words of the balcony scene (which predictably drew laughter from the cinema-goers of the 1990s) are strikingly presented as a mirror image of Shakespeare's act II, scene 2: no longer looking down from her balcony, Juliet is now placed beneath her Romeo. The question of whether existence precedes essence in the original tragedy, or whether the two lovers alight on Earth from a platonic, abstract, star-cross'd plane, is further, and reflexively, problematised by this reversal. Indeed, the idea of originality itself is satirised in the film's title: *Romeo and Juliet* is modernised with its '+' even as its lineage is preserved by the addition of Shakespeare's name. And this, of course, is then qualified by the implicit presence of Luhrmann's own name. The play was always designed to be played, but the acts of direction and performance are also actualisations of the playwright's blue-print. In other words, the reality comes from a *telos*. In Luhrmann's adaptation, this *telos* is continually doubled and mirrored. Indeed, the existentialist dichotomy (existence *versus* essence) set up in Shakespeare's

Romeo and Juliet is given so much emphasis that it is arguably transfigured beyond recognition. In Luhrmann's Red Curtain vision, existence and essence function more as partners in a frenetic dance.

Insofar as the nature of the being-for-itself is always to be a translation of self onto the world as it exists in real time, and thus into the continuously updated present moment, we can argue quite reasonably that the identity problems staged in *William Shakespeare's Romeo + Juliet*, expressed as its self-conscious translation onto the modern or present screen of a well-known tragedy, constitutes the film's nausea. And if we experience the film as being of our time – if it speaks to us – it is because we too are aware, often with the twenty-first-century nausea of computer stress and e-mail angst, of the viscosity of our own modern condition.

Modernisation has always brought with it its blend of progress and alienation. What we understand here by 'modernity', insofar as this term stands for a critical lens through which to see the new as problematically related to that which is gone and which must, therefore, be reconstituted through memories that are more mythologies than objective recollections of events past, is often intimately associated with mid-nineteenth-century France and, especially, Paris. For, nowhere was this new, confronting modernity more keenly felt than in the Paris of the 1850s and the bold swathes cut by Haussmannisation. Indeed, Charles Baudelaire's poetic response to the increasingly bewildering pace of life in Paris made his work something of an Ur-text of a French literature of modernity. And we should argue further that the description of the *flâneur*'s engagement with modern-day Paris, as given in Baudelaire's prose poetry, is a precursor not only (through its poetics of neutrality and its surnaturalistic overvaluation of all and anything, right down to the most commonplace events and lowliest bibelots) of Surrealism but also of Sartre's philosophical novel. For, the innovation of *Paris Spleen*, Baudelaire's collection of little prose poems, was to offer the reader an encounter with the streets of Paris as negotiated in real time by a poet who was present to the events being described. No longer was the art of poetry a belated and objective elevation of the real (put into verse from the comfortable retreat that was the artist's garret); now the stuff of poetry was brought down to street level and witnessed almost at first hand by the reader, with just the eyes of the *flâneur*-poet as mediating lens. And yet, the movement was double. Not only was poetry brought down to earth, but the prosaic was also elevated – the great Baudelairean abstraction of the Ideal is never far away. In fact, the encounter with Paris present is simultaneously doubled by the attendant aspiration towards representative (poetic, Ideal and, ultimately mythical) Paris. When the essential Venus, momentarily stranded in the street, meets with a motley fool, for example, there is pathos and tragedy, but communication is always impossible. Baudelaire's prose-poetic 'wherefore art thou?' is a reminder of the constant, ghost-like presence and contemporary applicability of Shakespearean tragedy in any self-referential vignette of modernity.

The disconnection that sees Paris cleaved into itself and an eternal Other is echoed in Luhrmann's party scene, where the role of Shakespeare's Paris is both played and broken by Paul Rudd's portrayal of 'Dave' Paris, who is made to stand out (whilst being left in the background) in his dashing astronaut suit, in which he has come to claim his star-cross'd love. The party is a Bacchanalian frenzy in which Romeo is enticed (by love as a drug) and repelled. This is Luhrmann at his reflexive best: it is the viewer that Mercutio (Harold Perrineau) lures into a passive reading of the party (here metonymic of Luhrmann's world) while, at the same time, forcing her to see it for – and actively question – what it is. Ecstasy here combines the pleasure and pain of inversion and adaptation.

From Romeo's perspective, the party unfurls before him like Paris before the poet-narrator in Baudelaire's prose poems, who seeks momentary respite in 'an orgy of silence' away from 'human holidays' and the tawdry mundanity of the 'universal ecstasy of things' (Baudelaire [1869] 1970: 10). Whereas Romeo moves from a human orgy towards ethereal abstraction, in the form of Juliet, 'Venus and the Motley Fool' begins in full poetic flight, its movement upwards towards ethereal abstraction. But even as it soars 'like youth under Love's dominion', the ecstasy of 'things' is always already present, proleptically sealing the poem's fate, which is to crash back down to the prosaic fool. This encounter between the human fool and the goddess Venus adds grief to joy and reminds us that, for Romeo too, essential and existential love are mirror images, separated, even as they are joined, by a barrier of glass.

When Romeo first sees Juliet in Luhrmann's film, it is across just such a divide. The glass fish tank mirrors the party outside; its coloured fish 'rival the azure' of the earthly revellers, who themselves ape the gods with their own 'gaudy costume[s]' (Baudelaire [1869] 1970: 10). The binaries of the human *versus* the divine and the existential *versus* the essential, which are overarched in Baudelaire's Parisian poetics by the tension between prose and poetry, are thus problematised in an overtly Parisian manner in *William Shakespeare's Romeo + Juliet*. Just as this film functions as a transition (as the second of Luhrmann's Red Curtain Trilogy) between the heavily Parisian Australia of *Strictly Ballroom*, with its dance-hall rooftop adorned by a Hills hoist erected against the backdrop of a neon Coca-Cola sign (Australia meets the roof of the Moulin Rouge),[11] and the Australianised Paris of *Moulin Rouge* (with Nicole Kidman as an unlikely new Marianne), it also operates a perpetual movement across binaries. It is in this prose-poetic oscillation that *William Shakespeare's Romeo + Juliet* sets up the opposition that is its title.

The party scene is the convulsive meeting of various contradictory forces, foremost amongst which is that of Surrealism's predisposed subject and existentialism's situated freedom. This is the nauseous underside of ecstasy. It is also the ecstatic underside of *Nausea*, whose own prose poetics lies in its status as philosophical novel. In other words, Sartre's text is always already both treatise on contingency and novel. In the analysis of Luhrmann's party scene that follows, therefore, we shall establish that the layers of inversion, and the movement between them, on which Romeo and Juliet's cataclysmic union is predicated are all present in *Nausea*.

Nausea's otherness is multiple. In addition to being a diary as well as a novel and a philosophical treatise, it is also, like *William Shakespeare's Romeo + Juliet*, a musical score structured around one particular song. For, *Some of These Days* is more than a simple tune that Antoine Roquentin listens to in order to seek solace from the nausea. It is more, too, than a simple graft of pre-ordained and immutable sequencing onto the contingency of the present moment. In fact, the song functions fetishistically as *Nausea's* other. It is the story between the lines, a parallel song-text, whose lyrics merge, in continual surrealist moments of objective chance, with Roquentin's prosaic tale of everyday life in Bouville. As a fetish, *Some of These Days* simultaneously symbolises and screens what Roquentin knows to be true: it serves to suppress the nausea, therefore, at the same time that it points to its cause, in this case an absence.[12] For, as we shall shortly see in the case of the love theme in *William Shakespeare's Romeo + Juliet*, *Some of These Days* is itself only ever manifest in *Nausea* as absence or as a memory of a song once sung (differently) and now gone. As Roquentin states:

> I recognise the tune from the very first bars. It's an old rag-time tune with a vocal refrain. I heard some American soldiers whistle it in 1917 in the streets of La Rochelle. It must date from before the War. But the recording is much more recent.
> (Sartre [1938] 2000: 36)[13]

The song operates, therefore, as the fetish of a fetish, a symbol of an absence symbolising another absence. For, the words fetishistically screened by the soldiers' whistling in 1917 tell the story of a boy who leaves his beloved. Heartbroken, the girl decides also to leave. On hearing that his beloved is herself leaving, the boy returns only to run to the train station to see her train pulling away from the platform. Not only does this 'other version' tell the story of Roquentin and Anny's distant, lost love, but it is also the story of their meeting in *Nausea*. Thus, when they are again present to each other in Paris, it is in a retelling of this story of absence; and when Roquentin rushes down to see Anny before she leaves, he is just in time to see her train pulling away. Their meeting is not simply a dream, then: it is a song. It is a screening of the otherwise screened text of *Some of These Days*. It is, then, a non-meeting, a series of non sequiturs and crossed wires. In other words, Roquentin plays the motley fool to Anny's Venus. And herein, too, is the relevance of the song to *William Shakespeare's Romeo + Juliet*, whose love theme, *Kissing You*, metonymically expresses the fundamental impossibility of synthesising the polarities their love seeks to cross and all the misgivings and instances of mistiming that flow from it.

The way in which *Some of These Days* operates as a *mise en abyme* of the prose-poetic tension of the philosophical novel is highlighted in its foundational role in *Nausea's* use of inversion. In the novel, Sophie Tucker, the white Jewish diva, becomes a black singer. The song's black composer Shelton Brooks, on the other hand, is transformed into a white songwriter in the New York Jewish tradition. This sets the stage, quite literally, for Mercutio's inverted party act in *William Shakespeare's Romeo + Juliet*. This time a black male dresses up in drag with a silvery white dress, wig and stockings. In the film, however, this colour-coded cross-dressing is only the beginning of the inversion; the party is, after all, designed to lead Romeo astray, to cause him to cross over. The party scene stages and enables this transition by showcasing the film's soundtrack, which moves from one song to another in a parody of adaptation. For, as Romeo moves away from the frenzy of the party into a chill-out space, there is a movement away from Mercutio's drag act, where he is obviously lip-synching *Young Hearts Run Free* (bright red lipstick stands out from his black beard, emphasising this disconnection), to Des'ree's quasi-live performance of *Kissing You*. The movement is thus from adaptation and inversion (of gender, and colour to the extent that Mercutio is dressed in white) to originality.[14] In addition to being lip-synched by a drag performer, *Young Hearts Run Free* is performed for the film by Kym Mazelle whereas it was 'originally' made famous by Candi Staton in 1976: the party theme is thus always already an expression of performance and artifice. For its part, the 'love theme' was written specifically for the film, and its effect is to slow down the tempo and create a moment of compelling 'reality'. The perversity of this is, of course, that the film's central truth is an abstraction. In existentialist terms, the real world is back at the party, and the movement made by Romeo towards Juliet is a poetic one, towards essence and real life's Other. Truth and authenticity here, despite their doffing of masks, bear all the characteristics of bad faith.

In terms of the film's narrative development, the transition is less a linear progression than a symptom of the underlying prose poetics of existent Love. Romeo seems to have found a space where communication with Venus is made possible, and yet the 'love theme' sings a different story. *Kissing You* is an expression of absence, a song of love stalled and divided (the lyrics are arguably even elided to sound like 'missing you' and thus, quite specifically, not 'kissing you'). If it seals Romeo and Juliet's union with a kiss, it does so, therefore, under the sign of absence. Like Roquentin and Anny's reunion in *Nausea*, this is a meeting in appearance only, an impossible juxtaposition. Right down to the statuary of the subsequent balcony scene (complete with the clam shell from which Venus emerges into the water, the key element in their meeting), we suspect that Romeo and Juliet are looking beyond each other, 'at I know not what' (Baudelaire [1869] 1970: 10).

For their part, when Roquentin and Anny meet, the diary entry (for Saturday) is preceded by two short references to the former's decision to leave for Paris on the train, the second of which (marked Friday) makes little attempt to disguise its abuse of copyright. It is a simple reworking of *Some of These Days*: 'At the *Rendez-vous des Cheminots*. My train leaves in twenty minutes. The gramophone. Strong feeling of adventure' (Sartre [1938] 2000: 194). Surrealistically, this signals the dream state into which Roquentin is crossing and acts as a prolepsis for the post-meeting *dénouement*, when the song is again played out with fetishistic overtones. As does the lover of *Some of These Days*, Roquentin arrives at the station too late, missing his opportunity. And when he sees Anny, she is clothed, like his desires, in fetishism: 'She was wearing a heavy fur coat which made her look like a lady' (Sartre [1938] 2000: 220). She thus looks like a woman, giving form to her function as signifier of absence. She is wearing a veil, too, adding the death of love to mere distance in time and place. We are left with a vision of Anny as fetish, an image capable of bringing together two diametrically opposed forces.

Whilst *Some of These Days* is a song of trains running out of synch and in different directions, *Nausea* is a story of trains going to and coming from Paris. On the one hand, there is Anny, a symbol of absent love (a 'naked rump' always at one remove), and on the other hand there is the *patronne*, whose own naked rump is always veiled by the desire for her abstraction into a dream of Anny. Indeed, the *patronne's* last words to Roquentin before, the reader assumes, they have sex for the first time in the novel are: 'If you don't mind, I'll keep my stockings on' (Sartre [1938] 2000: 17). The very next line ensures that the sexual act is buried beneath fetishistic desire: 'In the past – even long after she had left me – I used to think about Anny.' And while Anny will always be there, always missed and never rediscovered, the *patronne* is always being left and returned to, even if the reader comes to realise that the unromantic and existentially real sex that she offers never actually happens at all. In *William Shakespeare's Romeo + Juliet* Mercutio's drag act at first seems to give Romeo what he wants. If Mercutio keeps his stockings on, it is to perform and repackage Romeo's lost love (that of the noticeably absent lady Rosaline).[15] But while the stockings soon come off, Romeo exits reality for a space where desire is simultaneously actualised and virtualised. That is to say that he becomes the very embodiment of translation, and Rushdie's suggested adaptive gain occurs at a site of paradoxical juxtaposition.

As Gilles Deleuze discusses in relation to the contours that separate and conjoin the Figure and the material structure in Francis Bacon's paintings, 'the contour is like a membrane through which [this] double exchange flows' (Deleuze 2003: 12). Everything in Luhrmann's party scene, from Mercutio's lipstick to the continual ingress and egress through doors and lifts, functions like these contours, facilitating the transcendence of the existential and its paradoxical corollary, the grounding of the essential. According to Deleuze's analysis, the movement in Bacon's paintings happens in two phases. The first lends to Romeo an athleticism whose particularity is that 'the source of the movement is not in itself' but, 'instead … goes from the material structure, from the field, to the Figure' (Deleuze 2003: 14).[16] This is where Deleuze's schema diverges from the Sartrean model of transcendence, according to which the intentional consciousness is projected continuously out across the negating contour of human corporeality onto the world (thus situating the being-for-itself). For, whilst this intentionality is always already halted and recoiled into the self, the opposite movement – of the world into the body – does not occur; consciousness of the world is, as we have already mentioned, not a digestive process. That is not to say, however, that such double movement is not present in the Sartrean text, and it is precisely in the way that *Nausea* solicits the reader's writerly engagement with it that it effects its ongoing reconstruction as text and erotically enacts this particularly Sartrean lovers' discourse.[17] In *William Shakespeare's Romeo + Juliet* the movement of the world into Romeo (as abstract star-cross'd lover) is present as the first movement of Baudelairean prose poetics; the elevation of the mundane through poetic expression. Romeo is so bombarded by the material world at the party that he seeks solace in the bathroom, which is the very place where the second movement – 'toward the material structure, toward the field of colour' (Deleuze 2003: 15) – takes place in Deleuze's schema.

This time Romeo's gestures are more obviously in accordance with the traditional phenomenological analysis of a bout of nausea. As Deleuze notes of Bacon's *Figure at a Washbasin*, 'now it is inside the body that something is happening; the body is the source of movement' (Deleuze 2003: 15). And it is precisely 'clinging to the oval of the washbasin' that Romeo, like Roquentin, experiences his face as an alien presence.[18] Romeo's gaze, however, returns to the field of colour, in this case the tank of brightly coloured fish. And it is through this mediating strip, or aqueous contour, that Romeo's externalisation of his consciousness as Other meets Juliet's actualisation of ethereal Love. In terms of the adaptive process, this is where Luhrmann's modernising movement is confronted by the power of the Shakespearean original.[19] *William Shakespeare's Romeo + Juliet* is nowhere more reflexively both itself and (its) other. Thus, a double space, of ingress and egress, is opened here, across which the film moves outwards towards external text and other texts penetrate it. This is adaptation as intertextuality.

Intertextual athleticism is certainly easily attributed to written works, such as *Nausea*, and Bacon's paintings. The idea of a simultaneous and universal mobility in stillness underpins Julia Kristeva's notion of the singular intertext, for example, where the contours that make each individual 'text' recognisable and autonomous also function as permeable membranes, as discussed by Deleuze above, facilitating movement between texts and within the virtual Text (Kristeva 1969). Furthermore, this frenetic movement expressed through the stillness of the literary work (i.e. the creative death of the text at the moment of its completion by the author, at which time, in a sense, it coincides with the total of the parts of the writing process) recalls the convulsive beauty of the surging train that does not leave the station platform in André Breton's famous surrealist image (Breton [1928] 1964: 189). And it is just such an image that completes the fetishistic fantasy into which Roquentin withdraws during (or in place of) the first sexual act with the *patronne*:

> On Saturday, about four in the afternoon, on the short wooden pavement of the station yard, a little woman in sky-blue was running backwards, laughing and waving

a handkerchief. At the same time a Negro in a cream-coloured raincoat, with yellow shoes and a green hat, was turning the corner of the street, whistling. Still going backwards, the woman bumped into him, underneath a lantern which hangs from the fence and which is lit at night. So there, at one and the same time, you had that fence which smells so strongly of wet wood, that lantern, and that little blonde in a Negro's arms, under a fiery-coloured sky.

(Sartre [1938] 2000: 18)

Saturday again, the same day that Roquentin and Anny meet each other some 170 pages later. As a surrealist vignette, this moment of objective chance represents the collision of the otherwise parallel spaces of the dream and the waking moment. This lends a depth to *Nausea* that existentialist phenomenology, with its refusal of anything beyond conscious perception, denies. There is another space, then, in which Roquentin and the *patronne* are having sex; indeed, they are both having and not having sex 'at one and the same time'. This space is obviously afforded by the actualisation of writerly text. In psychoanalysis the unconscious is written in by the analysand's active talking to the passively listening analyst. In the production of the writerly, the text's meaning is abandoned by the author (wilfully made passive) and is (re)produced by active reading. As a work, the Sartrean novel is a being-in-itself, finished and self-coinciding. As a text, on the other hand, it is not only incomplete but intentional, offering itself up – through an array of self-reflexive techniques – for the freely given interpretation of the reader. The text's movement through stillness is effected by the curiously passive activity of 'being read'.[20] As an adaptation, this scene is *Some of These Days*, transposed and played backwards but still recognisable with its motifs of departure and railway platforms, and its inversion of black and white. This time, of course, when the song is played in reverse, historical reality collides with the work of fiction; the man is again black and the woman white. Thus, *Some of These Days*, whose chorus holds the nausea at bay, also functions as a fetish, its suppressed verses both symbolising and screening sex with the *patronne* and Anny's absence.

In the cinematic text, Luhrmann is able to express convulsiveness through movement.[21] In *William Shakespeare's Romeo + Juliet* this is made especially transparent through the use of transition across spaces, genres, degrees of 'originality' (which term is then, of course, re-conceptualised) and dramatic changes in tempo. There is less need for the viewer to read in the other side of the fetish as film provides new possibilities to the double movement of prose poetics. And it is in this transitional space, where communication (be it in the form of a gaze, a letter or a train) is a tensely charged mediation of connection and dis-/mis-connection, that both *William Shakespeare's Romeo + Juliet* and *Nausea* end. Not for the first time the space of Parisian modernity, where Paris is always already both itself and Other, is translated onto a desert wasteland.[22] And in that space youth languishing under Love's dominion is ever young and ever condemned to death. For Romeo and Juliet, the final tableau is of an appointment both missed (with Love) and kept (with death). Roquentin, for his part, leaves on a similarly convulsive note: from a window of the house of departure and return he inhales the same strong smell of damp wood that previously infused the reversed collision of black and white. Whether he stays or goes, the novel he has planned is both virtual and actual, and the space he is in is both itself and other. For Sartre, as for Luhrmann, adaptation always has a distinctly Parisian flavour.

As I hope to have demonstrated through this comparative study, the movement from the real world towards the purity of art is always already reflected by art's own mirroring of reality. Sartre's Roquentin hopes to avoid the nauseous experience of the real world through immersion in literature only for his endeavour to be corrupted by the completion of his project in the form of a novel that bears the name of the very angst he seeks to escape. Similarly, Romeo and Juliet's kiss becomes a love theme that, in all but name, sings the very failure of union. Just as the existentialist novel *Nausea* always already 'exists' its own adaptation (both away from itself – as an account of *Nausea* – towards abstraction as literature, and, at its conclusion, back away from this salvation towards deconstruction as a text re-read), *William Shakespeare's Romeo + Juliet*, too, stages a frenetic movement away from and back to Shakespeare's tragedy. As such, both incarnate incompletion and disconnection. In this way, Luhrmann's Shakespearean world, again as before, recalls our own – right down to our reflection in the mirror: it is 'at once familiar yet distant and exotic'.

Notes

1. I should like to dedicate this chapter to the memory of my colleague and friend Dr Kenneth Woodgate. Our co-written interpretation of Luhrmann's film was the inspiration for this chapter (Rolls and Woodgate 2004).
2. http://www.bazthegreatsite.com/redcurtaintrilogy.htm (accessed 1 November 2009).
3. http://www.bazthegreatsite.com/redcurtaintrilogy.htm (accessed 1 November 2009).
4. Doorways are, of course, always double in function: they both close off space and open outwards and onto other space. In this respect, Sartre's concept of 'negation' operates like a doorway: the nothingness that exists, permanently and inevitably, between me and the world both separates me from and joins me to it.
5. According to Luhrmann, the 'Red Curtain' style involves a 'simple even naïve story based on a primary myth [which] is set in a heightened interpretation of a world that is at once familiar yet distant and exotic' (Luhrmann 2001: 9).
6. See Rolls and Rechniewski (2005: 1–12).
7. http://en.wikipedia.org/wiki/William_Shakespeare's_Romeo_%2B_Juliet (accessed 12 May 2009).
8. http://www.imdb.com/title/tt0117509/ (accessed 12 May 2009).
9. http://www.imdb.com/title/tt0117509/plotsummary (accessed 12 May 2009).
10. www.reelviews.net/movies/r/romeo_juliet.html (accessed 12 May 2009).
11. The image of this most American of signs, which functions as a perverse symbol of Paris to those familiar with Place Blanche and the environs of the Moulin Rouge, proleptically signals the trilogy's finale from the very outset, and the Coca-Cola sign is also picked up in passing on a neon billboard in *Romeo + Juliet*.
12. As such it functions at what Ellen Lee McCallum (McCallum 1999: xii) refers to as the 'unique intersection of desire and knowledge'.

13. As Debra Hely has noted, both versions are recorded by Sophie Tucker. The one that Roquentin would have heard in La Rochelle is likely to have been the version recorded in 1911, which has verses as well as the haunting refrain 'Some of these days / You'll miss me honey'. When the song is recorded by Tucker in 1926, the chorus is all that remains. (Hely 2005: 169–72).

14. Another inversion is noted in an online comparison of Luhrmann's film with Franco Zeffirelli's 1968 version of the same play, which records the role of the 'singer' in each film. In this comparison, Luhrmann's 'African American female' inverts Zeffirelli's 'White male'. See http://www.geocities.com/Hollywood/9251/table.html (accessed 12 May 2009).

15. Mercutio's drag also inverts another amorous woman, perhaps the character who most closely recalls Sartre's *patronne*: Lady Capulet (Diane Venora), whose costume is the mirror image of Mercutio's own. While he sports a white wig over black hair, she covers her own blond hair with a black wig; she also wears a contour-restraining corset that flattens the length of her body rather than accentuating her waist, and which thus takes her one step closer to merging with Mercutio's gender-bending display; and finally, like Mercutio and the *patronne*, she is wearing stockings. Since her aim is to marry Juliet to Paris (or to cause the young girl to leave for Paris, to tie in *Some of These Days*), her desire to counter Romeo's union with a young woman mirrors Mercutio's own role in the film. Both are perverse; both encourage and facilitate love but seek to block the story's central union. In this way, Mercutio and Lady Capulet both express the prose-poetic tension of both the film and the play. Furthermore, the Egyptian theme of Lady Capulet's costume reinforces these paradoxes with the myth of Isis, who was herself spawned at the juncture of Earth and stars (as the daughter of Geb and Nut, the deities of the Earth and the Heavens, respectively).

16. This chapter of Deleuze's monograph is entitled 'Athleticism'.

17. The paradoxical way in which reflexive text prompts the reader to (re)make it, as the writerly, recalls the lover's attempts in *Being and Nothingness* to seduce the beloved into loving him freely (and thereby to capture this freely given consciousness in the form of love).

18. His movement towards abstraction – away from the crowd, towards Juliet – is experienced in just the way Deleuze describes: 'It is not I who attempt to escape from my body, it is the body that attempts to escape from itself by means of ... in short a spasm: the body as plexus, and its effort or waiting for a spasm' (Deleuze 2003: 15). Where Deleuze infers abjection, we should read a kind of nausea.

19. This is reflected in Shakespeare's own cameo role in the film: he is briefly shown urinating as Romeo enters the bathroom, in a scene redolent of Bacon's spasm series, which includes not only scenes of love but also 'of vomiting and excreting' (Deleuze 2003: 16).

20. In *Nausea* this is suggested by the double-sidedness of the pebble and the missing words that the reader is invited to fill in (Sartre [1938] 2000: 9–11). Sartre also proves himself capable of performing the same analysis as we have just offered of Luhrmann's fish tank. In his commentary on *The Stranger*, for example, he discusses Camus's image (from *The Myth of Sisyphus*) of a man talking on a telephone behind a glass partition. This image is, for Sartre, only 'relatively absurd, because it is part of an incomplete circuit' (Sartre [1946] 2007: 90–91). The transparent partition is doubly permeable, and the author meets the reader across it in the completion of the textual communication.

21. A nice example of convulsive movement is Capulet's (Paul Sorvino's) dance and singing out of '*amore*' during the party. This will remind those who have seen Louis Malle's inspired filmic adaptation (1960) of Raymond Queneau's *Zazie dans le métro* (1959), in which Trouscaillon frenetically professes his love of Albertine (Marceline in the novel). His dance of love serves, fetishistically, to screen and symbolise the dance of Albertine's partner Gabriel; it also acts as a moment of transition whilst Albertine changes into Albert and the cross-dressing Gabriel assumes more profoundly his performative identity as Gabriella.

22. We might think of Boris Vian's *L'Automne à Pékin* (1947), for example, in which a bus departs from Paris only to terminate in the 'Exopotamian' desert. Such instances draw on such mythical expressions of French Otherness as the Foreign Legion.

Bibliography

Baudelaire, C. [1869] 1970. *Paris Spleen*, trans. L. Varèse. New York: New Directions.

Breton, A. [1928] 1964. *Nadja*. Paris: Gallimard.

Cohen-Solal, A. 2007. 'Introduction', in Jean-Paul Sartre, *Existentialism Is a Humanism*, trans. C. Macomber. New Haven, CT and London: Yale University Press, pp. 3–15.

Deleuze, G. 2003. *Francis Bacon: The Logic of Sensation*, trans. D.W. Smith. London, New York: Continuum.

Harvey, D. 2003. *Paris, Capital of Modernity*. New York, London: Routledge.

Hely, D. 2005. 'Fact or Fiction? Reading through the Nothingness behind *Nausea*'. A. Rolls and E. Rechniewski (eds), *Sartre's 'Nausea': Text, Context, Intertext*. Amsterdam, New York: Rodopi, pp. 165–81.

Horowitz, D. 1965. *Shakespeare: An Existential View*. London: Tavistock Publications.

Kristeva, J. 1969. *Semiotikè: Recherches pour une sémanalyse*. Paris: Seuil.

Luhrmann, B. 2001. 'Foreword', in *Moulin Rouge: A Film Directed by Baz Luhrmann*. Crows Nest, NSW: Allen and Unwin, pp. 8–9.

McCallum, E.L. 1999. *Object Lessons: How to do Things with Fetishism*. New York: State University of New York Press.

Queneau, R. 1959. *Zazie dans le métro*. Paris: Gallimard.

Rolls, A. and E. Rechniewski (eds). 2005. *Sartre's 'Nausea': Text, Context, Intertext*. Amsterdam, New York: Rodopi.

Rolls, A. and K. Woodgate. 2004. 'Mercutio's Dance: Aspects of Inversion in Luhrmann's Film *William Shakespeare's Romeo + Juliet*', *Inter-Cultural Studies: A Forum on Social Change & Cultural Diversity* 4(1): 65–79, Special Issue: 'Queer Studies – Out from the Centre'.

Rushdie, S. 2009. 'Lost in Translation', *The Weekend Australian*, 28–29 March, 4–6.

Sartre, J.-P. [1938] 2000. *Nausea*, trans. R. Baldick. London: Penguin.

———. [1946] 2007. *Existentialism Is a Humanism*, trans. C. Macomber. New Haven, CT: Yale University Press.

Shakespeare, W. [1594] 1991. *Romeo and Juliet*. Leicester: Bookmark. Reprint of 1905. *William Shakespeare, Complete Works*. Oxford: Oxford University Press, 764–94. Date of the first performance of Romeo and Juliet estimated as 1594 according to http://absoluteshakespeare.com/trivia/bibliography/bibliography.htm (accessed 5 August 2009).

Thody, P. and H. Read. 1998. *Introducing Sartre*. Cambridge: Icon Books; New York: Totem Books.

Vian, B. 1947. *L'Automne à Pékin*. Paris: Editions de Minuit.

Filmography

Luhrmann, B. (dir.). 1992. *Strictly Ballroom*. M & A.

———. 1996. *William Shakespeare's Romeo + Juliet*. Bazmark Films.

———. 2001. *Moulin Rouge*. Angel Studios.

NOTES ON CONTRIBUTORS

Jean-Pierre Boulé is Professor of Contemporary French Studies at Nottingham Trent University and the author of a number of books, notably on Sartre, including *Sartre médiatique* (1992) and *Sartre, Self-Formation and Masculinities* (2005). He is the co-founder of the U.K. Sartre Society and executive editor of *Sartre Studies International*. He is co-editing with Benedict O'Donohoe, *Jean-Paul Sartre: Mind and Body, Word and Deed* (2011) and preparing with Ursula Tidd a companion to this volume, *Existentialism and Contemporary Cinema: A Beauvoirian Perspective* (2013).

Sarah Cooper is Reader in Film Theory and Aesthetics and Head of Film Studies at King's College London. She is the author of *Relating to Queer Theory* (2000), *Selfless Cinema?: Ethics and French Documentary* (2006), and *Chris Marker* (2008). She is working currently on a book on film theory and the soul.

Michelle R. Darnell holds a Ph.D. in Philosophy from Purdue University, where she completed a dissertation primarily on Jean-Paul Sartre. Her research is in the intersection between existentialism and ethics, including applied ethics, though she has published in the more general field of existentialism. She is currently a lecturer at the University of Florida.

Christopher Falzon teaches Philosophy at the University of Newcastle, Australia. He has published in the areas of continental philosophy and philosophy and film. He is the author of *Foucault and Social Dialogue* (1998) and *Philosophy Goes to the Movies* (2002, 2007).

Tom Martin is Head of the Department of Philosophy at Rhodes University, South Africa. He has published journal articles and book chapters in a range of fields, including philosophy and film, philosophy and literature, and philosophy of racism, and he is the author of *Oppression and the Human Condition: An Introduction to Sartrean Existentialism* (2002).

Enda McCaffrey is Reader in French at Nottingham Trent University. He is the author of a number of books including *Octave Mirbeau's Literary and Intellectual*

Evolution as a French Writer 1885–1917 (2000), *The Gay Republic: Sexuality, Citizenship and Subversion in France* (2005) and *The Return of Religion in France: From Democratisation to Postmetaphysics* (2009). He is currently working on a new monograph called *Ethical Responses to the Crisis of the Universal: A French Perspective.*

Tracey Nicholls is Assistant Professor of Philosophy and Co-director of the Women's Studies Program at Lewis University, in the Chicago area of the United States. She is a co-editor of *Fanon and the Decolonization of Philosophy* (2010), and is currently working on a manuscript, *Aesthetic Possibilities for a Political Future*, that explores connections between improvised music, aesthetic pluralism, and social justice, and considers how music-making can help build more responsive political communities. She is co-editing two volumes: with Bettina Bergo of the Université de Montréal, interrogating white privilege; and with Eddy Souffrant of the University of North Carolina at Charlotte, exploring possibilities for cosmopolitan peacebuilding.

Alistair Rolls is a Senior Lecturer in French at the University of Newcastle, Australia. He is the author of *The Flight of the Angels: Intertextuality in Four Novels by Boris Vian* (1999) and co-author with Deborah Walker of *French and American Noir: Dark Crossings* (2009). He has also edited a number of volumes, including, with Elizabeth Rechniewski, *Sartre's 'Nausea': Text, Context, Intertext* (2005).

Mark Stanton is an independent researcher and Editorial Manager at Berghahn Books where he is responsible for commissioning on the Film and Media Studies list. He has studied the works of Sartre for many years and is currently working on Sartre's *The Imaginary* and the relationship between film and imagination.

Kevin L. Stoehr is Associate Professor of Humanities at Boston University. He is the author of *Nihilism in Film and Television* (2006) and co-author of the forthcoming *Ride, Boldly Ride: Aspects of the Western in American Cinema*. He edited the books *John Ford in Focus: Essays on the Filmmaker's Life and Work* (2008), *Film and Knowledge: Essays on the Integration of Images and Ideas* (2002) and *Philosophies of Religion, Art, and Creativity* (1999).

Patrick Williams is Professor of Literary and Cultural Studies at Nottingham Trent University. His publications include *Colonial Discourse and Post-Colonial Theory* (1993), *Introduction to Post-Colonial Theory*, (with Peter Childs) (1996), *Ngugi wa Thiong'o* (1999), *Edward Said* (2000), *Postcolonial African Cinema* (with David Murphy) (2007). Forthcoming books include *The Routledge Companion to Diaspora Studies*, (edited with Alison Donnell and John Noyes), and a collection on Orientalism in Routledge's 'Major Works' series. He is on the editorial boards of *Theory, Culture and Society, Journal of Postcolonial Writing* and *Maghreb Journal of Cultural Studies and Translation.*

INDEX